On Holy Ground: The Theory and Practice of Religious Education

Religion has had notable and renewed prominence in contemporary public and political life. Religious questions have also been freshly examined in philosophy and theology, the natural sciences, the social sciences, psychology, phenomenology, politics and the arts. These fields reflect complex, multidisciplinary understandings of religion, some hostile, some accommodating. For religious education, this has all contributed to its own international renaissance. Religious education, in ensuring that it is contemporary, shares with these fields the same criticality, the same distance between the study of religion and the religious life.

Yet what are the *grounds* of this modern religious education? Through a systematic historical and contemporary cross-disciplinary analysis, answering this question is the ambitious task of the book.

Chapters include:
- 'Philosophy, theology and religious education'
- 'The natural sciences and religious education'
- 'The social sciences and religious education'
- 'Psychology, spirituality and religious education'
- 'Phenomenology and religious education'
- 'The politics of religious education'
- 'The aesthetics of religious education'.

The central problem of all modern religious education remains this: what are the *grounds* of religious education when religious education is no longer grounded in the religious life, in the *life* of the holy? Although this primarily appears to be an epistemological problem, it soon becomes a moral and existential one. The book will be of key interest to teachers, theorists and researchers working in religious education.

Liam Gearon holds the University Lectureship in Religious Education in association with a Senior Research Fellowship at Harris Manchester College, University of Oxford, UK. He is also Adjunct Professor at the Australian Catholic University, Australia, and Conjoint Professor at the Humanities Research Institute, Newcastle University, Australia.

On Holy Ground:
The Theory and Practice of Religious Education

Liam Gearon

 Routledge
Taylor & Francis Group

LONDON AND NEW YORK

First published 2014
by Routledge
2 Park Square, Milton Park, Abingdon, Oxon OX14 4RN

Simultaneously published in the USA and Canada
by Routledge
711 Third Avenue, New York, NY 10017

Routledge is an imprint of the Taylor & Francis Group, an informa business

British Library Cataloguing in Publication Data
A catalogue record for this book is available from the British Library

Library of Congress Cataloging in Publication Data
Gearon, Liam.
On holy ground : the theory and practice of religious education / Liam
Gearon.
pages cm
1. Religious education–Philosophy. I. Title.
BV1464.G43 2014
207'.5–dc23
2013003833

ISBN: 978-0-415-51710-2 (hbk)
ISBN: 978-0-415-85787-1 (pbk)
ISBN: 978-0-203-11757-6 (ebk)

Typeset in Galliard
by FiSH Books Ltd, Enfield

Contents

1   On holy ground

Introduction

The Book of Genesis narrates a curious and seemingly ludicrous tale of a plot to storm heaven by the construction of a tower. The core passage reads as follows:

> Now the whole earth had one language and the same words. And as people migrated from the east, they found a plain in the land of Shinar and settled there. And they said to one another, 'Come, let us make bricks, and burn them thoroughly.' And they had brick for stone, and bitumen for mortar. Then they said, 'Come, let us build ourselves a city and a tower with its top in the heavens, and let us make a name for ourselves, lest we be dispersed over the face of the whole earth.' And the Lord came down to see the city and the tower, which the children of man had built. And the Lord said, 'Behold, they are one people, and they have all one language, and this is only the beginning of what they will do. And nothing that they propose to do will now be impossible for them. Come, let us go down, and there confuse their language, so that they may not understand one another's speech.' So the Lord dispersed them from there over the face of all the earth, and they left off building the city. Therefore its name was called Babel, because there the Lord confused the language of all the earth.
>
> (Genesis, 11: 1–9, Revised Standard Version)

God, we note, is displeased with this storming of heaven. In order to lay waste to these human assaults, God destroys first the tower. He then uses the confusion of human language to limit the prospect of any such plans in the future.

If the inhabitants of Earth can no longer assail heaven, God seems happy to visit Earth. In addition to justified wrath wrought upon the godless and immoral, the Old Testament charts the appearance of God on Earth to converse with the faithful and to make promises or covenant with them. Although in post-lapsarian exile, many seek God, it is thus only God who initiates encounter, as with Noah, Abraham, Moses and, later, the prophets. Encounter with the holy, from which after the fall humans are separated, is made manifest in the temporal and immanent, the unholy with the holy.

Moses' first encounter with God is framed in these terms. Tending a flock of sheep on the edge of a desert wilderness, at Horeb, the mountain of God, we read how

> the angel of the Lord appeared to him in a flame of fire out of the midst of a bush. He looked, and behold, the bush was burning, yet it was not consumed. And Moses said, 'I will turn aside to see this great sight, why the bush is not burned.' When the Lord saw that he turned aside to see, God called to him out of the bush, 'Moses, Moses!' And he said, 'Here I am.' Then he said, 'Do not come near; take your sandals off your feet, for the place on which you are standing is holy ground.'
>
> (Exodus, 3: 2–6, Revised Standard Version)

Moses, we read, hid his face, for he was afraid to look at God.

In *Das Heilige und das Profane* (1957) translated in 1959 as *The Sacred and the Profane: The Nature of Religion*, Mircea Eliade (1907–1986) terms such encounters with the holy, *hierophany*, 'to designate the act of manifestation of the sacred' (Eliade 1959: 11). They are heightened by distinctions of sacred time and profane time (Eliade 1959: 20–65), sacred space and profane space (Eliade 1959: 68–113), nature from the supernatural (Eliade 1959: 116–59), a 'chaos' becomes a 'cosmos' (Eliade 1959: 116), 'the supernatural is indissolubly connected with the natural' yet 'nature always expresses something which transcends it' (Eliade 1959: 118). Human existence opens the possibility of the 'sanctified life' (Eliade 1959: 162–213) 'so the whole of life is capable of being sanctified', 'life is lived on a twofold plane; it takes its course as human existence and, at the same time, shares in a trans-human life, that of the cosmos'.

The religious life – of '*homo religiosus*' – is the path to sanctification. Holy in the Latin is *sanctus*, in the Greek *hagios*. The life of sanctification is the life of the holy. Eliade, drawing from a range of religious traditions, seeing in religion these essential components and paths – recognizing the means by which 'sanctification' is brought about are various, but the results are always the same (Eliade 1959: 167) – approaches in a strange way the narrower theological orthodoxy of St Thomas Aquinas (1225–1274). In the *Summa Theologica* (II–II: 81: 8), Aquinas answers the question as to 'Whether religion is the same as sanctity?' There is in reply an equation between the religious life and the path of sanctification, the holy life. If the outward form of religious belief is practice, 'it is by sanctity that the human mind applies itself and its acts to God: so that it differs from religion not essentially but only logically' (Pope 1910). In this meaning it is a life which is set apart, it is a call by God and to God (Leviticus, 11: 44), a call to perfection (Matthew, 5: 48), it is the narrow gate (Luke, 13: 24; Matthew, 7: 13). Interpreted in different ways across Christian traditions (see Alexander, 1988), it is that holiness without which no one will see God (Hebrews, 12: 14).

This notion of separateness between the holy and unholy, sacred and profane, permeates Durkheim (2001), its loss the source of *anomie* or meaninglessness, a key factor in Durkheim's work on suicide (Durkheim 2006; also Pickering and Walford 2000). It was this sense of loss which was described by Weber (2004, 1994) as a characteristic of rationalized modernity, the disenchantment of the modern world. For Eliade, it is a complex *forgetting*; and here we might return to the post-lapsarian context with which I opened, for Eliade sees the modern forgetting of the sacred, the holy, as a second fall: 'After the first "fall", the religious sense descended to the level of the "divided" consciousness; now, after the second, it has fallen even further, into the depths of the unconscious; it has been "forgotten"'. Eliade argues at the end of his book that this is where his task, the task of the historian of religion ends, and then 'begins the realm of problems proper to the philosopher, the psychologist, and even the theologian' (Eliade 1959: 213).

On Holy Ground examines the re-reading of the holy through the texts of modernity, not simply in its rejection of revelation as a source of knowledge but, more widely, the loss of the sacred and the conscious removal of sacred–profane, holy–unholy distinctions. The book demonstrates how such readings have been refracted, have become a coda for a modern religious education, for the re-reading of religious texts has become as integral a part of modern religious education as it was integral to the coda of modernity.

Indeed, the story of Babel, like others in Genesis (a modern-day Ur-text of religious scepticism), confirmed certainly for Charles Darwin religion's implausibility:

> Whilst on board the Beagle I was quite orthodox, & I remember being heartily laughed at by several of the officers (though themselves orthodox) for quoting the Bible as an unanswerable authority on some point of morality. I suppose it was the novelty of the argument that amused them. But I had gradually come by this time (i.e. 1836 to 1839) to see the Old Testament, from its manifestly false history of the world, with the Tower of Babel, the rain-bow as a sign &c &c, from its attributing to God the feelings of a vengeful tyrant, was no more to be trusted than . . . the beliefs of any barbarian.
>
> (Darwin [1876] 2008: 392)

And, he writes, 'by such reflections as these, which I give not as having the least novelty or value, but as they influence me, I gradually came to disbelieve in Christianity as a divine revelation' (Darwin [1876] 2008: 392; see Gearon 2013a, 2013b).

Darwin here demonstrates in a single instance a whole Western intellectual tradition which has needed to dispense with the holy in order to seek the legitimacy of new forms of knowledge, not to reach heaven but dismantle it.

Modernity began not with an assault on heaven to regain it but to remove it. Modernity is not an attempted recovery of holy ground but its eradication. In its originating impulse, modernity can be *negatively* defined as a cessation of the assault on heaven through the denial of the holy. In its originating impulse, modernity can be *positively* defined (against this cessation and denial) as a quest for earthly alternatives to heaven and alternative grounds for being in the world.

If, in its originating impulse, modernity can here be *negatively* defined as a cessation of the assault on heaven through the denial of the holy, *so too can religious education be read*. If in its originating impulse, modernity can be *positively* defined (against this cessation and denial) as a quest for alternatives to heaven and alternative grounds for what once both knowing and being in the world, *so too can religious education be read*.

Such a reading of modernity – and modern religious education – requires a close reading of the texts of modernity. As the tower of Babel narrative tells us and as postmodern interpretations of such texts concur (Derrida 2002; Ricoeur 1970, 1974, 1976, 1978, 1980), this reading of modernity is also a *profusion* of readings. I begin with one of the shortest and most defining. Despite its diverse origins, its aetiologies (Beiser 2000; Broadie 2003; Emerson 2003; Hampson 1990; Himmelfarb 2008), its multiplicity (Eisenstadt 2000, 2002), assimilations and reactions against it, this modernity is still shaped, is still being shaped, by the eighteenth-century movement called Enlightenment and one of its chief exponents.

On holy ground

In a short essay, written at Konigsberg in 1784, Immanuel Kant (1724–1804) presents an answer to the question: 'What is Enlightenment?' Freedom to think, to reason, to attain to a state of autonomy in thought and action are its fundamental principles: 'Enlightenment is man's [sic] emergence from his self-imposed immaturity.' This 'immaturity' is 'the inability to use one's understanding without guidance from another' and is 'self-imposed when its cause lies not in lack of understanding, but in lack of resolve and courage to use it without guidance from another'. For Kant, the motto of Enlightenment is, 'Have courage to use your own understanding!'

Kant recognizes that some 'gladly remain in lifelong immaturity', with the consequence that it becomes 'easy for others to establish themselves as their guardians'; 'If I have a book to serve as my understanding, a pastor to serve as my conscience, a physician to determine my diet for me, and so on, I need not exert myself at all.' Making an analogy between such people and domesticated animals, Kant argues that having 'first made their domestic livestock dumb, and having carefully made sure that these docile creatures will not take a single step without the go-cart to which they are harnessed, these guardians then show them the danger that threatens them, should they attempt to walk alone'. For those who would be free, the perceived dangers are 'not actually so great, for after falling a few times they would in the end certainly learn to walk'. In short: 'Nothing is required for this enlightenment, however, except freedom; and the freedom in question is the least harmful of all, namely, the freedom to use reason publicly in all matters.' It was this rationale of freedom which formed the basis for the Enlightenment. And it is freedom from religion with which Kant is above all concerned: 'I have focused on religious matters in setting out my main point concerning enlightenment, i.e., man's emergence from self-imposed immaturity, first because our rulers have no interest in assuming the role of their subjects' guardians with respect to the arts and sciences, and secondly because that form of immaturity is both the most pernicious and disgraceful of all.'

It is for this reason that, in the following century, Karl Marx (1818–1883) comments that 'the critique of religion is the prerequisite of all critique' (Marx 1977; Hegel 1991; see Ameriks 2000). It is why the Enlightenment spirit of enquiry across philosophy, the natural sciences, the social and psychological sciences, phenomenology, modern politics, aesthetics, amongst many forms of knowledge, are rooted in epistemological distance from religion as a form of knowledge.

The idea of the holy

This rationalization of the holy was a problem which preoccupied Rudolf Otto (1869–1937). Otto's 1898 dissertation on Luther's understanding of the Holy Spirit showed an early interest in religious experience, an intuitive trust in the presence of God. A second major influence was Schleiermacher; Otto edited a centennial edition of Schleiermacher's *On Religion* (1799) and gave the latter credit for stimulating reflections on religious experience. Otto's reputation persists for one short book, *Das Heilige* (*The Holy*) (1917). Here, countering what he determined as religion's over-rationalization, Otto reframed the debate around the holy, not to rid religion of its rational aspects but to counterbalance such interpretations with a reminder of non-rational elements which were, to his mind, its irreducible, *sui generis* essence (Harvey 1950: ix–xix).

Otto's claim is that the holy cannot be reduced by or to secondary rational frameworks. In the English translation of *Das Heilige*, *The Holy* becomes *The Idea of the Holy*. Otto's (1917) famed treatise has thereby the ironic distinction of manifesting in its English translation the very over-rationalization which he had sought to overcome.

Yet Otto opens with an argument for the necessity of reason in religion. He particularly refers to the theological conceptions of God by analogy to characteristics such as 'spirit, reason, purpose, good will, supreme power, utility, selfhood'; 'Now all these attributes constitute clear and definite *concepts*: they can be grasped by the intellect; they can be analysed by thought; they even admit definition.' An object that 'can thus be thought conceptually may be termed *rational*' (Otto 1950: 1). Although the book is permeated with comparative references to a range of religions, Otto's

Christian theological background gives prominence to this tradition. Christianity, he claims, from its various theological traditions, is a rational religion. It is precisely because it is rational, and makes claims to truth, that those sciences which emerged with full force after the Enlightenment were so able fully to critique it.

Otto underlines this rationality in contrast to feeling and emotion. On such rational grounds is '*belief* possible in contrast to mere *feeling*' (emphasis in original). 'We count,' Otto writes, this reasoned conception of God as the ground of all belief as the 'very mark and criterion of a religion's high rank and superior value – that it should have no lack of *conceptions* about God; that it should admit knowledge – the knowledge that comes by faith – of the transcendent in terms of conceptual thought' (Otto 1950: 1). Otto's claims made about the abundance of these concepts in Christianity being a sign of self-evident superiority of Christianity itself. Otto makes reference to such superiority throughout *The Idea of the Holy*, in part because his comparison of Christianity to other religions was theologically sensitive.

After undergirding his thesis on the rationality of Christian theology, of its concepts, with the caveat that the knowledge derived is aided by faith, Otto nevertheless argues that to stress only the conceptual in any religion is to miss much that is not rational: 'we have to be on our guard against an error which leads to a wrong and one-sided interpretation of religion' (Otto 1950: 1). This is the view that the essence of God can be exhausted by its conceptual or rational elaboration.

Where do we strike the balance between reason and that which lies outside of it? For Otto, 'All depends on this: In our idea of God is non-rational overborne, even perhaps wholly excluded, by the rational? Or conversely, does the non-rational preponderate over the rational?' And, 'So far from keeping the non-rational element in religion alive in the heart of the religious experience,' he writes, 'orthodox Christianity manifestly failed to recognize its value, and by this failure gave to the idea of God a one-sidedly intellectualist and rationalistic interpretation'. This 'bias to rationalization', he argues, 'still prevails, not only in theology but in the science of comparative religion in general'. 'This attempt we are now to make,' suggests Otto is 'with respect to the quite distinctive category of the holy or sacred'.

> 'Holiness' – 'the holy' – is a category of interpretation peculiar to the sphere of religion. It is, indeed, applied by transference to another sphere – that of ethics – but it is not itself derived from this. While it is complex, it contains a quite specific element or 'moment', which sets it apart from 'the rational' ... which remains inexpressible – ineffable – in the sense that it completely eludes apprehension in terms of concepts.
> (Otto 1950: 5)

These statements, he suggests, would be untrue from the outset if 'the holy' 'were merely what is meant by the word, not only in common parlance, but in philosophical, and generally even in theological parlance' (Otto 1950: 5).

The meaning often ascribed to the holy as being of a moral attribute, as 'completely good', 'the absolute moral attribute' is 'inaccurate'. Otto's task is an examination of the holy beyond mere goodness:

> For this purpose I adopt a word coined from the Latin *numen*. Omen has given us 'ominous', and there is no reason why from *numen* we should not similarly form a word 'numinous'. I shall speak, then, of a unique 'numinous' category of value and of a definitely 'numinous' state of mind, which is always found wherever the category is applied. This mental state is perfectly sui generis and irreducible to any other; and therefore, like every absolutely primary and elementary datum, while it admits of being discussed, it cannot be strictly defined.
>
> (Otto 1950: 6–7)

'Our X,' writes Otto, 'cannot, strictly speaking, be taught, it can only be evoked, awakened in the mind'. The holy is *mysterium tremendum et fascinans*: the *mysterium* is 'wholly other', while the *tremendum* evokes awe, fear, terror, and the *fascinans*, attraction, love. Identifying religious experience as the ground of religion itself, Otto identifies this experience as the 'numinous', from the Latin *numen*. For Otto, understanding the holy is integral to understanding religion, it is its ground, that component of religion which is its ground, its fundamental experience which is 'irreducible to any other' (Otto 1950: 7).

However, since Otto approached his study through the isolation and thus ultimately rational elaboration of the holy, he arguably succumbed to the very critique he was making. Kant suggested that which is transcendent cannot be known by reason and, although Otto is opposed to the rationalization of religion (or an interpretation of religion which rests too heavily on rationalization), we find in Otto differently and more favourably expressed a similar recognition of the limits of reason. Revivals of interest in Otto (for example, Smith 2009) thus centre on debates on religion as ultimately concerned with that which cannot be rationally conceived. For Ware (2007), Otto's idea of the holy, in its emphasis on alterity or otherness, the breakdown of subject–object, means his analysis is more applicable to non-theistic religious traditions (cf. Wach 1951).

The Idea of the Holy was one of the most influential studies of religious experience in the twentieth century. The influence can be said to be threefold. First, identifying the core, the ground, of religion, Otto led to an emphasis on a wider comparative study of religions. Second, though in *The Idea of the Holy*, Otto makes plain that Christianity is, in a hierarchy of religions, somewhere near an imagined peak, in works such as *Mysticism East and West* (Otto, 1987) we see him move to a more egalitarian religious pluralism (Almond 1984; Bastow 1976; Davidson 1947). Three, Otto saw religious experience as an irreducible *sui generis* feature of all religion.

Emphasising the experiential as religion's essence became an influence directly apparent in Smart's (1969) *The Religious Experience of Mankind*.

Streetman (1980) asked, 'That Otto made has made an impact on religious studies in undeniable, but whatever became of him?' The answer at least for religious education ironically lies in those rational interpretations which were Otto's principal concern.

The theory and practice of religious education

The problem of modern religious education remains how to ground the subject when it is no longer grounded in the religious life, in the *life* of the holy.

Willaime thus identifies as a 'double constraint' the extent to which models of religious education today are compelled to compliance with international standards:

> a *sociological* one, in that the religious and philosophical pluralisation of European societies obliges them to include ever more alternative religions and non-religious positions into their curricula, and . . . a *legal* one, through the importance of the principle of non-discrimination on religious or philosophical grounds (as well as others such as gender or race) in international law, especially in the European Convention on Human Rights.
>
> (Willaime 2007: 65; emphasis in original)

This 'double constraint' has resulted, in Europe, as Willaime (2007) notes, three models of religious education: (1) 'no religious instruction in schools'; (2) 'confessional religious instruction'; (3) 'non-confessional religious education' (Willaime 2007: 60). Similarly, Ferrari (2012: 100–3) suggests three models of religious education which are reflective of the European situation: '1) disallowing religious education within the formal curriculum in schools opened by the state (e.g. France); 2) providing non-denominational teaching about religions; and 3) providing denominational teaching of religion for prevailing religion(s) within the country'. Despite national historico-legal and policy differences, Durham suggests 'these appear to be the major options not only in Europe, but worldwide' (Durham 2012: 4).

I am concerned throughout this volume with what Willaime calls 'non-confessional religious education' and what Ferrari calls 'non-denominational teaching about religions'. The solution has been the seeking of grounds for such religious education when religion is no longer rooted in the pursuit of the holy life. The argument is that such religious education has sought alternative grounds in modern, Enlightenment and post-Enlightenment forms of knowledge. Since these have their origins in the critique of religion, modern religious education presumes a critical distance from the holy life. These grounds then are epistemological. How do we understand the holy? The holy is understood through rational grounds, a multitude of rationalizations. To understand the holy, religious education has appropriated frameworks which have their origins in the critique of religion.

While inter- and multi-disciplinary research makes rigid boundaries untenable, I identify the following forms of knowledge as having had an especially critical relationship with religion: philosophy, the natural sciences, the social sciences, psychology, phenomenology, politics and aesthetics. In each case, disciplinary identity emerged in relation to, often a reaction against, those forms of knowledge held to be sacred, revealed truth.

The ambitious task was to examine how precisely these forms of knowledge have come to ground modern religious education. Each chapter considers, then, a twofold relationship: first, between religion and each respective discipline – philosophy, the natural sciences, the social sciences, psychology, phenomenology, politics and aesthetics; second, broad parameters established, then outlined are the various *appropriations* of these disciplines within religious education. In Chapter 2, then, I consider the relationships between philosophy, theology and religious education. In Chapter 3, the impact of the natural sciences on religious education; in Chapter 4, the social sciences; in Chapter 5, psychology; in Chapter 6, phenomenology; in Chapter 7, the politics of religious education; in Chapter 8, the aesthetics of religious education. Each of these respective forms of knowledge – philosophy, the natural sciences, the social sciences, and so forth – have each in their own ways impacted on religious education.

In each case, I identify two *ideal types* responsive to religion: the adversary and the advocate. The *adversary* is not content simply to observe religion. They want something done about it, preferably its removal. Indeed, it has been a characteristic of the adversarial position that religion, once its delusions are highlighted, will remove itself. Yet there are, we might note, occasions in the history of ideas when even those most antagonistic to religion, though they abandon distinctions between sacred and profane, holy and unholy, are loathe to rid themselves of the terms of religion, and we see this in Rousseau's (1997a, 1997b) 'civil religion', Kant's (1996a) hopes for the 'founding of the Kingdom of Heaven on Earth' and Dewey's (1991) 'common faith'.

The *advocate* seeks not removal but better understanding of religion. The advocate can, however, also be antagonistic to certain forms of religion. Thus, advocates use frameworks more closely to observe and understand, to interpret religion. Religion, in other words, is interpreted and seen through the lens of a particular discipline – philosophy of religion, the natural sciences and religion, and so on. Advertently or inadvertently, these interpretive frameworks are advocatory of religion insofar as religion mirrors their interpretation. If religion is seen as an epiphenomenon of social or psychological factors, the model of religion favoured is one which contributes to social or psychological well-being, and so forth.

In each chapter, then, using a reading of classic sources, I address

adversarial and advocatory responses to religion through respective disciplinary lenses. Given the disciplinary range this is necessarily a *sketch* of
respective theories of religion. I then examine the extent to which these disciplinary perspective's understandings of religion have been appropriated
within religious education.

This is evidenced in two aspects, *themes* and *methods*. The first aspect is
evidenced in the manner in which religious education has been cognisant of
the *themes* of the respective disciplines (philosophy, the natural, social and
psychological sciences, and so forth). The second aspect is evidenced where
religious education adopts the respective (philosophical, etc.) disciplines as a
pedagogical *method*. Since themes often elide into methods, these developments I identify as *appropriations*.

In examining these appropriations, I turned to book and journal articles
in education but also, given the approach, beyond education. Reviews of
literature were thus central aspect to this study but extended beyond education narrowly defined. The study particularly necessitated a history of *ideas*
as much as narrow educational inquiry. While acknowledging the necessity of
historical inquiry in a limited (educational) sense (Sawicki 1987; Copley
2000, 2004, 2005; Freathy and Parker 2010; Veverka 1987), such studies
are ultimately insufficient unless supplemented by a more general history of
ideas.

To identify patterns of appropriation within religious education, keyword
searches were undertaken in subject specific and generic education journals,
where the respective disciplines (philosophy, science, and so forth) interface
religious education. Thus, standard means of identifying research in education were inappropriate. A database such as ERIC (the Education Resources
Information Center), for instance, limits searches to those article and book
publications narrowly defined as educational. This highlights, as Furlong and
Lawn (2010) have shown, an ever-increasing separation of educational
research from base disciplines of history, philosophy, psychology, sociology.
Researchers for example in the latter fields may be working in education
independent from 'educationalists'; educationalists may be using historical,
philosophical, psychological or sociological frameworks though former levels
of integration if not lost, are loosened. It can be noted that there is by
contrast wide, current interest in religion across disciplines which reflects
historical preoccupations.

To demonstrate the appropriation of various frames of knowledge in religious education specifically, particular attention was paid to two transatlantic
journals in the subject whose provenance extends for the longest period of
time within the field: in the United States (since 1903) *Religious Education*
and (since 1934, as *Religion in Education*, from 1964 until 1981, as *Learning
for Living*) the *British Journal of Religious Education*. As leading journals of
religious education their contributors also reflect worldwide developments in
the subject. These searches indicated a long provenance to diverse disciplinary
(philosophical, scientific, etc.) influences on religious education.

Others have, of course, undertaken meta-analyses of one or both of these journals to identify trends within and across disciplines. Greer (1984a, 1984b), for example, examined the influence of psychology in the first 50 years of the *British Journal of Religious Education*. But there have been a variety of disciplinary influences. That no consensus over which predominates, or should do so, is evidenced (a year after Greer) by Day (1985). Examining the history of the subject, Day identified 'a permanent identity crisis'. In the mid-1990s, Copley (1996) reviewed editorials in *Learning for Living* and the *British Journal of Religious Education*, 1971–1996. English *et al.* (2003) undertook a '10 Year Retrospective of the *British Journal of Religious Education*' examining contents and disciplinary approaches of contributors. English *et al.* (2005) also analysed contents, contributors and research directions in *Religious Education*, 1993–2002.

A longer perspective came from Jackson's (2008) 'The evolution of the *British Journal of Religious Education*: 30th and 74th birthdays' (the current journal and its earlier forms). Of particular note is the increasingly international focus of the journal but also the concerns of modern religious education itself:

> The *BJRE*'s increase in international visibility and participation has been facilitated through links to international professional bodies such as the International Association for the History of Religions (IAHR), the European Association for the Study of Religions (EASR), the American Academy of Religion (AAR), the International Network for Inter-religious and Inter-cultural Education (bringing together European and southern African researchers), the Co-ordinating Group for Religious Education in Europe (CoGREE), the European Network for Religious Education through Contextual Approaches (ENRECA), the Australian National Symposium on Religious Education and the Nordic Conference on Religious Education, to inter-governmental organisations such as the Council of Europe, the European Commission (via funded research projects on religions education such as the Framework 6 Project REDCo), UNESCO and the Office for Democratic Institutions and Human Rights of the Organisation for Security and Co-operation in Europe and to international non-governmental organisations, notably the Oslo Coalition on Freedom of Religion or Belief.
>
> (Jackson 2008: 184)

Some argue for comparative studies of the journals themselves:

> Researching religious education journals could also become a step towards a more extensive discussion on religious education as an academic discipline, in terms of its understanding of research, its methodologies, its academic standards, etc. In this respect, the

advantage of using journals as an object of study can be seen in reference to existing work rather than to mere ideas, claims or wishes for the discipline.

(Schweitzer *et al.* 2012: 92)

In terms of findings, Schweitzer *et al.* identify five trends: (1) 'Social and cultural modernization'; (2) 'the professionalization of the religion teachers ... the academization of religious education'; (3) 'increasing influence of scientific methods – of empirical research but also of the impact of natural science and of the social sciences – ... scientification'; (4) 'the changing religious landscape ... secularization' and 'the new pluralism observed in society'; (5) related to the latter, the increasing prominence of a political dimension to religious education (Schweitzer *et al.* 2012).

Useful as it appears as a method, there are some problems in limiting analysis of the developments in the field to comparisons of journals in the field not in rigour but in outcomes. First, Schweitzer *et al.* seem to enhance the epistemological confusion that their paper is designed to clarify, not least by adding further terms of jargon, 'scientification'; 'academization'. More importantly, however, the development of any field if restricted to the journals *in the field* risks a perpetual insularity, an enclosure within its own circle.

On the 100th anniversary of *Religious Education*, Buchanan (2005) discusses 'pedagogical drift', the 'evolution of new approaches and paradigms in religious education'. By contrast, Martin and de Pisón (2005) comment: 'The epistemological paradigm, known as *post-modernity*, challenges some of the presuppositions of educational systems in general, and of religious education in particular. One of these presuppositions is the exaggerated primacy given to knowledge attained through reason.' Martin and de Pisón argue that 'the paradigm shift invites us to make a transition from knowledge to wisdom' and 'to the integration and transformation of knowledge into human experience' (ibid: 157).

The result is an ongoing search which Seymour (2011a) has defined as a quest for the 'canon of religious education' (see also Baumfield and Cush 2012; Weiss and Cutter 1998). This includes key classic texts within a range of disciplines, which have historically informed and epistemologically formed the identity of religious education as a subject. Manifestly, the search for new epistemological grounds is as old as the modern subject of religious education itself. If the grounds themselves remain contested, from the earliest decades, a core effort has been to establish religious education *as education*. There are two reasons for this.

First, early on there was an unspoken premise amongst the professional community that religious education should be seen to be addressing the modern world. An early issue of *Religious Education* thus addresses 'the social situation' and the relationship between 'religious education and contemporary social conditions' (Addams 1911). *Religious Education* in the same decade explores science and religion 'as factors in progress' (Falconer

1913); the 'new world order' (Tracy *et al.* 1917), and so forth. Over subsequent decades was the ever-present pressure for religious education to be 'contemporary' (Deems 1949).

Second, the justification of religious education as *education* is seen as requiring the respectability of science, defined as a methodologically rigorous approach to knowledge, and religious education as a concern with theory and practice based on this rigour. Yet it is also one in which the religious educator early recognized the need to be aware of developments in science (Rolfe 1926). But which science is more suitable? Cavan and Cavan (1928) early identified 'rival disciplines aiming for control of child development': 'The past decade [the 1920s] has seen the development of movements to what is, after all, a single result, unfortunately those absorbed in one movement have often failed to take account of the others' (see, in the same period, Hartshorne 1922). Discussing sociology, psychology, psychiatry, political programmes of citizenship, they identify a growing insularity. Already, in 1928, a vast literature pertains to each, the 'total volume of writing in each of these fields is so large that no practical worker could be adequately familiar with it'. 'What,' they ask, 'can be done to make this huge accumulation of experience and science usable?' (Cavan and Cavan 1928: 482; see also Cavan 1932; Cavan and Cavan 1930; Smith 1928). By the early 1930s, Harner (1932) poses the question, 'Is religious education to become a science?' There is a 'new spirit' that 'breathes through' the subject (Harner 1932). An 'offspring of a union between religious idealism and scientific method', it is seen as imperative to examine such developments in their infancy: 'If we wait long, its character will be firmly set, and then it will be too late' (Harner 1932: 202).

As the grounds constantly shift, so too does the quest for stable epistemological foundations, in fundamental ways – meaning construction but also the means of living. Conroy *et al.* (2012) have thus identified, in Britain at least, contemporary 'failures of meaning in religious education'. Their substantial empirical study suggests that meaning generation in religious education attempts:

> (1) an insight into the meaning theological claims have for their adherents; (2) a coherent ground upon which the individual creates his/her own meanings rooted in something more substantial than oddly conceived personal preferences; (3) a transcendent ground for ethical attachment and moral behaviour.
>
> (Conroy *et al.* 2012: 317)

Conroy *et al.* argue that, 'In the end the enterprise of cultivating meaning is likely to fail as long as religious education, both theoretically and as a practice, continues to foreground purposes that perforce offer too many contradictions: e.g. between the intellectual and the affective, the public and the private, the metaphorical and the literal, self-determination and civic cohesion' (Conroy *et al.* 2012: 322; see also Baumfield *et al.* 2012; Lundie 2010; cf. Osbeck 2012). Attempts have been made to chart this pedagogical diversity (Grimmitt 2000), or what many see as increasing confusion (Teece 2010, 2011). Yet there is surprisingly little systematic effort to trace the epistemological roots of modern, non-denominational religious education, and the ways the subject attempts to re-ground itself using a range of academic disciplines and epistemological traditions.

The task, as outlined, is to review the key, critical sources of the construction of such diverse approaches to theory and practice in religious education. The argument is that the search for new epistemological grounds is the inevitable consequence of the separation of religious education from the religious life, once there is a separation of the holy from the idea of the holy, the idea of the holy and the holy life.

Despite Otto's attempts to separate the holy from the ethical, an epistemological problem soon becomes a moral and existential one. The problem of modern religious education remains in finding a ground when modern religious education is no longer grounded in the religious life, in the *life* of the holy. The solution has lain or has been sought then in the seeking of foundations. The grounds are primarily epistemological: how do we understand the holy? The problem is also moral: how do we live, how does religious education contribute to the educating, to the leading out from knowledge to life? Thus, again, an epistemological problem becomes a moral and existential one.

Summary

This volume, then, is an attempt to trace the epistemological grounds of religious education now religious education has separated from the religious life, once there been set a critical distance between the holy and the idea of the holy.

The Enlightenment is the chosen starting point, although I attempt throughout to show that it is neither a true beginning, nor, I argue by way of conclusion, can it ever be *an end*, a satisfactory end, literal or teleological. It is, however, a decisive historical marker, from which contemporary religious education begins to appropriate epistemological frames of reference from the modernity out of which it emerged.

Enlightenment, however, is as much an attitude as an epistemology. Søren Kierkegaard (1813–1855), in *Fear and Trembling* (Kierkegaard 2008), early in the century after Enlightenment, observed with dry irony the prevalent rejection of religious faith as a mere staging post in human progress:

> In our time nobody is content to stop with faith but wants to go further. It would be perhaps rash to ask where these people are going, but it is surely a sign of breeding and culture for me to assume that everyone has faith, for otherwise it would be queer for them to be going further.
>
> (Kierkegaard 1941: 1)

By contrast, in the century preceding Enlightenment – of Descartes (1596–1650), of Newton (1642–1727) – we see that humility and caution, even religious reverence, which is later absent. Blaise Pascal (1623–1662) – mathematician, philosopher, religious thinker (Hammond 2003; McKenna 2003; Rogers 2003) – defines a prescient caution as knowledge advanced:

> This is our true state; this is what makes us incapable of certain knowledge and of absolute ignorance. We sail within a vast sphere, ever drifting in uncertainty, driven from end to end. When we think to attach ourselves to any point and to fasten to it, it wavers and leaves us; and if we follow it, it eludes our grasp, slips past us, and vanishes forever. Nothing stays for us. This is our natural condition, and yet most contrary to our inclination; we burn with desire to find solid ground and an ultimate sure foundation whereon to build a tower reaching to the Infinite. But our whole groundwork cracks, and the Earth opens to abysses.
>
> (Pascal 1660: 14–15)

Following an accident in 1654, involving horse and carriage, Pascal took fright at the unexpected proximity of death. The experience for Pascal was life transforming. A religious believer already, this incident led to a yet more profound conversion (Moriarty 2003; Wetsel 2003). It prompted the polymath to make an irrevocable avowal of faith, stitching in the lining of his overcoat some fervent sentences of reminder of the day his life changed. It is from the consciously unsystematic *Pensées*, we launch into the certainties of systematization and seeming epistemological certainty of the centuries that followed.

2 Philosophy, theology and religious education

Introduction

In Gifford lectures delivered between 1930 and 1932, Étienne Gilson 1884–1978 made a then unfashionable attempt to restate the historically close relationship between philosophy and theology, a thesis beginning with figures of classical stature, Augustine, Anselm, Aquinas (Gilson 1990, 1994). Taking the same historical lineage as Gilson, MacIntyre (2011) similarly traces the lost relationship not only between theology and philosophy but an entire framework of modern-day 'knowledge construction'. For MacIntyre, the Academy has lost any unifying theme and knowledge generated across disciplines lacks an integrative purpose, and an epistemological fact becomes in consequence a moral problem (MacIntyre 2011). The sixteenth-century Reformation is in this regard, both Gilson and MacIntyre agree, part of the story of the separation of philosophy and theology which would subsequently define eighteenth-century Enlightenment, although, as MacCulloch (2009) has argued, all the elements needed for such a movement to flourish were in place by the end of the seventeenth century.

Protestantism's self-imposed separation of philosophy from theology gave both their independence. Theology was free to reflect on scripture; philosophy could guide those spheres of human activity outside or beyond revelation. The philosophers of the sixteenth and seventeenth centuries took less interest in theology as a result: *qua* Locke, de Montesquieu – and directed attention to the secular. Since the separation of philosophy from theology meant a disentanglement of theology from those spheres it had influenced – in the medieval world, everything – philosophy's role became increasingly important. The responsibilities of philosophy became greater, and were especially notable where ecclesiastical and political authority had been intertwined. By the eighteenth century, philosophy began to turn its attention to that sphere of enquiry which had given it its independence. Enlightenment philosophical attention was drawn not simply to those spheres of activity outside of revelation but to the truths of revelation itself. Human reasoning alone could not come to the truths which had been revealed and as such the truths of revelation could be dismissed as valid claims to knowledge. Critical philosophy was *critical* first and above all else of theology.

Philosophy and theology

The power of ecclesiastical authority to challenge the orthodox limits of knowledge was particularly evident from the thirteenth century onwards, even as the ability to maintain that control was slipping from the powers which sought to maintain it. Fourteenth and fifteenth century inquisitors who persecuted John Wycliffe (1328–1384) and John Huss (1372–1415) saw the direction of the new learning and sought to halt it. Change only intensified. Reformation and Counter-Reformation were attempts at an orthodoxy which only served to emphasize theological differences. Divergences in theology were mirrored in radical transformations of political as well as ecclesiastical structures (Calvin and Luther 1991). Ecclesiastical disunity created a political divide across Europe, which only further weakened religious authority. Declining doctrinal conformity coincided with historical closure on ecclesiastical authority and its usurpation by secular power, democratic and dictatorial. By the end of the sixteenth century Protestant conformity to doctrine was as little apparent it was impossible to determine. By the end of the eighteenth century, theological orthodoxy was looking philosophically implausible. Theological hegemony had given way to intellectual heterogeneity. Such radical theological and political change enabled epistemological challenges to theology itself. From the nineteenth century, philosophical assaults on religion were a commonplace.

The philosophical adversaries of religion

Writing of David Hume (1711–1776), Immanuel Kant used the language of rest to describe the philosopher who woke him from his dogmatic slumbers (Norton and Taylor 2008). Hume's (2009) *Dialogues Concerning Natural Religion* presents natural theology as mere speculation, outside the scope of empirical demonstration or rational proof and, if the truths of Christian revelation were to be believed as truths, they were to be believed on blind faith. Hume's *Dialogues Concerning Natural Religion* was only published posthumously. Yet the influential philosophers of that century saw no philosophical progress possible without the removal of theology and the metaphysics it carried. In the pursuit of truth, what was transcendental was beyond rational thought or empirical investigation. What was required in philosophy was not a modification of religion but its renunciation.

It is here, following not only Hume but a range of epistemological and theological positions, that Kant becomes a critical figure in philosophy of religion (Guyer 1992). Kant's writing on religion can be divided into pre- and post-critical periods; before, that is, and after the publication of *The Critique of Pure Reason* in 1781 (Kant 1998). In the pre-critical Kant, his concerns with philosophy of religion are primarily with the classical proofs for the existence of God, the ontological, the cosmological and the argument from design; for example, *A New Exposition of the First Principles of Metaphysical Knowledge* (1755); *Universal Natural History and Theory of the Heavens* (1755) and *The One Possible Basis for a Demonstration of the Existence of God* (1763). The latter work incorporates Kant's pre-critical conclusions that the only reasonable proof for the existence of God is the ontological; the idea that God is a being none greater than which can exist, and, since a being who exists is greater than one which does not, God is a being who must possess the quality of being and thus must exist. In the post-critical period, Kant dismisses again the argument from design and the cosmological but also dismisses his own former proofs for the ontological argument. But the post-critical Kant is important for the constructive interpretation he provides of what can be left of religion, 'within the bounds of reason'; notably, *Religion within the Boundaries of Mere Reason* ([1793] Kant 1996b), 'The End of All Things' ([1794] Kant 1996c) and *The Conflict of the Faculties* ([1798] Kant 1996d).

To grasp the implications of Kant's significance for much theory of religion in subsequent centuries, I outline the framework of knowledge, the epistemological project of the *Critique* and then review some of Kant's writings where he addresses the post-critical role and status of religion directly.

The Critique of Pure Reason is only concerned with religion in so far as its claims to knowledge are suspect. Kant is careful to affirm what may be termed true (epistemologically possible) as opposed to false (epistemologically untenable) religion. In the preface to the second edition (1787) Kant states:

> I cannot even assume God, freedom and immortality unless I simultaneously deprive speculative reason of its pretensions to extravagant insights; because in order to attain such insights, speculative reason would have to help itself to principles that reach only to objects of possible experience, and which, if they were to be applied to what cannot be an object of experience, then they would always actually transform it into an appearance, and thus declare all practical extension of pure reason to be impossible. Thus I had to deny knowledge in order to make room for faith.
>
> (Kant 1998: 117)

Kant accepts the presupposition that there are truths which cannot be demonstrated by reason but he rejects that they can be known at all.

The negative task is in fact a positive one. We need simply:

> to compare the culture of reason that is set on the course of a secure science with reason's unfounded groping and frivolous wandering about without critique, or to consider how much better young people hungry for knowledge might spend their time than in the usual dogmatism that gives so early and so much encouragement to their complacent

quibbling about things they do not understand, and things into which neither they nor anyone else in the world will ever have any insight.

(Kant 1998: 117–18)

Attention to the 'well-grounded sciences' thus results in putting 'an end for all future time to objections against morality and religion'. This is achieved following the Socratic or dialectical method:

> namely by the clearest proof of the ignorance of the opponent . . . Hence it is the first and most important occupation of philosophy to deprive dialectic once and for all of all disadvantageous influence, by blocking off the source of all errors.

(Kant 1998: 118)

The Critique of Pure Reason is therefore corrective of error but constructive or enabling us to be certain of knowledge, within the limits of pure reason. In the preface to the second edition, Kant outlines these major forms of errant thinking as philosophical as well as theological metaphysics, for, 'Through criticism alone we can sever the very root of materialism, fatalism, atheism, of freethinking unbelief, of enthusiasm and superstition, which can become generally injurious, and finally also idealism and scepticism' (Kant 1998: 119). The *Critique* then is a rejection of what Kant calls dogmatism, the perpetuation of unexamined assumptions. It is also a rejection of scepticism (that we cannot know anything) or that we can only know through our sense experience (empiricism). The complexities of the *Critique* arise in part from the ambition of the task but also for the manner in which it undertakes the critique simultaneously in corrective or more often consciously destructive and constructive modes.

Beyond the general remarks Kant makes about the errors of dogmatism (philosophical and theological) in the preface, the introduction is concerned to establish the nature of judgement as the basis of knowledge. He introduces the distinction between forms of cognition, the means by which we know and make judgement, according to the distinction of *a priori* and *a posteriori*, under the heading 'on the difference between pure and empirical cognition':

> There is no doubt whatever that all our cognition begins with experience; for how else should the cognitive faculty be awakened into exercise if not through the objects that stimulate our senses and in part themselves produce representations, in part bring the activity of our understanding into motion to compare these, to connect or separate them, and this to work up the raw material of sensible impressions into a cognition of objects that is called experience? *As far as time is concerned*, then, no cognition in us precedes experience, and with experience every cognition begins.

(Kant 1998: 116)

However, he continues, 'although all our cognition commences *with* experience, yet it does not on that account, all arise *from* experience':

> It is therefore at least a question requiring closer investigation, and one not to be dismissed at first glance, whether there is any such cognition independent of all experience and even of all impressions of the senses. One calls such cognitions, *a priori*, and distinguishes them from empirical ones, which have their sources *a posteriori*, namely in experience.
>
> (Kant 1998: 134)

The task of the remaining part of the introduction is to establish those categories by which cognition is grounded by the conditions or categories which provide the limits of thought. This is the justification of philosophy as 'a science which determines the possibility, the principles and the domain of all *a priori* cognitions' (Kant 1998: 139). In grounding this knowledge, Kant distinguishes between analytical and synthetic judgements:

> In all judgements in which the relation of a subject to the predicate is thought...this relation is possible in two different ways. Either the predicate B belongs to the subject A as something that is (covertly) contained in this concept A; or B lies entirely outside the concept A, though to be sure it stands in connection with it. In the first case I call the judgment analytic, in the second synthetic.
>
> (Kant 1998: 141)

The former, analytical judgement can also be termed 'judgements of clarification' and the synthetic 'judgements of amplification', since:

> through the predicate the former do not add anything to the concept of the subject, but only break it up by means of analysis into its component concepts...while the latter...add to the concept of the subject a predicate that was not thought in it all.
>
> (Kant 1998: 141–2)

Judgements of experience are all synthetic, for 'it would be absurd to ground an analytic judgement on experience, since I do not need to go beyond any concept at all in order to formulate the judgement' (Kant 1998: 142).

Reason then consists of two kinds of judgement: analytical (the logical) and synthetic (those which are based on and tested by evidence and logical contradiction). Human reason cannot know that which is beyond its mental capacity to experience. The major part of the remainder is the 'Transcendental doctrine of elements', in which first section is the defining *a priori* limitation of 'space' and 'time'; given the spatial and temporal limits of the mind itself, what is beyond space and beyond time the human mind cannot know. The 'transcendental doctrine of elements' is divided into 'transcendental *analysis*', which is concerned with the identification of the objects of analytical and synthetic judgement, the further limits of thought, the categories – quality, quantity, relation, modality (Kant 1998: 206, 212) – and the 'transcendental *dialectic*', in which Kant formally applies the principles of pure reason to the former errors of philosophy as well as theology. The latter includes the formal dismissal of three classic proofs for the existence of God: the ontological (the argument that God by necessity must be the greatest being that exist, since if God did not exist God would be a lesser being); the physical–theological (the argument for existence of God from the evidence in nature) and the cosmo-logical (the argument for the existence of God from the evidence of causes, there must be a first cause). Kant thereby dismisses a rational theology but also defines the limits of critical philosophy and curbs the natural tendency of human reason to extend beyond its own capacities.

Constructively, then, Kant admits that the critical project is to establish the relationship between the analytical and the synthetic, which makes knowl-edge possible, 'a special science which can be called the critique of pure reason'. Pure reason 'is that which contains the principles for cognizing something absolutely *a priori*' (Kant 1998: 149). In Kant's own terms, this is metaphysical, as Rohlf (2010) comments:

> The main topic of the *Critique of Pure Reason* is the possibility of meta-physics, understood in a specific way . . . metaphysics for Kant concerns a priori knowledge, or knowledge whose justification does not depend on experience; and he associates a priori knowledge with reason. The proj-ect of the *Critique* is to examine whether, how, and to what extent human reason is capable of a priori knowledge.
>
> (Rohlf 2010)

Guyer and Wood (1998) emphasize the task as moral as well as epistemo-logical: 'The *Critique of Pure Reason* was the work in which Kant attempted to lay the foundations both for the certainty of modern science and the possi-bility of human freedom' (Guyer and Wood 1998: 2).

Thus, an epistemological (and theological) problem soon becomes a moral one. Kant makes the connection explicitly. It is a restatement of one the oldest of epistemological problems (from Plato's metaphor of the cave onwards), of our knowledge of reality as opposed to its appearance. For Kant, the epistemological distinction between the phenomenal (things as they appear) and the noumenal (things as they in themselves) has a moral dimension which is integrally connected to the notion of freedom; that is, our freedom to act as moral creatures:

> if the critique has not erred in teaching that the object should be taken in a twofold meaning, namely as the appearance or as thing in itself; if its deduction of the pure concepts of the understanding is correct, and hence the principle of causality applies only to things taken in the first

sense, namely in so far as they are objects of experience, while things in the second meaning are not subject to it; then just the same will is thought of in the appearance (in visible actions) as necessarily to the law of nature and to this extent *not free*, while yet on the other hand it is thought of as belonging to a thing in itself as not subject to that law, and hence *free*, without any contradiction hereby occurring.

(Kant 1998: 116)

If all of our knowledge points to a world in which all is determined, we are not free and no morality, in the sense of free action, can be possible. Kant continues:

Now suppose that morality necessarily presupposes freedom (in the strictest sense) as a property of our will, citing a priori as data for this freedom certain original practical principles lying in our reason, which would be absolutely impossible without the presupposition of freedom, yet that speculative reason had proved that freedom cannot be thought at all, then that presupposition, namely the moral one, would necessarily have to yield to the other one. Whose opposite contains an obvious contradiction; consequently *freedom* and with it morality... would have to give way to the mechanism of nature.

(Kant 1998)

The 'doctrine of morality' thus 'asserts its place and the doctrine of nature its own'. Critical philosophy enables this – it 'would not have occurred if criticism has not first taught us of our unavoidable ignorance in respect of the things in themselves and limited everything that we can cognize theoretically to mere appearances' (Kant 1998). Critical philosophy is thus not simply a path to knowledge but to freedom.

For Kant, this epistemological clarity grounds not only knowledge but a freedom that allows for faith, even of doctrine: 'Just the same sort of exposition of the positive utility of critical principles of pure reason can be given in respect to the concepts of God and of the simple nature of our soul' (Kant 1998: 116–17).

Yet we cannot *know* these things. We cannot know what cannot be thought but this does not leave us without assurances about faith. The only ones affected by the critique are those who have made useless speculations about what cannot be known:

I ask the most inflexible dogmatist whether the proof of the continuation of our soul after death drawn from the simplicity of substance, or the proof of freedom of the will against universal mechanism drawn from the subtle though powerless distinctions between subjective and objective practical necessity, or the proof of the existence of God drawn from the concept of a most real being (or from the contingency of what is alterable and the necessity of a first mover), have ever, after originating in the schools, been able to teach the public or have the least influence over its convictions?

(Kant 1998: 117)

It has, he says, 'never happened, and it can never be expected to happen'. For each of the latter three points, Kant shows how the critique leaves true faith undisturbed:

> if rather the conviction that reaches the public, insofar as it rests on rational ground, had to be effected by something else – namely, as regards the first point, on that remarkable predisposition of our nature, noticeable to every human being, never to be capable of being satisfied by what is temporal (since the temporal is always insufficient for the predispositions of the our whole vocation) leading to the hope of a future life; in respect of the second point the mere clear exposition of our duties in opposition to all claims of the inclinations leading to the consciousness of freedom; and finally, touching on the third point, the splendid order, beauty, and providence shown forth everywhere in nature leading to the faith in a wise and great author of the world – then this possession . . . remains undisturbed.

(Kant 1998: 117–18)

The 'schools' – of rational theology – then 'are instructed to pretend to no higher or more comprehensive insight on any point touching the universal human concerns than the insight that is accessible to the great multitude (who are always most worthy of our respect) and *to limit themselves to the cultivation of those grounds of proof alone that can be grasped universally and are sufficient from a moral standpoint* (Kant 1998: 118, emphasis added).

Metaphysics, in philosophy as well as theology, as Kant affirms in the *Prolegomena to Any Future Metaphysics* (Kant 2004), will always fail to find God *ens realissimum*, as God is in reality, by the limitations of reason. In outlining Kant's theoretical philosophy after 1781, Guyer and Wood (Kant 2002), show how Kant, his philosophical reputation established, sought in works like the *Prolegomena* to popularise his thinking (Kant 1997, 2004). It is in these texts that Kant argued that any attempt to identify what is said of God with God becomes an idolatry, to give the qualities of the God to that which is not God. Biblical revelation becomes anthropomorphism and any notion of divine intervention in human history delusory. What remains of religion is a practical matter (Kant 1999a, 1999b).

In the *Critique of the Power of Judgment* (1790) Kant will acknowledge that the God that cannot be known by reason can be expressed, however distantly through a sense of the sublime. In *The Critique of Practical Reason* (1788) Kant retains a *moral* sense of God which hints of a sublime. This moral sense he links to the wonder that was once directed to the transcendent now limited to nature:

> Two things fill the mind with ever new and increasing admiration and awe, the oftener and the more steadily we reflect on them: the starry heavens above and the moral law within. I have not to search for them and conjecture them as though they were veiled in darkness or were in the transcendent region beyond my horizon; I see them before me and connect them directly with the consciousness of my existence.
>
> (Kant 1909: 111)

This moral sensibility becomes Kant's categorical imperative, the rule of conscience, and the basis for Kant's moral argument for the existence of God. But this sense of God and this morality do not need religion or its institutions. Rather, self-perpetuating ecclesiastical institutions are a social and moral evil. The churches are purveyors of ignorant superstitions and, in maintaining influence over an ignorant and susceptible populations, are guilty of deception, which hampers rather than enables natural, moral development. Morality 'stands in need neither of the idea of another Being' for a person to apprehend their duty, nor 'an incentive other than the law itself' to impel duty. As Kant will note in *Religion within the Boundaries of Mere Reason*, 'Hence, for its own sake, morality does not need religion at all' (Kant 1996b: 39–216).

Kant's post-critical works show an ever-confident dismissal of religious practice and a growing disdain for scriptural and clerical authority. If, as Wood (1992) tells us, Kant was 'a man of scientific temperament, concerned with the intellectual development and moral progress of humanity', he was also 'deeply sceptical of popular religious culture, severely disapproving of the traditional activities of prayer and religious ceremonies and downright hostile to ecclesiastical authority' (Wood 1992: 413–14). Thus, as we have noted, Kant regarded religion as 'the most pernicious and disgraceful of all' unenlightened states. In *Religion within the Boundaries of Mere Reason* ([1793] Kant 1996b) – the three *Critiques* having now consolidated a towering reputation – Kant delivers his most systematic analysis of the implications of a critical philosophy for religion. Wood (1992) identifies the specific targets for Kant's philosophy of religion, which can be seen as a middle ground between the abandonment of all consideration of religion and the pretences of rational theology.

The first of these was *Pietism*, founded by Philipp Jakob Spener (1635–1705):

> The Pietists regarded Christian faith not as a set of doctrinal propositions but a living relationship with God. They stressed above all the felt power of God's grace to transform the believer's life through a conversion of 'born again' experience. Pietism was hostile to the intellectualization of Christianity. Like Lutheran orthodoxy it exalted scriptural authority above natural reason, but for Pietism the main purpose of reading scripture was inspiration and moral edification. The experience of spiritual rebirth must transform the believer's emotions and show itself in

outward conduct. Within the universities, the Pietists favoured cultivation of piety and morality in life rather than theoretical inquiry.

(Wood 1992: 394)

The other current that fed the Enlightenment was rational theology. Wood identifies this with Christian Wolff (1679–1754) but the scope of Kant's assault was broader. If Wolff regarded scriptural revelation as 'distinct from rational theology, but wholly consistent with it' (Wood 1992: 394–5), new developments in Biblical criticism would undermine the reasonableness of rational theology based on revelation and thus for many any plausibility to a rational theology which claimed consistency with biblical revelation. This was all the more significant at the time since Biblical criticism was assimilating linguistic and historical analysis. J. A. Ernesti (1707–1781), J. D. Michaelis (1717–1791) and H. S. Reimarus (1694–1768) laid the foundations in Kant's time for a re-examination of scripture, which had been read as inerrant and inviolable. The uncovering of inconsistency, contradiction and historical unreliability led to a doubting of the foundational text of Christian belief as a ground for understanding the world and human purpose in it (Kant 1996a, 1996b, 1996c).

This, as I suggested, was especially important in a Protestant context, since the doctrine of *sola scriptura*, scriptural revelation, provided the ground for faith and since faith (*sola fide*) was the means to salvation, this provided self-evident problems for faith as conceived in Protestant tradition. In part, Kant is a reaffirmation of the separation of philosophy from faith which became systematized in the Reformation. Kant is reaffirming an attack not only on the tradition of philosophical theology in his own time but also the entire tradition of theology as faith seeking understanding, which found its apogee in figures from Augustine and Anselm to Aquinas. Some version of this tradition was prevalent in Protestant form in Kant's own century. Yet it is ironic – given the Protestant emphasis on faith not works – that Kant's defence of faith argues the *moral* as its only justification and ground.

God is not only unknowable, but – by the means associated with traditional practice – unreachable. Kant's most systematic philosophy of religion and his view of the moral as the sole basis for religion, as noted, is found in *Religion within the Boundaries of Mere Reason* (Kant 1996b). The work is divided into four parts – each part of 'The Philosophical doctrine of religion': Part 1 Concerning the indwelling of the evil principle alongside the good, or, Of radical evil in human nature; Part II Concerning the struggle of the good with the evil principle for the dominion over the human heart; Part III Concerning the victory of the good over the evil principle and the founding of the Kingdom of Heaven on Earth; Part IV Concerning the service and counterfeit service under the dominion of the good principle, or, Of religion and priestcraft. Kant gives attention to religions in general: 'The acceptance of the principles of a religion is pre-eminently called faith (*fides sacra*)' but, in relation to Christianity, he makes his most refined judgements:

> We shall have to consider the Christian faith, therefore, on the one hand as pure rational faith, and on the other as revealed faith ... the first may be considered as a faith freely accepted by everyone (*fides elicita*), the second a commanded faith (*fides imperata*)'
>
> (Kant 1996b: 184)

Philosophy, he claims, is not at odds with revealed faith although in his main arguments about religion adherents of such faith might differ. His persuasiveness would be evidenced in many subsequent developments, at least in liberal Protestant theology, which rid Christianity of the necessity of doctrinal conformity and thus unwarranted claims to religious knowledge.

Thus, Kant's core argument is that the moral principle of religion – good opposed to evil – is opposed to its delusion: 'Apart from a good life-conduct, anything which the human being supposes that he can do to become well-pleasing to God is mere religious delusion and counterfeit service of God' (Kant 1996b: 190).

> Specifically there can be three kinds of *delusory faith* in overstepping the boundaries of our reason with respect to the supernatural (which according to the laws of reason is neither an object of theoretical or practical use). First, the belief that we have cognition of something through experience which we in fact cannot accept as happening according to objective laws of experience (faith in *miracles*). *Second*, the delusion that we must include among our concepts of reason, as necessary to what is morally best for us, that of which we ourselves form no concept through reason (faith in *mysteries*). *Third*, the delusion that through the use of purely natural means we can bring about an effect which is a mystery to us, namely the influence of God upon our morality (faith in *means of grace*).
>
> (Kant 1996b: 209)

There are four means whereby the devout try to effect the latter (faith in *means of grace*): 'praying', 'church-going', rites of initiation and communion. Church-going, for example,

> thought of as the solemn general external worship of God in a church, inasmuch as it is a sensuous display to the community of believers, is not only a means valuable to each *individual* for his own *edification* but also a duty obligating them collectively, as citizens of a divine state which is to be represented here on Earth.
>
> (Kant 1996b)

Yet church-going as

> a means of grace, as though God were directly served by it and had attached special graces to the celebration of these solemnities ... is a

delusion which might indeed suit the mentality of a good citizen in a political community, and external propriety, yet not only contributes nothing to the quality of the citizen as citizen in the kingdom of heaven but rather debases it.

(Kant 1996b: 212–13)

He makes similar assessments of rituals that bring the community together. For instance, that

oft-repeated solemn ritual of renewal, continuation and propagation of the church-community under the laws of equality (communion), which after the founder of such a church (and at the same time in memory of him) may well assume the form of a ritual communal partaking at the same table.

(Kant 1996b)

This 'expands people's narrow, selfish and intolerant cast of mind, especially in religious matters, to the idea of a cosmopolitan moral community'. But to boast that 'God has attached special graces' to this celebration 'is a delusion which cannot but work counter to the spirit of religion'. It is mere 'priest-craft', 'the dominion that the clergy has usurped over minds by pretending to have exclusive possession of the means of grace' (Kant 1996b: 213–14).

Kant reserves his most scathing remarks for those engaged in prayer. If God is unknowable, prayer and piety (the outward pretence of this knowledge) can be mocked. In what Kant considers the true spirit of prayer, a person will work on themselves; when prayer takes outward and ritual form, a person attempts to work on God. If someone is found perchance in the attitude of prayer, alone, 'Everyone will naturally expect, without my saying so that this individual will fall into confusion or embarrassment, as though caught in a situation of which he should be ashamed.' But why?

Because a human being found talking to himself immediately gives rise to the suspicion that he is having a slight fit of madness, and so we would also judge him (not altogether unjustly) if, though alone, we find him occupied in practices or gestures that we expect only of one who sees somebody else before him, whereas this is not the case in the adduced example.

(Kant 1996b: 210)

If persons cannot effect any support from a God who is beyond human knowledge and outside human experience, from the moral sense comes assurance of God's existence, a moral responsibility to use freedom for good moral ends. Thus, Kant presents a teleological summation in 'The End of all Things' (Kant 1996c):

> The end of all things which go through the hands of human beings, even
> when their purposes are good, is *folly*, i.e. the use of means to their ends
> which are directly opposed to these ends. Wisdom, that is, practical
> reason using means commensurate to the final end of all things – the
> highest good – in full accord with the corresponding rules of measure,
> dwells in God alone.
>
> (Kant 1996c: 238)

The 'only thing which could perhaps be called human wisdom is acting in a
way which is not visibly contrary to the idea of that [divine] wisdom'; that is,
the moral life. The moral life is the ground of the religious life and human
history, above all its political history, an uncertain movement towards that
final end of all things.

From these moral preoccupations are derived, however, not only the principles of the religious but also those of political life. Although his political
theory is less developed than his critical method and his pedagogy even less
so (Kant 1991, 2011), Kant's political ideals are developed in his *Idea for A
Universal History from a Cosmopolitan Point of View* (1784) and *Toward
Perpetual Peace* (1795). Humanity, freed from the constraints of stifling
tradition, could move forward towards its future destiny. In part three of *The
Conflict of the Faculties* (1996d), Kant thus conceives of this as 'An Old
Question Raised Again: Is the Human Race Constantly Progressing?'
(1798). By this time, the democratic revolutions of America and France may
have seemed the political realization of Enlightenment reason. In 'The
History of Mankind and Conjectures on the Beginning of Human History',
Kant exchanges theological, God-centred for human-oriented teleology
(Kant 1991).

Kant's (2007) lesser-known works on anthropology, history, as well as
education, show the implications that arose from his critical philosophy. If
Kant had described his first *Critique* as a Copernican revolution, this revolution would impact on human beings' self-understanding and their sense of
purpose and would provide new templates of education. In his posthumously
published 'Lectures on Pedagogy', beyond the inculcation of a moral sense,
Kant self-evidently saw no role for religion in an enlightened curriculum
(Kant 2007).

Such religiously critical philosophy would provide the ground for further
critiques. Some were positive, like that of Georg Wilhelm Friedrich Hegel
(1770–1831), who would see religion as an integral stage in the development
of human consciousness towards Absolute Knowledge, where human history
is an unfolding of the story of that consciousness (Hegel 1910, 1991, 1981;
also Beiser 1993, 2000, 2008). Ludwig Feuerbach (1804–1872), like Karl
Marx (1818–1883), would describe religion as a form of *false* consciousness,
which must needs be supplanted by philosophy. For Feuerbach, religion thus
always precedes philosophy. In *The Essence of Christianity*, Feuerbach (1854)
argues that philosophy's task is to demonstrate that the consciousness of God

is really a projection of human self-consciousness. It is not that, as in Kant, God cannot be known but that God is not there.

Since the idea of God had around it not only a theological but also a moral, social and political superstructure, all these elements of a civilization of the future would need to be rebuilt on different grounds. Friedrich Nietzsche (1844–1900) is most famous, even for those who have not read him, for declaring that 'God is dead'. The renowned or notorious expression is in *Thus Spoke Zarathustra* (1883–1885). Encountering a holy man praying in the forest Zarathustra asks of his purpose:

> The saint answered: 'I make hymns and sing them; and in making hymns I laugh and weep and mumble: thus do I praise God. With singing, weeping, laughing, and mumbling do I praise the God who is my God. But what dost thou bring us as a gift?'
>
> When Zarathustra had heard these words, he bowed to the saint and said: 'What should I have to give thee! Let me rather hurry hence lest I take aught away from thee!' – And thus they parted from one another, the old man and Zarathustra, laughing like schoolboys.
>
> When Zarathustra was alone, however, he said to his heart: 'Could it be possible! This old saint in the forest hath not yet heard of it, that God is dead!'
>
> (Nietzsche 1974: 41)

In his *On the Genealogy of Morals* (1887), Nietzsche, accepting the episte-mological ground of religious belief as illusory, shows that what follows is the collapse of a whole civilization of ethics (Nietzsche 2006). The death of God required a re-evaluation of ideas of responsibility, law and the political order-ing of society. Grounds however are easier to critique than replace. The new freedom based on a philosophical rejection of religion would be the episte-mological foundation for the social, psychological, political and other sciences. For Nietzsche, in *Beyond Good and Evil*, a 'prelude to a philosophy for the future', written around 1886, published posthumously (Nietzsche 2008), is a pattern for life untrammelled by the simple oppositions of moral-ity or arcane scholarly philosophy unrelated to life, a life of imagination and creativity, freedom, above all freedom from religion.

The philosophical advocates of religion

Philosophical advocates of religion arose alongside its most stringent Enlightenment critics. These advocates accommodated religion to philoso-phy rather than using philosophy for its removal. The required accommodations were often dramatic. The critical move was to identify theology and not religion as the problem.

It was thus in final years of the eighteenth century, amidst an increasingly confident dismissal of religion, Friedrich Schleiermacher (1768–1834), a young Calvinist chaplain in Berlin, wrote his first book, *On Religion: Speeches to its Cultured Despisers*, published in 1799 (Schleiermacher 1893). *On Religion* consists of five 'speeches': the 'Defence'; 'The Nature of Religion'; 'The Cultivation of Religion'; 'Association in Religion, or Church and Priesthood'; and the fifth, 'The Religions'. It made Schleiermacher an early international reputation and, for the next century, *On Religion* was one of the most influential, if unsystematic works of theology to arise from Enlightenment and a popular and accessible, even cheerful religious response to it.

Schleiermacher was socially well connected, mixed in economically affluent and cultured salons – gatherings that were the epitome of 'enlightened' Europe – for whom religion meant little. He saw at first hand the direct impact on the cultured and learned of the rational philosophy of Enlightenment. Although derided by conservative theologians, Schleiermacher's speeches to religion's 'cultured despisers' was a brave and individual work, for he was responding to a philosopher of far greater intellectual status and position than certainly he had at the time, writing as he was in the shadow of Kant. It was also politically courageous, for these were dangerous times to be defending religion. When Schleiermacher was writing his short work, the Revolution across the border in France had not yet failed and news of the Terror had spread. The fate of aristocracies and royalty in France would instil fear in the aristocracies and royalty across Western Europe.

On Religion was then of political as well as intellectual import. The national context was important to Schleiermacher. This historical and political context is often overlooked. Schleiermacher 'opens out ineluctably towards history, substantiating the complex conditionings of historical life rather than ignoring them' (Reynolds 2002: 51). For all its supposedly universal appeal, *On Religion* is a particularly local affair. 'If I am thus impelled to speak of religion,' writes Schleiermacher,

> and to deliver my testimony, to whom should I turn if not to the sons of Germany? . . . Where else is an audience for my speech? It is not blind predilection for my native soil or for my fellows in government and language, that makes me speak thus, but the deep conviction that you alone are capable, as well as worthy, of having awakened in you the sense for holy and divine things.
>
> (Schleiermacher 1893)

By contrast, he describes the English as '[t]hose 'proud Islanders whom many unduly honour' and considers them attendant to nothing but 'gain and enjoyment' who 'know nothing of religion, save that all preach devotion to ancient usages and defend its institutions' and see in religion little but 'protection wisely cherished by the constitution against the natural enemy of the state'. The success of Christian missionary activity through expanding British Empire is compared with a decline in belief in England. Missionary activity for the British is an aspect of the 'political and mercantile'; the 'pure interest of Christian piety does not dominate as appears in this, that the religious needs at home have been attended to much later and with much less brilliant result' (Schleiermacher 1893: 14).

Revolutionary France he dismisses for obvious reasons: 'On them, one who honours religion can hardly endure to look, for in every act and almost in every word, they tread its holiest ordinances under foot.' Rousseau's 'civil religion' nevertheless remains a tacit influence: 'Might it sometime arrive that this office of mediator cease, and a fairer destiny await the priesthood of humanity!' Schleiermacher emphasized feelings and emotions in defining and defending religion, 'a sense and taste for the Infinite in the finite' (Schleiermacher 1893: 15–16).

But he is scathing, too, of Germany. Here, the aesthetic and philosophical have replaced the divine: 'In your ornamented dwellings, the only sacred things to be met with are the sage maxims of our wise men, and the splendid compositions of our poets.' Here, 'Suavity and sociability, art and science have so fully taken possession of your minds, that no room remains for the eternal and holy Being that lies beyond the world.' Since, he suggests, his countrymen have succeeded in making their 'earthly life so rich and varied', they 'no longer stand in need of an eternity' (Schleiermacher 1893: 9).

To this point, condemning a this-worldly focus in religion, Schleiermacher can be loosely compared with Otto. However, although their premises may have been similar, their conclusions were very different. For where Otto sought the holy demarcated from social and political, Schleiermacher regarded the holy as integral to the commonplace, that 'sense and taste for the Infinite in the finite' (Schleiermacher 1893: 5).

Schleiermacher's adjustment to this rationalization of religion would, however, unintentionally prepare the ground for later psychological and social sciences:

> Those of you who are accustomed to regard religion simply as a malady of the soul, usually cherish the idea that if the evil is not to be quite subdued, it is at least more endurable, so long as it only infects individuals here and there.
>
> (Schleiermacher 1893)

Schleiermacher also presages a very modern-day social, psychological and political interpretation and use of religion, fearing that the damaging aspects of religion, if not corrected, might infect the body politic: 'On the other hand, the common danger is increased and everything put in jeopardy by too close association among the patients.' Schleiermacher writes of the need for 'due precautions against infection and a healthy spiritual atmosphere' that 'may allay the paroxysms and weaken, if they do not destroy, the virus ... The evil would be accompanied by the most dangerous symptoms and be far more deadly being nursed and heightened by the proximity of the infected'.

For Schleiermacher, this debased religion requires a wholesale redress of ecclesiastical influence: 'Hence your opposition to the church, to every institution meant for the communication of religion is always more violent than your opposition to religion itself, and priests.' The latter he describes as 'the most hated among men' (Schleiermacher 1893: 104).

The future of religion, rid of institutional hampering, would be 'quiet', allowing each to 'would illumine himself and others'. There would be 'communication of holy thoughts and feelings' through 'an easy interchange'. A 'whispered word would then be understood, where now the clearest expression cannot escape misconception'. Freed from the need for clerical interference, the people 'could crowd together into the Holy of Holies' where once they stood only in 'the outer courts'. Religion must therefore seek 'refuge from the coarse barbarism and the cold worldly mind of the age' (Schleiermacher 1893: 13). There is no solace to be found in scripture since, of the 'true work of religion, you would find little even in the sacred books' (Schleiermacher 1893: 15). 'Belief' must be distinguished from 'a mixture of opinions about God and the world'. Religious *practice* cannot be infected by doctrine: 'Piety cannot be an instinct craving for a mess of metaphysical and ethical crumbs' (Schleiermacher 1893: 13):

> To a pious mind religion makes everything holy, even unholiness and commonness, whether he comprehends it or does not comprehend it, whether it is embraced in his system of thought, or lies outside, whether it agrees with his peculiar mode of acting or disagrees.
>
> (Schleiermacher 1893: 50)

'These charges' he proposes 'do not touch religion'. They rest rather 'upon the confusion between religion and that knowledge which belongs to theology'. Knowledge 'whatever be its value . . . is to be always distinguished from religion' (Schleiermacher 1893: 50). We are dealing with, he writes, 'action as an exercise of feeling, not with any symbolical or significant action meant to represent feeling'. The effects of 'those dogmas and opinions that would join themselves more closely to religion than is fitting' are apparent. They 'are only designations and descriptions of feeling'. They are 'knowledge about feeling and in no way an immediate knowledge' (Schleiermacher 1893: 53). Schleiermacher envisages a future 'happy time' when 'everyone can freely exercise and use his sense, at the very first awaking, of the higher powers, in sacred youth, under the care of paternal wisdom, all who are capable will participate in religion' and with 'sacred reserve' lay 'bare everything of the relations of the Universe'. Here, 'All that is human is holy, for all is divine' (Schleiermacher 1893: 144).

What Schleiermacher conceived as a sense that 'All that is human is holy, for all is divine', Hegel raises to a system. Where, for Schleiermacher, the divine is sensed, for Hegel it is known. Georg Wilhelm Friedrich Hegel (1770–1831), German idealist philosopher, was born only a decade before

Kant's first work of critical philosophy and he was educated in the philosophical tradition which Kant had come to dominate. Training initially as a seminarian at Tübingen, it was here he met Hölderlin, the poet, and Friedrich Schelling, the philosopher. He was completing his studies during the early years of the French Revolution, which he regarded with more idealistic fervour than had Schleiermacher. Tutoring for a living for his early adult years, it was not until 1801 when he obtained the post of lecturer at Jena University before, in 1805, obtaining a professorship. In 1807, he published his first major work, *Phenomenology of Mind*, which contains the essence of a philosophy and a view of history which would have nearly as much influence as Kant and, in the political sphere, more so. Human consciousness is a journey towards Absolute Knowledge. For the human consciousness, the highest mark of which is reason, is Spirit becoming conscious through human being. Science is the systematic realization of this consciousness, which does not see reason as veiling but revealing religion. Contra Kant, reason is not the limiting of religion but its fulfilment; contra Schleiermacher, feeling is not separate from concept but an aspect of it. Scientific knowledge incorporates all knowledge and the ultimate aim of the Hegelian system is Absolute Knowledge. It is a philosophy that does not simply extend epistemology to teleology, the path towards knowledge is teleology. Thus, in the preface to the *Phenomenology of Mind*: 'The systematic development of truth in scientific form can alone be the true shape in which truth exists' (Hegel 1910: 70).

Hegel comments that, for many (indirectly countering Schleiermacher), the Absolute 'is not to be grasped in conceptual form but felt, intuited; it is not its conception but in the feeling of it and intuition of it that are to have the say and find expression'. Philosophy is thus expected not so much 'to bring chaotic conscious life back to the orderly ways of thought' but 'restore the feeling of existence'. It wants from philosophy 'not so much insight as edification': 'The beautiful, the holy, the eternal, religion, love – these are the bait required to awaken the desire to bite: not the notion, but ecstasy, not the march of cold necessity in the subject-matter, but ferment and enthusiasm' (Hegel 1910: 72).

'Now', however, Hegel suggests, human interests are 'so deeply rooted in the earthly that we require a like power to have them raised above that level'. Like 'a wanderer in the desert craving for the merest mouthful of water', by 'the little which can thus satisfy the needs of the human spirit we can measure the extent of its loss'.

This path 'does not suit the character of science'. The person 'who only seeks edification, who wants to envelop in mist the manifold diversity of his earthly existence and thought, and craves after the vague enjoyment of this vague and indeterminate Divinity – he may look where he likes to find this' (Schleiermacher's 'all is divine'). Philosophy 'must beware of wishing to be edifying': 'Still less must this kind of contentment, which holds science in contempt, take upon itself to claim that raving obscurantism of this sort is something higher than science.'

Moreover, when this unreflective emotional knowledge makes a pretence of having immersed its own very self in the depths of the absolute Being and of philosophizing in all holiness and truth, it hides from itself the fact that instead of devotion to God, it rather, by this contempt for all measurable precision and definiteness, simply attests in its own case the fortuitous character of its content and, in the other, endows God with its own caprice.

(Hegel 1910: 74–5)

When such minds 'commit themselves to the unrestrained ferment of sheer emotion, they think that, by putting a veil over self-consciousness, and surrendering all understanding, they are thus God's beloved ones' (Hegel 1910: 75).

For Hegel, nothing less than knowledge of Absolute Truth will suffice and this age of reason is the time when we realize the possibility. For 'it is not difficult to see that our epoch is a birth-time, and a period of transition', a time when the spirit 'has broken with the old order of things hitherto prevailing, and with the old ways of thinking, and is in the mind to let them all sink into the depths of the past and to set about its own transformation'. It is 'never at rest, but carried along the stream of progress ever onward'. Enlightenment is a disintegration of the old, the renewal of all:

This gradual crumbling to pieces, which did not alter the general look and aspect of the whole, is interrupted by the sunrise, which, in a flash and at a single stroke, brings to view the form and structure of the new world.

(Hegel 1910: 75)

Phenomenology of Mind (Spirit) from this beginning develops a system which begins with the question of how we can be certain of truth (in chapter 1, Hegel discusses consciousness in relation to sense experience; in chapter 2, perception and the possibility of deception; in chapter 3, 'force' or nature and the place of consciousness within it). From here (in chapter 4), he develops the nature of self-certainty and forms of consciousness in historical context. In chapter 5 is developed the certainty of 'truth of reason' as the realization of consciousness, Spirit. Guided by this certainty, Spirit finds itself in 'self-estrangement', expressed through and yet restrained by 'the discipline of culture and civilization': 'Spirit comes into being, *History,* is the process of becoming in terms of knowledge, a conscious self-mediating process – Spirit externalized and emptied into Time'. In the final chapters, Hegel discusses the role of religion in this evolutionary development (chapter 7, religion in general, that is natural and revealed religion) towards (in chapter 8), 'Absolute Knowledge'. Philosophy is the realization that

This immediate existence is at the same time not solely and simply immediate consciousness; it is *religious* consciousness. This immediacy means

not only an existent self-consciousness, but also the purely thought-constituted or Absolute Being; and these meanings are inseparable.
(Hegel 1910: 122)

Being is ultimately thought, consciousness and philosophy the realization, the moving toward that knowledge of Absolute Being.

Liberal theology originates here. What begins as an accommodation of religion with reason in Schleiermacher is elevated to a religion of reason in Hegel and a religious pluralism which sees truth everywhere manifest at differing levels of evolutionary consciousness. If, for Hegel, Christianity is a peak of such consciousness, it remains revealed religion and revealed religion is an evolutionary stage, a passage from those distinctions between the sacred and the profane, the holy and the unholy. Human beings can reach directly in the here and now to the divine, the holy; if Schleiermacher declares 'all that is human is holy, for all is divine', Hegel systematizes it, provides the narrative of Absolute Being raised to conscious in *human* being.

From this arises diverse forms of theology unified by a spirit of accommodation with modernity. From its leading late nineteenth to early/mid-twentieth century exponents like Adolf von Harnack (2009) and the demythologizing theology of Rudolf Bultmann (1953), the path is to Bonhoeffer's (2001) 'religionless Christianity', *The Secular City* of Harvey Cox (1965), Paul Van Buren's (1963) *The Secular Meaning of the Gospel*; the self-proclaimed 'new morality' of Joseph Fletcher's (1997) *Situation Ethics*; the systematic existentialist 'death of God' theology of Paul Tillich (1973, 1975, 1976); to more modest but no less influential efforts such as John Robinson's (2001) *Honest to God*, Don Cupitt's (2003) *Sea of Faith* and Brian Mountford's (2011) *Christian Atheist*.

There were many counter-responses. The long nineteenth century saw a prolonged, systematic and outright rejection of the Enlightenment and all it stood for, most famously in Pius IX's *Syllabus of Errors*, officially 'A Syllabus containing the most important errors of our time, which have been condemned by our Holy Father Pius IX in Allocutions, at Consistories, in Encyclicals, and other Apostolic Letters', which had been prefaced by the encyclical *Quanta Cura (Concerning Current Errors)* (EWTN, 2013; Haag, 1912; Vatican 1864a, 1864b). These errors were reaffirmed in Leo XIII's *Inscrutabili Dei Consilio* (Vatican 1878) and most notably in Pius X's *Pascendi Dominici Gregis* (Vatican 1907) Modernism, wrote Pius X, was a 'synthesis of all heresies'. The same tradition today seeks no separation of faith from reason but gives as ever a primacy to revealed truth, as in John Paul II's encyclical *Fides et Ratio*, on faith and reason (Vatican 1998).

Protestant theology also resisted the radical accommodation to reason and modernity, reaffirming Biblical inerrancy and resisting the natural theology, which, it perceived, had led to this undermining of revealed truth. The first systematic Protestant reaction was defined by *The Fundamentals* (Torrey 1917), and later by Karl Barth's (2012) *Church Dogmatics*. Torrey's *The*

Fundamentals: A Testimony to the Truth, published between 1910 and 1915, reaffirmed what can be safely considered as the Reformation's founding orthodoxy, the inerrancy and ultimate authority of the Bible. Barth's *Church Dogmatics*, his 'theology of crisis', was a redressing of the imbalances brought about by liberal Protestant theology and distanced his position from any natural theology. When Emil Brunner, a Barthian ally, asked whether God was revealed in nature as well as Scripture, the vehemence of Barth's response is apparent in his 1934 rejoinder: 'No! An Answer to Emil Brunner' (Barth 1934). Natural theology was regarded as the undermining source not a solution to a theology grounded in revealed truth.

Postmodern philosophy, especially philosophy of language, provided other sources for the defence of the liberal position, both in affirming that religion was still possible if narrow doctrinal alliances were modified. The succour came from a surprising source, from within philosophy itself. From the hermeneutics of Dilthey (2010), through Gadamer (2004) to Ricoeur (again, for example, 1974, 1978) and Derrida's (1984) 'deconstruction', all provided a re-examination of language which undermined the certainties of Enlightenment reason. Modern philosophy of language opened philosophy itself to autocritique – what Ricoeur called the 'conflict of interpretations'. Derrida's (1984) *Margins of Philosophy* illustrated this by examining the use of metaphor in the classical Greek tradition of philosophy, which is the root of the modern (Socker 2006). This was most obvious in the use of the metaphor of the cave in Plato's *Republic*. This language was contained by its very use of metaphorical imprecision. Derrida (2001), in *Writing and Difference*, argued that language always is once removed from meaning; language as a *sign* has within itself an inbuilt distance from that to which it is referring, providing a perpetual epistemological distance between that to which it was referring and the reality it hoped to express (Stocker 2006). Such analyses allowed philosophy to take new metaphorical turns which rein-vigorated theology (Caputo 2002; Caputo and Vatimmo 2009).

The argument which undergirded theology was this: if modernity was based upon a critique of the pre-modern, the traditional, *religious* under-standings of the world, then the critique of modernity allowed some post-modern reassessment of the sacred (Ricoeur 1980). If the *critique* of *critical* philosophy provided a post-modern reinstatement of the sacred, theology potentially has renewed epistemological legitimacy.

Hart (2000) tells this story of theology's appropriation of deconstruction and postmodern philosophy. Taylor (1987) shows that the implications for theology are not so simple: theology becomes 'a/theology', the borderline between belief and unbelief blurred. For conceding the imprecision of language undermines doctrinal certainty every bit as much the theological critiques of modernity. Derrida argued that the Babel narrative 'does not merely figure the irreducible multiplicity of tongues; it illustrates an incom-pletion, the impossibility of finishing, of totalizing, of saturating, of completing something on the order of edification, architectural construction, system, architectonics' (Derrida 2002; cf. Bartholomew 1998). Not all did so. This is evident in the emergent divide between 'analytical' ('Anglo-Saxon'/British American) philosophers, who disregarded such post-modern developments as nonsense, retaining faith in logic and reason, and 'continental' philosophers who embraced new ways of doing philosophy. Nevertheless, 'post-modern' philosophy of language provides no lesser theological difficulties than those critiques that Schleiermacher took so seriously from his contemporary Kant. These are all matters with which philosophy in religious education has had to contend.

Philosophy and religious education

Philosophy's various rejections of and reorientations towards theology and religion *per se* are mirrored in similarly diffuse ways in religious education. Philosophical *themes* haves long featured in religious education, as the history of ideas makes plain. Only in recent decades have philosophical *methods* been appropriated as an underpinning of religious education. By presenting religions rationally, assessing their claims to knowledge, their truth claims, we can justify the place of religious education as a subject along the lines of any other subject in a liberal education.

Religious education and the appropriation of philosophy

In the philosophy of education, John Dewey (1859–1952) would exert some of the most significant impact, both in philosophy of education narrowly conceived but also in the relation of a critically engaged education to political structures (Dewey 2008a, 2008b; for an overview, see Phillips 2008). *Democracy and Education: An Introduction to the Philosophy of Education* exemplifies this (Dewey 1916). It is also notable for its neglect of any aspect of religion as part of a liberal, that is, enlightened education. In this regard, where the rise of philosophy gave education a distinctly critical as well as political flavour, the traditions from which Dewey principally draws are obviously excluding of religion; in his analysis of the lineage of a philosophically critical and democratically engaged education, his historical account begins (obviously) in Greek antiquity and leaps nearly two millennia to the eighteenth-century Enlightenment, citing Jean-Jacques Rousseau (1712–1778) as a particularly important, formative influence on his thinking.

For religious education, this has presented palpable problems. Evans (1944), in examining religious education and some of its critics, identifies the philosophical critics as amongst the most vociferous. In the 1940s and 1950s, philosophical rationalism and scientific empiricism were presented as an established faith (cf. Dewey 1980) and amongst many challenges to the validity of – the grounds and justifications for – religious education (Harner 1950).

Seymour (1995) here identifies a major shift in the theory and practice of religious educators in 'normal' schools. Between the nineteenth century, when Christianity, 'albeit a strictly Anglo-Protestant variety', framed aims, purposes and values of education, to the twentieth century when, with increased urbanization and secularization, the philosophy of education took on what was perceived as a more value neutral role: 'If, in the nineteenth century normal school, religion was expected to supply its purpose and basic values, in the early twentieth century school of education, educational philosophy was expected to fill this role'. As Seymour points out, philosophy of education would become a subfield in its own right, yet 'There was a time in the history of educational thought when philosophy of education and religious education were close allies' (Seymour 1995: 318).

If, however, the early decades of the twentieth century marked a separation of philosophy and religious education, towards the end of the century, certainly by the late 1970s and the early 1980s, critical philosophy was seen as having potential value to and within religious education (see, for example, Berry 1983). The philosophy for children movement might be said to have inadvertently facilitated this development (Kennedy 2012).

The initiative to include more philosophy in schools, as conceived by Lipman and Sharp (1978; Lipman *et al.* 1980; also, Golding 2011; Vansieleghem and Kennedy 2011a, 2011b) would see children as having the capacity for critical thinking beyond that assumed by developmental psychologists (Vermeer 2012). For others, philosophy for children is about 'accomplishing modernity' by providing children with the philosophical tools young enough to enable them to achieve real autonomy of thought and choice in later life (Oliverio 2012). A 'humanistic practice with roots in the Hellenistic tradition of philosophy as a way of life given to the search for meaning', 'its emphasis on qualitative experience, collaborative inquiry and democratic society', its roots lie in shared agnostic and atheistic traditions of Western philosophy from antiquity through Enlightenment and, in twentieth century, to 'American pragmatism with its emphasis on qualitative experience, collaborative inquiry and democratic society, and in American and Soviet social learning theory':

> The programme has attracted overlapping and conflicting criticism from religious and social conservatives who do not want children to question traditional values, from educational psychologists who believe that certain kinds of thinking are beyond children of certain ages, from philosophers who define their discipline as theoretical and exegetical, from critical theorists who see the programme as politically compliant, and from postmodernists who see it as scientistic and imperialist.
>
> (Gregory 2011: 199; also Gregory and Granger 2012)

Approaches using philosophy in religious education emerged almost simultaneously (Hand 2006; Hobson 1999; Holley 1978; Sealey 1982). Philosophy for children also emphasizes 'dialogue' in ideas, aesthetic, affective and cognitive (Bleazby 2012). Just so Puolimatka and Tirri (2000) argue for 'intelligent belief' that unites 'thinking and feeling'. Philosophy for children encourages dialogical engagement sensitive to epistemological disagreement:

> Dialogical enquiry in religious education in our classroom communities, where there can be conflict over truth claims, has an especially valuable part to play in helping young people develop their own sense of identity and belonging. Through helping them to work out, with their peers, their values and beliefs about questions relating to the origin of things and what things really matter to them, philosophical enquiry in religious education facilitates a growing appreciation of belief and culture in the world today.
>
> (Lewis and Chandley 2012)

Dialogical thinking emerges as central to inter-religious education (Hull 1997; Lied 2009a, 2009b). The religious educator is facilitator, providing bridges between religious difference (Engebretson *et al.* 2010).

Biesta (2010) argues that this risks relativism – not elucidating but compromising truth. Since philosophy for children inclines to an engagement with the secular through publicly acceptable reason, it risks an 'instrumentalism' in being used for promoting liberal secular or other political goals (Biesta 2011). Both problems – of epistemological relativism and political manipulation – have parallels in religious education. For some, it is an unacceptable means of promoting particular political ways of thought through teaching religion. As Pike (2008) puts it, (critically) religious education seems increasingly to encourage 'faith in citizenship', all the more potent under the guise of critical, philosophical engagement with political ideas, a process of the societal inculcation of political value through education which has a very ancient history (Heater 2004).

The problem of *relativism* is especially apparent where discussions of conflicting *religious* truths are the focus and one of the resolutions is a religiously pluralistic understanding of truth (see for example, Davis 2010). Wright's (2003a) *Religion, Education and Post-Modernity* is a systematic attempt to counter these post-modern challenges to truth in religious education. In a religiously plural world of competing truth, sociocultural as well philosophical–theological, truth claims become a problem for resolution in religious education (Wright 2007, 2008).

Strhan (2010), however, argues that a narrowly conceived, critical philosophy fails to take seriously the developments in philosophy that engage with different ways of knowing. She argues against the most systematized approach to doing philosophy in religious education, critical religious education (on philosophy and post-modern epistemologies in religious education, see Cooling 2005; again, Wright 2003a).

For Wright, the 'questioning of the existential relevance of academic knowledge has its roots in the Enlightenment's ideal of a pure objective knowledge untainted by the vagaries of subjective opinion'. Wright argues that the 'truth' encountered operates on two levels: immanent and transcendent. In the immanent, it is a 'pragmatic approach to truth, in which religion is taught not as an end in itself, but as a tool for encouraging tolerance and mutual understanding in a culturally divided society'. In the transcendent: 'insofar as religion is viewed as a human response to transcendence, the only valid theological option is that of a universal theology in which all traditions are regarded as being equally true' (Wright 2003: 287–8). Astley *et al.* (2012) argue:

> It is no longer sufficient to teach about the history of religions: religion is not relegated to the past. It is no longer sufficient to teach about the observable outward phenomena of religions: religion is not restricted to practices, artefacts, and buildings observable in the outside world. It is also necessary to take seriously what religions believe about themselves, and what religions believe about other religions. Seen from the inside, religions deal in the currency of truth. For the religions themselves, truth matters. Truth-claims can lead to harmony and peace, but they may also engender discord and violence. What ultimately counts is how one set of truth-claims confronts or embraces the truths claimed by other, different voices.
>
> (Astley *et al.* 2012)

Similarly, Astley's 'Theological Reflection on the Nature of Religious Truth' (2012) examines this in terms of how difference in theological understandings of truth or the bases (in reasoning, authority, revelation) might allow for their resolution. However, no satisfactory answer has as yet been provided as to what ground there is for resolution of the claims of religious truth through philosophy in the classroom.

As Carr (2012) points out, simply because, or even if, we live in a post-secular world (which Carr doubts) the cultural, sociopolitical reassertion of religion does not mean that religion has found renewed epistemological justification (for a wide discussion, see Radford 2012). Thus, Hyslop-Margison and Peterson (2012) challenge the idea that study of religion in education could be legitimized by examination of epistemic truth claims. They suggest such approaches face three 'insurmountable hurdles to become an achievable education objective': first, a failure to articulate 'how religious claims might be evaluated epistemologically'; second, given that there are no clearly identifiable standards by which to measure these sorts of theological claims epistemologically, 'an untenable situation is created for schools, parents, students and teachers' which may enhance, rather than resolve, religious conflict; third, the epistemic foundations, the *ground*, 'required to support religious truth claims is itself epistemologically problematic' (see also Rosenblith 2012).

Two contrasting solutions have been proposed. Hand (2007) provides a philosophical defence, although on intriguingly interesting grounds, asking whether religious education is possible. Examining whether what is taught in religious education is a distinct form of knowledge, he argues that, if it were, then it would be difficult to teach this from a secular liberal perspective, since to do so would be to give credence to that which (by the philosophical tradition from Kant onwards) cannot be taught, since it cannot be known. Since, Hand argues, religion does not constitute a distinct form of knowledge, it is possible to teach it within said secular liberal education. Those opposed to the argument (Barnes 2007a; cf. Hand 2007; McKinney 2011) suggest that religion *is* a distinct form of knowledge but claim that it may *nevertheless* be taught. Philosophical tradition, their argument goes, allows for the interrogation of truth claims and therefore religious truth claims. These *are* distinctive claims – doctrines, metaphysics, views of the world and the afterlife, religious experience – which, as truth claims, can even in secular liberal education be subject to open and critical, that is, philosophical scrutiny. The other response, from a critical religious educator, is by Barnes (2006), whose assertion is that the answer is not found in the resolution of epistemological difference but in its acceptance. That said, there are in this debate often references to critical philosophical approaches as being opposed to those models of thinking which resist them; those forms of religious belief and practice which stress personal experience. Wright (2003a), for example, dismisses whole swathes of Protestant tradition, such as the Great Awakenings in America, pietism too, and utterly ignores whole traditions of Catholic mystical tradition. But, more obviously, the philosophical, the 'reasonable' approaches to religion and religious education are presented – *qua* their place in liberal education – as a bastion against 'fundamentalism' of all kinds (Streib 2001b).

There is another aspect to philosophical perspectives becoming a vital part of religious education. Philosophers of education have also been some of the most adamant objectors to religious education, in most part because moral or ethical education fulfils any valid role that religious education might have in liberal education (see, for example, White 2004; cf. Wright 2005; Carr 1994; 2007; Strhan 2010; Tilson 2011); but, more significantly, the opponents of religion have also found a direct stronghold within religious education itself.

Critical philosophical engagement now means the inclusion of religiously sceptical philosophical stances, which, historically and in contemporary context, remain hostile to religion. Religious education has thus witnessed growing attention to atheism, agnosticism, secular humanism, and so forth. Philosophies adversarial to religion have become integral to teaching about it. Some regard this positively; one advocate argues 'that children and young people can learn from atheistic beliefs and values for their spiritual and moral development' (Watson 2008a, 2010). Through two figures antagonistic to religion – Bertrand Russell (1872–1970) and Jean Paul Sartre (1905–1980) – Watson explores atheism as 'faith' and 'illustrates atheism's spiritual and moral potential'. Religious education should transmute 'preferably under a new name' so that it can 'continue to be a valuable curriculum subject' as long as it offers 'a broader, more inclusive spiritual education which includes positive accounts of atheistic beliefs' (Watson 2008a: 49).

Chater and Erricker's (2012) *Does Religious Education Have a Future?* is based on a not-dissimilar premise. Indeed, it sees philosophical scepticism not as an element of religious education but, if it is to survive, as its future, arguing for a radical reform of religious education in which the subject is set free from 'religious concerns', enabling religious educators philosophically to engage with religion in political context.

As we note of the Enlightenment, the philosophical invariably becomes indistinguishable from the political. In modern times, these philosophical–political developments are also as political as they are philosophical or theological. Their lineage is in, of all conflicts, the Cold War, to an even greater extent than the origins of the United Nations. Their moment of formal appearance, though, can be as precisely identified as 1981, the year of the United Nations' (1981) *Declaration against Declaration on the Elimination of All Forms of Intolerance and of Discrimination Based on Religion or Belief.*

The incorporation of agnostic, atheistic, humanistic understandings of ('or belief') within religious education curricula today arises here, at least in terms of international human rights. Since that time (the early 1980s), atheism and agnosticism have increasingly been recognized as forms of belief and a source of scientific study as a belief system within state-sponsored atheistic regimes (see, for example, Binns 1982). With the end of the Cold War, unforced non-belief has new-found educational legitimacy. In a special issue of the *Journal of Contemporary Religion* on *Atheism and Secularism*, religiously sceptical and even religiously antagonistic 'beliefs' are given the same scholarly weighting as religious faith itself (Keysar 2012; Zuckerman 2010). Cimino and Smith (2011) examine how 'the new atheist phenomenon' has been 'interpreted and appropriated by those involved in atheist and secular humanist organizations' to form not the isolated views of individual atheists but an ever more organized social and community-oriented phenomenon directed to 'the publicly emerging needs and desires of secularists'. For Cimino and Smith, 'a highly diverse population of secularists with a common and general set of issues and ideas' are now themselves a 'community'. Epistemologically, liberal theologies have divested belief of credal commitment; we ironically now talk of *The Atheist's Creed* (Palmer 2010).

For good or ill, philosophical approaches legitimize critical engagement in religious education. This critical engagement has its origins in philosophical stances often but not always entirely hostile to religion. Such attitudes to religion were amongst the most formative influences in many of the disciplines which emerged from the Enlightenment. As a notable theorist of religion comments: 'The social "scientific"; study of religion originated in atheism and the basic theses pursued today, especially by psychologists and anthropologists, are little changed since they were first proposed by militant opponents of religion in the seventeenth and early eighteenth century' (Stark 1999a: 41). Atheism itself has become a form of collective identity as much as individual belief. Studies of atheism, once restricted to state-sponsored forms of non-belief, have now become part of the scientific study of 'religion' through a range of disciplines, from the sociological to the psychological (Beit-Hallahmi 2012; Bullivant and Ruse 2013; Hunsberger and Altemeyer 2003; Martin, 2007). Thus the scientific study of atheism has now become prevalent in sociology (Bullivant 2008) and mainstream psychology (Wildman *et al.* 2012). In psychotherapeutic practice, atheism and agnosticism as much as religious faith are shown as factors – for psychotherapists and patients alike – often exposing unresolved conflicts between atheism, agnosticism and religious belief (Magaldi-Dopman *et al.* 2011). Atheism has now not only its own creeds but also an increasingly formalised history of its own evolution (Joshi 2011). Through such pathways, religiously sceptical philosophies now have more than a foothold in religious education. They have attained a legal as well as epistemological legitimacy, as law legitimizes religion *or* belief.

It seems that Feuerbach (1854) was prescient in declaring that 'what is regarded as atheism today will be religion tomorrow'. It might have bemused him to think that religious education was one of the means by which this transformation was facilitated.

Summary

Philosophy in religious education is, then, associated with not simply the encounter of philosophical themes – philosophical arguments for or against God, religious experience, and so forth – but a *method* of making judgements on religious truth, however this truth is conceived. Religious education has focused on the reintegration of philosophical themes and methods as a way of doing religious education.

Critical, philosophically engaged religious engagement is certainly the sort of religious education within the bounds of reason of which Kant might have approved. Although it is unlikely, too, if we read his *Lectures on Pedagogy* that Kant (2007b) would have approved of any religious education. Yet such approaches can also be and even inevitably are self-limiting. Kant argued that there can be no way of knowing the transcendent. Claims that personal prayer or religious experience represent such knowledge are false. Epistemologically, religious claims to knowledge or truth are simply nonsensical. The transcendent is as far beyond human experience as it is beyond human knowledge. Essential as philosophy has been to theology throughout the history of ideas, any claim therefore to ground religious education *simply* on critical philosophy seems, in its own terms, curiously self-defeating.

3 The natural sciences and religious education

Introduction

The common lineage of philosophy and the natural sciences is apparent in science's origins as 'natural philosophy' (for a critical historical overview, see Harrison 2010; Heilbron 2003). In this vein, Aristotle wrote on biology and physics, as well as ethics and metaphysics. In the Christian tradition, natural philosophy, like natural theology, was a way of understanding a world whose first cause was God. Hannam (2010) takes the argument to a further extreme, that medieval philosophy and theology were the foundations of modern of science. Hannam's trail through the medieval world draws together Boethius' (480–525) *The Consolation of Philosophy* (Boethius 2012), Gerbert of Aurillac, later Pope Sylvester II (c. 940–1003), Anselm (1033–1109), and Peter Abelard (1079–1142). Hannam takes a conventional view of the natural theology in the High Middle Ages where observation of the world is a means of knowing of God's existence and operation in creation, knowledge of God confirming of but in no way inconsistent with the revealed truths of scripture (see also Brooke 1993; Lindberg 2008). Here, Thomas Aquinas (1225–1274) is the theologian who integrated Catholic Christianity with classical, especially Aristotelian, philosophy during the Renaissance in ways managed by no other Scholastic philosopher. Natural philosophy and natural theology were subdisciplines of the one integrated science. Other Renaissance figures that Hannam covers are: Roger Bacon (1214–1292), Richard of Wallingford (1292–1336), William of Ockham (1287–1347), Nicolaus Copernicus (1472–1543), Johann Kepler (1571–1630), Galileo Galilei (1564–1642). The history of modern science is complex with ongoing entangling and disentangling of epistemological relations with religion. Given the social and political context of science and religion in history, inevitably, such epistemological disputes often for all sides become fevered moral arguments.

The natural sciences and religion

The history of science and religion in the modern world is often and rightly conceived as a history of conflict, which divided natural philosophy and natural theology, imprecisely and messily, in the lives of individual scientists. Nicolaus Copernicus (1473–1543) and Galileo Galilei (1564–1642) are the two figures who stand out. 1543 saw publication of Copernicus' *De Revolutionibus* (*On the Revolutions of the Heavenly Spheres*), conceiving, *contra* Ptolemy, not an Earth- but a sun-centred solar system. Copernicus's title would indicate a revolution not only in physical but also in theological understandings of the universe.

Galileo's *Dialogue Concerning the Two Chief World Systems* (1632) is a shorter and, although technical, more accessible work than *De Revolutionibus*. *De Revolutionibus'* accessibility drew attention to the profound implications of its thesis. Unlike Copernicus, Galileo had the advantage of the telescope and, with empirical measurement, supported the sun-centred view of the solar system. Galileo's appearance and ultimate submission before the Grand Inquisition for heresy is now *par excellence* the epitome of conflict in religion and science. The former is obscurantist, knowledge denying; the latter is truth and knowledge seeking. Of the penitential Psalms, Galileo was required to recite was Psalm 102: 'In the beginning you laid the foundations of the Earth, and the heavens are the work of your hands'. Galileo ironically never denied these truths but he had undermined a view of the universe in which the Earth and therefore human beings were not at its centre.

The scientific adversaries of religion

Sir Isaac Newton (1642–1727), a deist, believed that there was a Creator but not necessarily one who took an interventionist interest in the workings of the universe. God made the laws but he did not break them. (In eighteenth century philosophy this became a critical discussion about miracles, and Hume's attack on their possibility.) If God does not intervene in the universe, it raises questions fundamental to Biblical revelation based on such intervention. If the Bible is the story of God's intervention in the world and, through the incarnation to save it, the idea of a Creator who did his work and then stood back to watch its operations unfold can hardly be seen as theologically orthodox. Newton's position is ambivalent, since his pastimes were hardly *scientifically* orthodox either; notably his passion for alchemy (a love of gold marked by appointment as Master of the Royal Mint) and Bible reading, with a particular fascination with the prophetic books of Daniel and Apocalypse (Ackroyd 2008).

Copernicus and Galileo may have redrawn the Earth's place in the cosmos but they did not challenge its origins. Neither did the foundational biological scientists. Newton's deism, more presumed than articulated, suggested that God did not intervene in the universe he created. Pioneering studies in biology caused scandal, even when it was suggested that God did intervene. Carl Linnaeus (1707–1778), later *Count* Linnaeus, the pioneer of modern taxonomy in two key works, of which there were many editions – *Systema Naturae*

(1735) and *Species Plantarum* (1753) – formalized the binomial naming system, one name for genus and the other for species. He conceived of his work as simply recording the glorious diversity of God's creation. Linnaeus formalized natural history (itself a development from natural philosophy) through species classification, which would be unproblematic until the classification included human beings. A century earlier, it was the Reverend John Ray (1627–1705), a naturalist and minister of the Church of England, who placed human beings into a natural history from which Christian traditions had separated them. For Ray, human beings were primates, superior but nevertheless related 'wise man' or *homo sapiens* (Hancock and Skinner 2000).

No biologist until the early eighteenth century had systematized the view that species change over time. Genesis taught that the species were created on their respective days and this implied that they were created complete. Comte de Buffon (1707–1788) in a 44-volume natural history published over half a century, his *Histoire Naturelle* (1749–1804), had begun to suggest that species did change and develop. The work was published as a limited edition in the days when science was undertaken largely by those of private means. If the pressures of profit were not felt by many undertaking science then, the pressures of public opinion were. Even in a post-Reformation Europe of divided Catholic and Protestant loyalties, churches were united in a Biblical faith. Jean-Baptiste Lamarck (1744–1829), in *Philosophie Zoologique* (1809), theorized correctly that species inherited characteristics but had suggested that the factors of inheritance were entirely environmental (Hancock and Skinner 2000).

A leading critic of Lamarck was George Cuvier (1769–1832), who accounted for diversity of species by a theory of catastrophism. Periodic cataclysms wiped out species in specific physical regions and other creatures took the space. Scientists now tell us that the Earth has encountered periods of cataclysm but the theory only explains the disappearance and not the diversity of species. The English geologist Charles Lyell (1797–1875) concluded that the Earth must be very much older than the Biblical record attests. Lyell's (1990, 1991a, 1991b) *Principles of Geology* was published in three volumes between 1830 and 1833 and suggested a gradual geological formation (Hancock and Skinner 2000).

Geology and palaeontology seemed to show the Bible at least in need of reinterpretation. Geology and palaeontology thus unwillingly aided the accommodation of Biblical revelation and scientific discovery and challenged those who saw the latter as a threat to the former. Combined with the observation of species change over time, this made the nineteenth century a fertile ground for a (any) theory of evolution. *Vestiges* ambitiously attempted an early theory of everything, the birth and death of stars with the birth and death of species on Earth. The carefully guarded anonymity of a book published in 1844, *Vestiges of the Natural History of Creation*, showed however the level of sensitivity inherent in the book's subject matter (Chambers 1993). Yet though *Vestiges* found a large readership it had no great theological or scientific credibility; it was received as a scandal by clergy but condemned for its amateurism by the scientific establishment. The book was what Secord (2003) described as a 'Victorian sensation'. Only the 12th edition (1884) revealed the author as Robert Chambers, a Scottish journalist, a decade after his death in 1871. It is noteworthy that the scientifically less creditable *Vestiges* continued to so many editions after *Origin of Species* and that Chamber's anonymity was unveiled only posthumously. Originally entitled *The Natural History of Creation*, *Vestiges* gave resonance to a phrase offered by James Hutton, a fellow Scot and professional geologist, who suggested that the geological record showed 'no *vestige* of a beginning, no *prospect* of an end'.

Lamarck had already speculated on rudimentary evolutionary theory. Alfred Russel Wallace (1823–1913) can be credited too with the rudiments of a modern theory of evolution, at least a theory of natural selection that would be forever associated with Charles Darwin (1809–1882). Wallace had written to Darwin only a couple of years before publishing *Origin* explaining his own theory. The view expounded by Wallace was so similar to Darwin's that it spurred him with great nervous energy to write down hurriedly the ideas which had been germinating since his voyage on the Beagle 20 years earlier and the scandalous consequences of which he had long realized (see Shermer 2011). Publication of *Origin of Species* (Darwin 2011), combined with new knowledge from geological science, would provide a challenge of an order of magnitude far exceeding any other science, for the way in which it directly undermined the Biblical account of origins. With immediate public controversy (see Desmond 1995), subsequent relations around science and religion centre as frequently on evolution as they do on creation and cosmology.

While many Christians were able to accommodate the theory of evolution, many were sceptical and saw its dangers as irreconcilable with revelation. Creationism, the literal upholding of the Biblical account of Genesis, has become the centrepiece of 'New Atheist' critique, most prominently in Richard Dawkins' (2007) *The God Delusion* and *The Greatest Show on Earth* (2010). The conception of such religious views as epistemological obscurantism is also associated with Daniel Dennett's (2007) *Breaking the Spell: Religion as a Natural Phenomenon*. The political dangers of a world view committed to obvious falsehood is associated with Sam Harris' (2007) *Letter to a Christian Nation*, *The End of Faith: Religion, Terror, and the Future of Reason* (2006) and *The Moral Landscape* (2011); as well as Christopher Hitchens' (2009) *God is Not Great*.

The New Atheists form part of a mini-industry in scientifically informed religious scepticism. Some of these have provoked direct responses, such as Wilson's (2007) response to Harris in *Letter from a Christian Citizen*. More general polemical critiques include, for example, Beattie's (2007) *The New Atheists: The Twilight of Reason and the War on Religion* and Day's (2008) *The Irrational Atheist: Dissecting the Unholy Trinity of Dawkins, Harris, and Hitchens*. Critics point out that the New Atheist assumption that religious faith is irrational is at odds with a long philosophical history, from Augustine (2008; Stump and Kretzmann 2001) through Anselm (Davies and Leftow 2004; Williams and Visser 2009) and Aquinas (2002) as faith seeking understanding (Kretzmann and Stump 1993).

The mere mention of God by scientists does not often imply a faith position, often rather the opposite. Einstein's oft-quoted remark on quantum mechanics, that 'God does not play dice' does not imply any religious system *per se*. Stephen Hawking's (1998) *Brief History of Time* claims that physics can know 'the mind of God' but it is not intended as a proof of God's existence. Such theological language in science resurfaced on 4 July 2012 at the European Centre for Nuclear Research (CERN), with experiments observing particles consistent with the long-sought Higgs boson. Religion would have not featured to the degree that it did had this particle not been nicknamed 'the God particle', a term originating with Lederman (1993). Peter Higgs, the British physicist whose hypothesis the particle was, although an atheist, has been averse to the term, concerned not only with its inaccuracy but to avoid offence to those who are religious.

The same fractures between philosophy and religion are evident, then, in those between philosophy and the natural sciences. At the end of the *Critique of Practical Reason*, Kant maintains an interrelated vision of philosophy, science and morality, and a foundational role for philosophy, where, 'Philosophy must always continue to be the guardian of this science; and although the public does not take any interest in its subtle investigations, it must take an interest in the resulting doctrines, which such an examination first puts in a clear light' (Kant 1788: 166). In modern times, the same nuclear science that had provoked the talk of the God particle had been, earlier in the twentieth century, the centre of moral debates around the potentiality of the atom as a source of destructive, military power. At the beginning of the 'atomic age', one of the pioneers of the quantum physics, the German physicist Werner Heisenberg (1901–1976), famous for developing the 'uncertainty principle', contributed to the Gifford lecture series, later published as *Philosophy and Physics* (Heisenberg 2000). The moral dilemmas of science are nowhere better illustrated than in the secret 1941 meeting between the German Heisenberg and his former friend and scientific colleague the Danish Niels Bohr (1885–1962), whose country was then Nazi occupied. Historians of science still debate the nature and purpose of the meeting. David Cassidy's (1992) *Uncertainty: The Life and Science of Werner Heisenberg* deals with the science and the speculation, which centred around whether Germany would have or had the capacity to develop an atomic bomb (for related documents of the incident and the wider see the exhibit by the Center for History of Physics, available online at www.aip.org/history/heisenberg/bohr-heisenberg-meeting.htm). Michael Frayn's (1998) play *Copenhagen* dramatizes the events and shows one powerful instance of the unambiguous moral implications or the intended moral consequences of modern science.

Yet another notable quantum theorist and cosmologist, Stephen

Hawking, in *The Grand Design* (Hawking and Mlodinow 2011) promotes a view of scientific determinism in which science is the means to explain and understand the operation of the laws of nature. The first chapter ('The Mystery of Being') of *The Grand Design* opens nevertheless with a personal and reflective tone, reminiscent of Kant's *Critique of Practical Reason*:

> We each exist for but a short time, and in that time explore but a small part of the whole universe. But humans are a curious species. We wonder, we seek answers. Living in this vast world that is by turns kind and cruel, and gazing at the immense heavens above, people have always asked a multitude of questions. How can we understand the world in which we find ourselves? How does the universe behave? What is the nature of reality? Where did all this come from? Did the universe need a creator? Most of us do not spend most of our time worrying about these questions, but almost all of us worry about them some of the time.
>
> (Hawking and Mlodinow 2011: 13)

The book is also a tract on why religion is no longer needed as a source for explaining the universe. As for many socio-anthropological and psychological theories of religion (which I examine in later chapters), for Hawking, religion is a form of proto-science which had tried to explain the universe without the necessary (scientific) tools to do so. But nor, importantly however for Hawking, is philosophy any longer an adequate (or fully adequate) source of explanation. Philosophy, it is true, had inculcated in human beings a capacity to wonder and inquire, which had been essential to the historical development of science, but philosophy's tools (critical reasoning alone), like theology's, are too limited to be of use if we wish truly to know the world. If religion here is a form of primitive science easily dismissed, Hawking admits of the historical importance of philosophy in relation to science but not its contemporary or future relevance. In relation to the questions of meaning and being he posed in the opening paragraph of his book, he states:

> Traditionally these are questions for philosophy, but philosophy is dead. Philosophy has not kept up with modern developments in science, particularly physics. Scientists have become the bearers of the torch of discovery in our quest for knowledge.
>
> (Hawking and Mlodinow 2011: 13)

'Philosophy is dead.' The natural sciences in this view have as little need for philosophy as they do for religion.

The natural scientific advocates of religion

As Eliade remarks: 'The science of religions, as an autonomous discipline devoted to analysing the common elements of the different religions and seeking to deduce the laws of their evolution, and especially to discover and define the origin and first form of religion, is a very recent addition to the sciences' (Eliade 1957: 216). Some sense of this evolution can be traced through the history of the Gifford lectures, a legacy dating from the nineteenth century (Gifford 2013). Crediting William Paley's *Natural Theology* (2008) as the beginnings of a modern (natural) theology, this provides the framework for the legacy of Lord Adam Gifford:

> The Knowledge of God, the Infinite, the All, the First and Only Cause, the One and the Sole Substance, the Sole Being, the Sole Reality, and the Sole Existence, the Knowledge of His Nature and Attributes, the Knowledge of the Relations which men and the whole universe bear to Him, the Knowledge of the Nature and Foundation of Ethics or Morals, and of all Obligations and Duties thence arising.
>
> (Gifford 1885)

Gifford thereby institutes a series of lectures. The lecturers may be of 'any denomination' or 'no denomination at all', 'of any religion' or 'of no religion', with the proviso that they be 'reverent', 'true thinkers, sincere lovers of and earnest inquirers after truth' (Gifford 1885):

> I wish the lecturers to treat their subject as a strictly natural science, the greatest of all possible sciences, indeed, in one sense, the only science, that of Infinite Being, without reference to or reliance upon any supposed special exceptional or so-called miraculous revelation. I wish it considered just as astronomy or chemistry is.
>
> (Gifford 1885)

The lectures themselves:

> shall be public and popular, that is, open not only to students of the Universities, but to the whole community without matriculation, as I think that the subject should be studied and known by all, whether receiving University instruction or not. I think such knowledge, if real, lies at the root of all well-being.
>
> (Gifford 1885)

The lecture series reads now as a 'who's who' of philosophy, theology and the natural sciences. The first series of lectures (1888–1889) by Friedrich Max Müller (1823–1900) remain foundational in methodological as well as in historical priority. It is through Müller that natural theology becomes the study of religion. Müller was a Sanskrit scholar and philologist and a pioneer in the fields of Vedic studies, comparative philosophy, comparative mythology and comparative religion. In 1851, he was appointed Professor of Modern European Languages at Oxford and was made full Professor in

1854. Empire had stimulated interest in the ideas as well as the economics of the east. In Victorian England, he was a leading public figure.

Müller's prominence was also at a time of unprecedented challenge to Christianity's intellectual credibility. The decade in which Müller achieved the academic position which was the fount of his prodigious output was also the decade of Darwin and Huxley and an unprecedented public interest in science. In 1868, the University of Oxford created a new Chair of Comparative Philology, which Müller won. In 1878, Müller inaugurated the annual Hibbert lectures on the science of religion at Westminster Abbey. In 1888, Müller began his first course of Gifford Lectures in Natural Theology at the University of Glasgow on the subject of 'natural religion'. Müller's four volumes of Gifford Lectures (*Collected Works*, vols. 1–4): *Natural Religion* (1889), *Physical Religion* (1891), *Anthropological Religion* (1892), *Theosophy, or Psychological Religion* (1893) provide epistemological ground and method for the study of religion (Müller, 1889–1893).

Such multidisciplinarity and epistemological hybridity encouraged a range of approaches to the study of religion. The field's breadth would arguably contribute to a dissolution of the foundational distinction between the sacred and the profane, for religion, through such study, began to be reduced to the terms outside and often critical of it. Thus, an idea which pervades Smart's work is precisely the breaking down of boundaries between religious and secular worldviews: 'I believe there are sufficient affinities between religious and secular worldviews (such as applied Marxism and nationalisms) to include secularism in the scope of this work' (Smart 1999: 2). The scientific advocates of religion facilitated a disciplinary proliferation that would shape not only the academic study of religion but religious education in schools.

The natural sciences and religious education

From its inception, the American journal *Religious Education* reflected the epistemological challenges for religion from science. Beyond those appropriations of science within religious education were those findings from the natural sciences which seemed to undermine religion itself as a form of knowledge. Thus, Falconer (1928) writes of the 'difficulties for religion in an age of science', science and the religious education curriculum (MacLean 1928), Ames (1931) of the 'machine age', Aubrey (1928) of the implications of science for Biblical revelation. Science also presented problems for Christian anthropology or understanding of the person, and his or her action in the world, and indeed for the sources of moral authority; as in Ross's (1932) 'Sin and Salvation in an Age of Science', and its related symposium on 'Sin and Salvation in an Age of Science and Machinery' (Freehof *et al.* 1932). Science clearly presented here alternative forms of understanding of the world which religious educators were beginning to take seriously. Ross identifies 'two quite distinct lines of thought':

One might consider, for instance, the changes that science and machinery can introduce into our conception of what is sinful. For just as other times and peoples have had ideas differing from ours as to what is sinful and what is not...so the change in social and economic conditions together with the revolution in intellectual outlook introduced by science, may alter the idea of what is right and wrong.

(Ross 1932: 234)

Referring to the novelist Aldous Huxley, a contemporary of Ross, the latter suggests:

The Decalogue may be discarded or re-interpreted, and new sins may be created. Aldous Huxley, in his *Brave New World,* has shown us what certain tendencies of a scientific and mechanical age, if unchecked, will ultimately produce – a Model T Fordian universe, where the morality and immorality of today largely change places.

(Ross 1932: 234)

Thus, 'Anyone interested in that line of thought can read Huxley instead of *Religious Education*'. On the other hand,

one can take sin in its old-fashioned sense as an offence against God, a violation of His Commandments as summed up in the Decalogue, and then consider what effect science and machinery as we know them today have in decreasing or increasing such violations...Following this latter line of thought, it is perfectly evident that science and machinery have only an indirect and accidental bearing on sin. In themselves, science and machinery are neither moral nor immoral. But machines can be used for immoral purposes, while as a byproduct they may produce social conditions increasing temptations, weakening resistance, and making it easier to yield to the allurements of sin. At the same time, certain conclusions from scientific data may blur the consciousness of a personal God, reduce the sense of one's own responsibility, and empty morality of any...meaning.

(Ross 1932: 234)

By the mid-twentieth century, along with the rise of Nazism, Fascism and Communism, developments in and the influence of philosophical rationalism and scientific empiricism, were presented as an emergent, new faith and a challenge to established religious faith (Harner 1950). These represented for religious education a problem: were such perspectives to be a source of conflict or an opportunity for incorporation? Subsequent decades have seen the same tensions.

The response of religious education today, however, for those committed to a secular outlook, provides no great difficulties. Those positions antagonistic to religious belief in those forms outlined above are incorporated into religious education. Thus, religion and science are commonly taught as core topics in religious curricula worldwide. As Michael Reiss discovered in suggesting that creationism had a legitimate role in science education when, in 2008, he was forced to resign his role as Director of Education at the Royal Society, it is easier on occasion to comment on science in religious education than on religion in science education (Independent 2010). The exception might be when science is being contrasted with theology in historical perspective (de Berg 2011). De Berg thus assesses the work of Joseph Priestley (1733–1804) as chemist and educator, and as a scientist engaged in theological reflection (de Berg 2012). The Michael Reiss episode marks an unusual and thus headline worthy case because Reiss was speaking on behalf of an official scientific body. It may betray less an attitude of scientists to religion than scientists attitudes to certain types of religion and a need to differentiate more fully disciplinary boundaries. On more general grounds, the strongest case for accommodation between the natural sciences and religion – and the appropriation of the natural sciences within religious education – arises when creditable scientists also hold a religious, even theologically orthodox faith. Modern and prominent exponents of the latter case make a potentially stronger case for the appropriation of the natural sciences in religious education when believing scientists are also committed in the broadest sense to this as a programme of apologetics or education (for example, McGrath, 2007, 2010, 2011a, 2011b; Polkinghorne 2003, 2007, 2012).

Religious education and appropriation of the natural sciences

In the fiftieth anniversary year of *The Origin of Species*, Dawson's (1909) 'The Biological Sciences and Religious Education' had marked Darwin as one of the most significant challenges for religious education. Yet, if *The Fundamentals* (1910–1915) presented the case for the defence of a Biblically oriented Protestant theology only a decade after their publication in 1925, the trial of a science teacher, John Scopes, in Dayton, Tennessee, would show just how the real divide was not between liberal and conservative theologies but between Biblical Christianity and the natural sciences.

In 'Teaching God to Students of Science', Rolfe (1924) declares that the author 'is the daughter of an eminent geologist'. Her opinions are forthright: 'Our Liberals explain and apologize and try to adjust, but the bare fact remains that our young people are Godless to their best knowledge'. The solution, suggests Rolfe, is 'to sail uncharted waters to a new conception of God'.

What was thought formerly to be confined to American education in the early years of the third millennium also surfaced in Europe. The dangers of creationism in education were raised in a report of the Council of Europe Committee on Culture, Science and Education (Council of Europe 2011). 'The theory of evolution,' it stated, 'is being attacked by religious fundamentalists who call for creationist theories to be taught in European schools alongside or even in place of it'. The Council of Europe is a human rights organization with a 47-state membership. The draft resolution was careful to highlight the political implications of this scientifically derisory religious standpoint. The Draft Resolution went on to detail the 'total rejection of science' as 'one of the most serious threats to human rights and civic rights': 'The war on the theory of evolution and on its proponents most often originates in forms of religious extremism which are closely allied to extreme right-wing political movements'. The Creationist movements possess 'real political power' and 'this has been exposed on several occasions...The fact of the matter...is that the advocates of strict creationism are out to replace democracy by theocracy'. The report excludes Pope Benedict XVI and his predecessor Pope John-Paul II from the Creationist position, showing how the Vatican has moved from a formerly antagonistic stance to the theory of evolution. The teaching of evolution 'as a fundamental scientific theory' is therefore 'crucial to the future of our societies and our democracies'. The draft report argues that the Council of Europe 'firmly oppose the teaching of creationism as a scientific discipline on an equal footing with the theory of evolution by natural selection and in general resist presentation of creationist theories in any discipline other than religion'. The report was, however, rejected. The report's socialist lead author was outraged, claiming that creationism had the 'makings of a return to the Middle Ages'.

Midgley (2007) has attempted to moderate the extremes. She claims creationism's influence as growing rapidly but also transmogrified into the moderated form of Intelligent Design. This approach is less concerned with the literal interpretation of origin stories, such as Genesis, than with an assertion of their underlying principles of an intelligent designer behind them, a position favoured by the natural theology of William Paley and given Biblical and theological reinforcement for the present day. Yet, for Midgley,

> The theory does not, as one might expect, merely aim to add a spiritual dimension to supplement accepted biological views, which would be quite unobjectionable. Intelligent Design (ID) is presented firmly as a scientific theory to displace existing ones. Its central point is that living things are so 'irreducibly complex'. The disturbing feature about ID theory is its open imperialism. It inserts a Creator not as a metaphysical background but as a necessary part of the physical process.
>
> (Midgley 2007)

Midgley sees the debate between science and religion, in this instance, in political as much as epistemological terms, as 'the old idea of a stark epistemological Cold War, a contest for dominance between science and religion'. Science and religion are, in this regard, a clash 'not of epistemologies but functions, the former deals in facts, the latter in meaning'. She cites Einstein's adage that religion without science is lame, while science without religion is blind: 'Any apparent clashes between the two must therefore arise either from faulty religion or faulty science, or both. They don't call for war, but for a better understanding'. But she sees flaws on both sides:

> For instance, believers celebrating God as Creator need not be trying to smuggle an illicit set of dubious variables into the realm of scientific facts. They may simply be trying to show the whole natural realm in a different light, as pervaded by the divine. Insights like this are, of course, somewhat mysterious, which is why... religious experiences vary widely and why different cultures express them differently. The parties in today's Cold War will, however, accept no such awestruck open-mindedness. Both opt for simple and final certainty.
>
> (Midgley 2007)

On the religious side, 'fundamentalists stand by the stark claim which they first made just over a century ago – that the Scriptures, literally read, are infallible' (see Torrey 1917). She calls this 'a deep devotion to the Bible going far beyond what has been normal in Protestantism'. She identifies this as 'characteristically American' and provides a curiously sociological as well as political reading of the epistemological-theological dispute:

> This devotion probably arose at first because so many immigrants to the US had been persecuted for their religion before leaving Europe, and their religion was one of the few things they had to sustain them in their stressful new life.
>
> (Midgley 2007)

Today, the 'conditioned anti-religious response ... distorts the whole controversy... It should surely be obvious that there is nothing *scientific* about atheism. God's existence is not a question for the tests of physical science; it belongs to metaphysics'. As for fundamentalism, this she describes as a perverse attempt to use

> a particular, bronze-age Hebrew vision of God to resolve factual questions in science and history... Opponents who answer fundamentalism on its own terms by arguing against this mixed project as a package-deal merely perpetuate its characteristic confusion between the realms of fact and meaning.
>
> (Midgley 2007)

On epistemology and meaning making Conroy *et al.* (2012), as we have seen, identify this as central to the core purposes of religious education. The natural sciences and religion have been seen in such historical opposition that making the case from one side to the other is often dependent – as Midgley elaborates – on establishing the reasonableness of either case. A special issue of the *British Journal of Religious Education* in 1990 included contributions on 'Biotechnology and Religious Education' (Riggs 1990), 'Science and Religion: A Challenge for Secondary Education' (Poole 1990), the epistemologies of religion and science as narrative in Yates' (1990) 'True Stories: Science and Religion in Education', Stannard's (1990) 'Science and Religion: How to Start an Argument'; and Cooling's (1990) restatement of an old opposition, 'Science and Religious Education – Conflict or Cooperation?'. Nearly two decades on, Midgley demonstrates that new and perceived as unreasonable uses of science or religion – 'scientism' or 'fundamentalism' – have no role in religious education.

Conflicts and accommodations continue within the subject and, not unnaturally, impact upon and are reflected in students' attitudes to religion and or science, as studies of religious education classrooms have shown for some time (Bausor and Poole 2002; Francis *et al.* 1990; Reich 1989, 1990; Barendt 2011). For Astley and Francis (2010), it is a critical task for religious education to encourage student openness to religion in a 'scientific age' and to counter the narrow oppositions identified by Midgley. Astley and Francis (2010) took a sample of 187 female students attending a sixth-form study day on religious studies and asked them to undertake a questionnaire assessing four attitudes towards: theistic religion, science, scientism and creationism. They found a negative correlation between attitudes towards religion and attitudes towards science. This negative correlation became, they found, a positive one, when the extremes of 'scientism' and 'creationism' – the exclusive view of science or religion – were accounted for. This led the researchers to call for science and religious education to make combined efforts to further understanding on both sides, to understand the respective roles and limits of scientific method and to promote the idea that 'religious belief about creation should be recognized as essentially a claim about the ontological dependence of nature rather than about the details of its origins and development' (Astley and Francis 2010: 189).

Summary

From nineteenth-century Darwinian theory to twentieth- and twenty-first century advances in biology, chemistry, physics and cosmology, discoveries in the natural sciences have affected discourse in religion and theology more drastically even than philosophical rationalism. The most significant influence of the natural sciences upon religious education has, however, been the inclusion of scientific themes rather than scientific methods. Arguably, these are twofold, epistemological and existential: first, scientific knowledge and method and the implications for religion as a way of knowing the world; second, scientific method and the implications for religion as a way of being in the world. Insofar as scientific advances have ethical implications – environmental, medical and military – these are arguably of secondary concern to the more fundamental questions that both sides claim, in adversarial or accommodating ways, about the meaning and purpose of existence itself.

The natural sciences had from the Enlightenment onwards a role in shaping not only knowledge of the world but the shape of society. Seeking to imitate the impressive advances of scientific knowledge in the natural sciences, the formation of the social sciences was derived from an impetus to uncover the laws which govern society to better guide its improvement. In their origins, the social sciences share with their natural scientific counterparts attitudes to religion which are equally as conflictual.

4 The social sciences and religious education

Introduction

The eighteenth century foundations of the social sciences owe a debt to the principles of the natural sciences in the seventeenth century. Newton was here the pivotal figure in uncovering the inalienable mathematical and physical laws that were universal and, crucially, could be determined without recourse to that Biblical revelation of God's law. The discovery of laws governing the natural world was a founding principle for uncovering the laws of society. The idea that the universe was ruled by unalterable laws was applied to society. It was the task of the new social sciences to determine what these laws were.

Discovering the laws of society was critical to the Enlightenment idea of human progress. Such progression was the unifying idea of Enlightenment, even conceived as an inevitable pattern of history, marked by an inexorable path towards personal and collective perfectibility. For social scientists, like other Enlightenment thinkers – philosophers and scientists as well as political revolutionaries – there was a presumption of a forward movement of society.

Although this optimism would be belied by subsequent centuries, so confident were many of the inevitability of such progress that the political changes needed to sustain it were often forced. This is why the century of Enlightenment was also the century of revolution, the patience of scientific enquiry often being inversely proportionate to the social impatience for political change. With this presumption of the forward movement of society, uncovering the laws which determined the direction of this path was crucial to its realization.

Just as the natural sciences gave little credence to revelation in determining the laws of nature, so the social sciences would give little credence to notions of human history dependent on God's intervention in it. Indeed, such interpretations of history were themselves seen as an intractable obstacle to human and social progress. For Enlightenment thinkers, this made the engagement with the origins of Christianity in history itself important. Since Christianity had risen in the context of the Roman Empire and since

Christianity's ascendancy as a faith, historians often made the rise and fall of Rome a central part of their evaluation of Christian history. Charles de Montesquieu's (1689–1755) 'Considerations on the Causes of the Greatness and Decline of the Romans' is an early elaboration (de Montesquieu 1999).

Edward Gibbon's *The Decline and Fall of the Roman Empire* presented the thesis on a magisterial scale (six volumes, published 1776–1789). Progressive as the time was, in his dying months, Hume read the first volume of Gibbon's work and warned the young historian of the likely public outcry. The most contentious aspects of Gibbon's thesis were in blaming the decline and fall of Rome on the rise of Christianity, its other-worldly preoccupations being key to its lack of imperialist ambitions, its moral outlook out of synch with the military might needed to sustain an empire. Gibbon does not therefore see in the foundations of Christendom the hand of God guiding salvation history. Christian theology had seen Christendom as evidence of the 'great Author' of history. For Gibbon, that transcendental realm was beyond the scope of historical analysis. Lamenting the fall of Rome, for Gibbon Christianity's ascendancy was a victory of superstition over reason.

This required a new teleology of history; what were its aims and purposes if not divine or if the divine aims and purposes could not be discerned? It was the task of the enlightened historian as much as the philosopher to discern these aims and purposes. The sciences of society that simultaneously emerged sought to determine not simply the patterns in historical events but the laws that governed them. Inevitably, the laws became the means by which not simply to observe but guide society and, thus, social laws would become integral to political process. De Montesquieu's (1989) *The Spirit of the Laws*, first published in French in 1748 and first translated into English by Thomas Nugent in 1750, was a paramount example: 'Laws, taken in the broadest meaning, are the necessary relations deriving from the nature of things'. From this principle, in a work that took two decades to write, he systematically shows how these laws penetrate all aspects of the political and social order and their histories, as much as the natural order and its history. 'Those who have said,' he wrote, 'that *a blind fate has produced all the effects we see in the world* have said a great absurdity' (de Montesquieu 1989: 3). As did Rousseau and Paine, and later Hegel and Marx, de Montesquieu saw in human history a natural evolution. Political progress had all the necessity of physical law. The revolutionary inclinations of America and France in his century were regarded as the fulfilment of such laws (de Montesquieu 1989), as would many later revolutions.

That history had a predetermined and natural course which would inevitably be fulfilled was applied in economics by Adam Smith (1723–1790). The foundations of modern capitalism rest on *The Wealth of Nations*, published in 1776 (Smith 2008). Smith's study was a theory of society as much as of economics. He observed that some societies succeeded in wealth creation but others did not. While this was for a range of factors – social, political, scientific, technological – the decisive factor was the degree to which free markets prevailed. The intellectual flourishing of Enlightenment sciences, the Industrial Revolution and the growth of colonial power, were seen as evidence of success not only of a free market of capital but of ideas.

If Hegel saw history as the movement of ideas, Marx saw history as the momentum of material conditions. Marx, by this account, would take a diametrically opposed view of economics. Regarding from the nineteenth century the revolutions of the eighteenth, Marx saw these as having only inadequately fulfilled the ideals, especially of equality, that they sought to achieve. Capital was not freedom but slavery. More decisive revolution, a true revolution of the proletariat, would be needed to effect social structural change and to force what was an historical inevitability (Marx and Engels 2002; Marx 1994, 1996; for the collected works, see Marx and Engels 1975–2005).

If social and political theory saw a replacement of religion with laws guided by reason, others, such as Mikhail Alexandrovich Bakunin (1814–1876), saw an opportunity to abandon laws altogether. Bakunin's *Statism and Anarchy* (1873) predicted that Marx's dictatorship of the proletariat would become, as Shatz (Bakunin 1991) puts it, a dictatorship *over* the people. Bakunin more widely predicted the likely repressive uses of power when the state, whether Communist, Fascist or Nazi, became *all*-powerful. Bakunian analyses have their applications in modern-day politics, which sees the operation of such power as being not simply an outcome of modernity but its essence (see Arendt 2004; Voegelin 1995; Wolin 2008; Zizek 2011). The semblance of knowledge construction is simply a reflection of political order (Foucault 1994). The ultimate demonstration of power is not merely the construction of states but the construction of reality.

The social sciences and religion

All social scientific treatment of religion ultimately reduces religious belief and practice to terms relevant to society, to social relations and to culture. The terms of reductionist or functionalist are traditionally applied in the study of religion to theories which explain the underlying terms of religious belief and practice because (a) they *reduce* to a category outside of religion, or (b) theorize religion as a function of those terms. There are variations in each that are reflective of differing degrees of antagonism and empathy towards its religious subject matter. Increasingly, however, formerly reductive modes of interpretation seek not simply to reduce religion to a function but to adapt and utilize religion. This often, in turn, entails modifications in our understanding of the definition of religion. Social scientific advocates, for instance, will see religion as a useful means of attaining social and community cohesion but, in so doing, highlight those aspects of religion which are compatible with such social goals and exclude those which are not.

The sociological adversaries of religion

Born in Montpellier, France, in Year 6 of the Revolution's calendar, Auguste Comte (1798–1857) is credited with having coined the word 'sociology' as part of a philosophy of positivism. Educated at the École Polytechnique until its forced closure in 1817, it was here that Comte met the aristocratic but impoverished Henri-Claude Saint-Simon (1760–1825). The latter's 'Letters of an Inhabitant of Geneva to His Contemporaries' (Saint-Simon 1976) expressed the view that priests should be replaced by scientists (a view which, as we shall see, was an influential idea in the history of the social sciences) and he impressed the young Comte. He agreed to become Saint-Simon's secretary. Positivism was as much a view of the progressive history of humanity as it was a philosophy and history of science. The three stages of progress were envisaged first by Saint-Simon's 'Law of the Three Stages'. They were affirmed by Comte as part of a wider evolutionary model of human mental and social development. Comte's version of this model saw the three developments as, first, the theological (subdivided into animism, polytheism and monotheism), second, the metaphysical and third, the positive stage, the search for absolute knowledge. For each of these stages, a progressive development in intellectual insight was mirrored in the development of material progress (Comte 1998a, 1998b). Such ideas had been expressed by the French Encyclopedists, the founding editors of this project being Denis Diderot (1713–1784) and Jean le Rond d'Alembert (1717–1783) (Diderot and d'Alembert 1976; Diderot 1992). Beginning with the letter 'A' in 1751, the project was completed 28 volumes later, in 1765, with contributions from Condorcet, de Montesquieu, Voltaire and Rousseau (on Comte's intellectual context, see Pickering 1993, 2009a, 2009b).

In addition to his reading of the economics of Adam Smith and of David Hume, another major influence on Comte was the Marquis de Condorcet, Marie Jean Antoine Nicolas de Caritat Condorcet (1743–1794; Condorcet 2012). Condorcet's *Sketch for a Historical Picture of the Progress of the Human Mind* (1795), published posthumously, provides a model of human progress towards perfectibility which profoundly shaped Comte's thinking on nature, purpose and future direction of society. Condorcet, in training, education and early interest, was foremost a mathematician. He became, by force of circumstance, an individual of broader interests. The French Revolution made of him a political thinker and educational reformer. A friend of the leading intellectuals of his day – he wrote a life of his friend Voltaire (1694–1778), one of the most influential intellectuals of his age, politically he shaped the thinking of the Revolution in France, although he died a decade before it began (Voltaire 1994). It was Condorcet's model of a state education that was accepted by the National Convention in the early years of the Revolution. With the Revolution itself becoming divided – the ascendant Jacobins represented by Robespierre and (after the *département* of the Gironde) the more moderate and loosely organised Girondins, their most prominent figure Jacques-Pierre Brissot – Condorcet sided with the latter and was forced into hiding. He was arrested in March 1794. Two days later, he was found dead in his prison cell. In the time of his greatest trial, Condorcet wrote his most famous and profoundly optimistic work, *Sketch for a Historical Picture of the Progress of the Human Mind*. Sharing Condorcet's utopianism, Comte's methodology develops the means of studying yet also shaping human progress. This Comte achieved did in the six volumes of *Course of Positive Philosophy* (1830–1842). *The System of Positive Polity* (1851–1854) and *The Catechism of Positive Religion* (1852) followed but neither work captured an audience like the *Course of Positive Philosophy*. In this course, literally a curriculum, of positive philosophy, Comte attempted to demonstrate that each science is necessarily dependent on the previous science; that is, science can only be understood historically as the process of greater perfection (Comte 1998a).

Historical teleology is as old as history itself but the attempt to define it outside of a *theological* historiography and *as a science* is a part of the story of modernity (Hughes-Warrington 2007). In the seventeenth century, even those such as Giovanni Battista Vico (1668–1744) in *The First New Science*, ([1725] Vico 2002) defined this uncovering of meaning as a *science*. What might be said to distinguish the efforts of the seventeenth and eighteenth century is that the former still attempted to link the ancient and the modern, the theological and the secular as science (see for example, on Vico, Levine 1991), whereas in the later part of the eighteenth century, and certainly by the nineteenth century, theological interpretations were expunged from secular historiography. But perhaps what was significant about Comte was not the method but the *naming* of the science.

The ultimate science that Comte claimed to have discovered was sociology. It was sociology, he claimed, that would give ultimate meaning to all the other sciences. In the 47th lesson of the fourth volume of the *Course of Positive Philosophy*, Comte proposes to call the new science not *physique sociale* (or social physics), the term formerly used for the new science, but sociology. *Physique sociale* indicates the self-conscious intentions of early sociologist to mirror the natural sciences.

In the meeting between Comte and Sainte-Simon, we see the political implications of sociology. If progress was inevitable, hastening it required revolution. From the eighteenth, nineteenth and twentieth to the present century, we see this revolutionary impetus in large part motivated by ideals that emerge from a single source of belief, the idea that change and transformation of society, even its fundamental structures, are possible. Both Comte and Saint-Simone saw the agents of change as primarily scientific and technical, requiring political order, but above all being grounded in rational knowledge of the world and the technological means to control it. For this reason the creation of a technical-scientific elite was envisaged who would oversee the development of pure as well as applied sciences. The École

Polytechnique was formed in 1794 for this purpose, directed to the training of military engineers, which remit extended when it became a school for the advanced sciences. Under Napoleon, the École Polytechnique emerged as the foremost French scientific institution and a model for a future society ordered and sustained by a technocratic elite. Scientific knowledge conjoined with and a means of social progress is an ideal retained today across all political perspectives (Comte 1998a, 1998b).

The sociological advocates of religion

A field dedicated to the study of religion is unlikely to want to see its disappearance. The emergence of the sociology of religion is thus a consequence of the founding of sociology as a scientific discipline. Its formation, though, marks a less polemical phase in the development of sociology's study of religion. Not all early sociological analysis of religion was therefore as scathing as Comte, Condorcet or Marx. E. B. Tylor (1832–1917) transformed and did much to form the field of anthropology. Tylor's (1871) *Primitive Culture* was a landmark anthropological study, which would also impact psychological and especially psychoanalytical interpretations of religion. *Primitive Culture* identified the origins of religion in animism, dreams and the spirit world. With the evolutionary spirit of its century, *Primitive Culture* considers religion in terms of historical development:

> Having thus traced upward from the lower levels of culture the opinion of mankind as to the souls, spirits, ghosts or phantoms, considered to belong to men, to the lower animals, to plants and to things, we are now prepared to investigate one of the great religious doctrines of mankind, the belief in the soul's continued existence in a Life after Death.
>
> (Tylor 1871: 1)

As Comte had developed a science of society, Tylor would develop the history of anthropology to focus on the 'science of culture'. In this context, Tylor relates primitive culture to more advanced state of 'civilization': the 'Culture or Civilization taken in its wide ethnographic sense is that complex whole which includes knowledge, belief, art, morals, law, custom, and any capabilities and habits acquired by man in society' (Tylor 1871: 1). Tylor was interested, however, in the links between primitive culture and advanced civilization, especially the notion of 'survivals'; that is, those traces of ancient thinking and practice which persist concealed in modern times. For example, when someone sneezes and the phrase 'bless you' is said, this indicates the persistence of such survivals. The subliminal ways in which survivals persist would assist the development of Freud's theory of the unconscious. Freud makes his debt explicit by drawing in many works – especially those such as *Totem and Taboo*, which deal with religion and culture – by drawing significantly upon the anthropological literature (Freud 1990).

Tylor conceived of religion, especially the myths associated with it (for example creation and human origin stories) as a form of primitive scientific theorising. Thus, Tylor examines, in his chapters on myth, accounts of geological formation: 'myths of relation of apes to men by development or degeneration'. *Primitive Culture* unites this notion of myth as primitive theorizing with stories about belief in a world of spirits. Herein arises a definition of religion as a 'doctrine of spiritual beings here termed animism'. Animism is a doctrine of souls and other spirits. Because these are psychic entities, often manifest in dreams, Tylor again anticipates a connection between anthropology and the rise of psychoanalysis.

Similar psychoanalytical and psychological significance was drawn from another late nineteenth/early twentieth century anthropologist, J. G. Frazer (1854–1941). He is renowned for *The Golden Bough* ([various editions from 1890] Frazer 1993). Frazer identifies an evolutionary progression of religious belief from magic (a theory not only of the world but of how to influence it). In this framework, religion in its (rationally, theologically) developed forms is more advanced than magic but science is a direct advance on both. *The Golden Bough* exerted an influence on Freud, who read it as a treasure trove of exemplars that demonstrated religion as primitive thinking and justifying the ascent of reason to supplant it.

Tylor had focused his analysis on primitive culture without making explicit connections to Christianity. To include this would be, he realized, to make the latter simply a stage in the development of primitive belief. Frazer had no such compunction. In 1915, on first publication *The Golden Bough* was regarded scandalously by devout Christians for the manner in which Frazer considered Christianity itself as a form of story, which was, apart from its rich theology, little different from other myths. Narrative theology is now commonplace but, then, Frazer's suggestions that fundamental Christian doctrines – Jesus as the Lamb of God was a relic of similar other myths of sacrifice – were regarded as blasphemous. Extending this analysis to the crucifixion was a step too far and even Frazer bowed to the outcry and removed it to the appendix of later editions, in some editions omitting the comparison altogether. Regarding Christianity as advanced-primitive thinking was the anthropological equivalent of species classification, which placed human beings firmly within, although as the most highly evolved member, of the animal kingdom.

But even while these latter approaches were achieving recognition and notoriety, the category distinction between primitive and advanced peoples was becoming questioned within anthropology itself. Franz Boas' (1911) *The Mind of Primitive Man* was here notable: 'There is no fundamental difference in the ways of thinking of primitive and civilized man'. This statement was from an important 1938 edition of his earlier work, clearly cognisant not only of the Nazi repression of Jewish science but also of the segregationist racial policy in the United States. As Degler comments:

In the history of many fields of inquiry there comes a time when the standard or accepted modes of explanation or analysis shift fundamentally and dramatically. This occurred in the social sciences in the course of the first third of the twentieth century. Biology in the shape of racial explanations for human behavioural differences was replaced by a new explanatory mode: that of social environment or culture. By the 1930s it was about as difficult to locate an American social scientist who *accepted* a racial explanation for human behaviour as it had been easy to find one in 1900.

(Degler 1989: 1)

In arguing for a cultural determination and not a biological superiority-shaped culture, Boas 'not only provided the catalyst for change, but also shaped the content of the concept of culture, a concept that became fundamental in twentieth-century social science' (Degler 1989: 1; see also Degler 1992; Degler *et al.* 1989).

Boas, and other anthropologists such as E. E. Evans-Pritchard and Malinowski, were to be distinguished from early anthropologists by undertaking work with the peoples they were writing about. This may seem like an obvious thing for anthropologists to do but then it was a methodological, if surprisingly late, innovation. Again, we might draw parallels with the natural sciences and imagine Darwin basing his theory of evolution on books sent back from the Galapagos, without having gone there. But the innovation in anthropology shows specifically a continued effort by social sciences to mirror of natural science colleagues and to defend against claims that the study of society could hardly be called in any truly empirical sense a science.

Evans-Pritchard's fieldwork was undertaken initially amongst the Azande, resulting in *Witchcraft, Oracles and Magic Among the Azande* (Evans-Pritchard 1937). His anthropological and ethnographic reputation, though, was based largely on the Nuer (Evans-Pritchard 1940) with a particular focus on Nuer religion (Evans-Pritchard 1956). But Evans-Pritchard's reputation endures for a final concise volume, *Theories of Primitive Religion* (Evans-Pritchard 1969). Here, he provides an overview of his anthropological predecessors, Tylor and Frazer, but also Durkheim and Malinowski. Like Boas, in *Theories of Primitive Religion*, Evans-Pritchard not only rejects the primitive–advanced distinction (despite using it in his title), he also argues that these foundational anthropological explanations of 'primitive' religion as proto-science was to impose categories of interpretation alien to the societies themselves.

Of all theorists of religion, few have had the impact of Emile Durkheim (1858–1917) and few works in sociology have gained the stature of *The Elementary Forms of the Religious Life*, first published in 1912 (Durkheim 2001). To understand the nature of religion, Durkheim sought its most primitive forms to trace back from its evolved forms to its origins. Reviewing the 'leading conceptions of elementary religion, including theories of animism, magic as a proto-scientific form of thought' (Durkheim 2001: 47–75), he identifies the religion of totemism as the most elementary *organized* form and its oldest manifestation in Australian aboriginal culture (Durkheim 2001: 76–83). This is the first of the two books which comprise the *Elementary Forms*. Books two and three make a systematic analysis of nature of totemism, its importance as a social phenomenon uniting aboriginal groups, its core beliefs (Durkheim 2001: 87–218) and how in its ritual forms (Durkheim 2001: 221–343) these practices reinforce in subliminal ways the idealization of society. Durkheim was dependent upon the secondary writings of accounts of the cultures he studied. He saw the significance of the totem but came to a different conclusion: prohibitions around and special sacred–profane demarcations around the totem were for Durkheim the means of tribal peoples representing their own society, sacralizing it through an object, revering in a way itself in objective form. The most notable conceptual contribution of Durkheim to sociology of religion is in delineating the critical distinction between sacred and profane (Eliade's later use of the distinction gives little credence to Durkheim), since this distinction is more elementary than specific (for example) theistic belief: 'religion is a unified system of beliefs and practice relative to sacred things, that is to say, things set apart and surrounded by prohibitions – beliefs and practices that unite its adherents in a single moral community' (Durkheim 2001: 46).

The sacred is that which is set apart from the profane by ritual, by worship, by a sense of awe. Through this distinction a thesis is elaborated which argues that religion is the means of society's representing that which it is of greatest significance, itself.

Max Weber's sociological reputation endures for an analysis of the socio-economic impact of religious belief and practice, *The Protestant Ethic and the Rise of Capitalism* (Weber 2002). Weber examined pietism, Calvinism, Methodism and Baptists in the light of 'the practical ethics of the ascetic branches of Protestantism' and the religious foundation of 'worldly asceticism'. Here, he found doctrines that embodied in these Protestant denominations a theological need for signs of justification. These Protestants' primary concern was for eternal salvation. This meant that worldly success was of little consequence in itself, except in so far as, and herein is Weber's thesis, such worldly success might be seen in itself as a sign of the assuredness of salvation.

Since salvation through faith was only through the grace of God, works or human effort towards personal salvation was of no effect. It was not through the law but through faith that we are saved. Would this mean that a Christian might act in any way he or she pleased? Not in the least; indeed, the living of a virtuous life was a sign of salvation and continuing to live a life of wickedness was a sign of damnation. The Calvinist interpretation of *sole fide* was integral to a theology of predestination. God's omniscience must mean that he knew from all eternity who would be saved and who would be damned. Did this mean that human beings had no freewill to choose salvation? Calvinist theology argued that God knew from all eternity who would freely choose the path of salvation and who would not. Work here and, as Weber would have it, in Calvinist-influenced Protestantism, gains special significance. Work itself took on the nature of vocation. Through work, 'the Protestant ethic', the Elect could find assurance that they were doing God's will and have assuredness therefore of salvation. The predestination of the Elect to heaven could be seen affirmed in material success of the Elect on Earth. Works or, in Weber's frame, *work*, was not a means but a sign of salvation. Protestant nations were the engine of modern-day capitalism. The theological value that Protestant nations place on work directly, if unintentionally, impacted on its development. Weber, rather than seeing religion as an anti-progressive force which needed to be abandoned before society could develop, saw rather a contrary impulse: modern, developed, industrialized societies formed through capitalist economic were forged not hindered by religion.

In his 'Science as a Vocation' however, Weber (2004) showed that the originating impulse of such theological values had been progressively lost, along with all other senses of the divine. The modern world, if formed by, no longer needed the religious impulse. The procedures and structures of capitalism could now work without recourse to anything but reason. This rationalization was a source of what Weber called disenchantment. Weber's 'Science as a Vocation' is a title that demonstrates a thesis:

> The fate of our times is characterized by rationalization and intellectualization, and, above all, by the 'disenchantment of the world.' Precisely the ultimate and most sublime values have retreated from public life either into the transcendental realm of mystic life or into the brotherliness of direct and personal human relations.
>
> (Weber 2004)

Weber suggested that modernity in its entirety was characterized by the malady of disenchantment.

Weber's disenchantment is then a loss of the sense of sacred through the rationalization of the modern world. Weber's disenchantment (like Tylor and Frazer) depends upon a view of religion as a proto-scientific-magical thinking. In *The Protestant Ethic and the Spirit of Capitalism*, Weber describes the priest as a 'magician'. The Protestant Reformation thereby gave the believer responsibility for working out that faith. This working out of faith required an independent, autonomous reasoning, which, where it met irresolvable conflicts, led many to another faith, that of Enlightenment rationalism itself. Protestantism contained in its origins the impetus that disenchantment which marks the modern world.

The social sciences and religious education

Classic reductionist accounts of religion across the social sciences, from Comte, Condorcet, Marx, through Tylor and Frazer to Durkheim and

Weber – adversarial and advocatory – did not systematically elaborate theories of secularization but they presumed it. Secularization is the theory that religion, once understood, would feature less and less as a determinant of social relations. However much formative influence religion had in the past, it would not feature in determining society's future. Classical sociological theory would thus frame the terms of debates later conceptualized around secularization by interpretive frameworks which sought not only to explain but also to explain religion away (Pals 2006). Secularization theory proper was framed by theorists such as Luckmann (1966), Berger (1967), Martin (1978), Wilson (1966) and revived by Taylor (2007, 2010). Renewed contemporary and historical interest around religion in public and political life (Burleigh 2006, 2007; Casanova 1994; Davis *et al.* 2005; Haynes 2008, 2009; Trigg 2007) has revitalized generalized assumptions about the marginalization of religion from the public to the private sphere, 'the process by which sectors of society and culture are removed from the domination of religious institutions and symbols' (Berger 1967: 107). Like Weber, Berger (1970) claimed that modern consciousness had itself become secularized.

Even amongst social scientists, secularization as a concept has however always been contested:

> Throughout the 1970s and 80s, a controversy has raged among sociologists of religion around the question of secularization. One of the most puzzling aspects of the discussion is that sometimes the issue has seemed to be not so much whether secularization actually occurred, but whether or not 'secularization theory' itself exists.
>
> (Tschannen 1991: 395)

Warner (1993) distinguishes between linear, non-dialectical and dialectical, non-linear models of secularization. The classic, linear model is associated with Talcott Parsons (1967), Robert Bellah (1967, 1968), Peter Berger (1967), Thomas Luckmann (Berger and Luckmann 1966), Bryan Wilson (1966), David Martin (1978; 2005) and Richard Fenn (1977, 1978). Warner argues that a new non-linear model of secularization is evident, which shows that the influence of religion ebbs and flows rather than retreats. Goldstein (2009, also 1999) challenges this view, arguing that the classic linear model fails by not identifying what is meant by linear and neglecting to acknowledge the dialectical non-linear aspects of the classical secularization theory. For Goldstein, no classic sociological theory of the role of religion argued that the path of its declining influence would be unimpeded.

Goldstein (2009) finds further support for this position in the way that secularization theorists themselves have moderated their formerly held position. Although many secularization theorists have not abandoned long-held positions (Bruce 2002, 2003; Martin 1978, 2005), some have. Significant is Bellah's conceptualization of religion as an integral part of human – biological as well as social evolution (Bellah 2011, 2012). Often cited as a notable retraction is the shift from a trenchant secularization by Berger's (1967) to a pronounced retraction in favour of a 'de-secularization' position (Berger 1999; see also Berger *et al.* 2008). Stark (1999b) puts it plainly: 'Secularization RIP'. Davie (2001) never thought that religion was dead in the first place.

Many prominent theorists of religious education suggest that the increased prominence of religion in education is indicative itself of a wider reversal of secularization in society. This I review elsewhere (Gearon 2012) in regard to the European Commission's largest-ever funded research initiative on religion in education, an eight-country study investigated whether religion in education is a source of conflict or dialogue, the REDCo project (Religion in Education. A Contribution to Dialogue or a Factor of Conflict in Transforming Societies of European Countries) (Jackson 2011a, 2011b). A foundational claim of REDCo researchers has been that current patterns in (European) religious education present decisive evidence of counter-secularization:

> In most European countries, we have assumed for a long time that increasing secularization would lead to a gradual retreat of religion from public space. This tendency has reversed itself in the course of the past decade as religion has returned to public attention.
>
> (Weisse 2011: 112)

Given the plethora or inter-governmental, that is political initiatives around religion in education, which I deal with in a later chapter, these international developments in religious education cannot be said to reflect counter-secularization if they are themselves driven by secular political forces, which it seems they are. Nevertheless, social scientific approaches to interpreting religion would seem to be highly appropriate here, that is, to serve such social and political prominence, and this remains one of the prime justifications for the appropriation of social scientific interpretations and methods religious education.

Religious education and the appropriation of social science

The educational impact of sociological understandings of religion is found most obviously in the educational system of France, where its founding thinkers arose – Comte, Condorcet, Rousseau and Durkheim – that is, by its absence (Dericquebourg 2012). The Cold War curricula of a good proportion of the world's population excluded religion in part on the basis of such sociological analysis. The absence of religious education is these cases was arguably a mark of success for the adversaries. But Grace (2004) found contemporary sociology of education discontinuing classical sociological interest by failing to take 'religion seriously'. Grace argues that contemporary sociology of education operates within a 'secularization of consciousness paradigm' that has limited both the depth and the scope of its intellectual enquiries', that sociological writing and research follows contemporary intellectual culture in the West by the 'secular marginalisation' of religion. Religion, it is true, features little in modern analyses of Durkheim in education (Durkheim 2009). Drawing on the historical canon of sociology – and citing Durkheim, Weber and Marx – Grace maintains that discussion of religion that once permeated discussion of social and economic relations no longer does. For Grace eighteenth- and nineteenth-century polemics against religion are now replaced 'by a cultural form of marginalisation and silence'. Grace explains his thesis by suggesting that, while the

> formation of many sociologists of education in the 1960s and 1970s involved some encounter... with the classic sociological discourses in which religion was implicated in various ways with social institutions and social processes... This grounding in 'grand theory' became progressively weaker in the 1980s and 1990s as sociology of education as a discipline became marginalised and reduced to technical service functions in the 'training' of teachers. A larger analytical vision of the historical and religious cultures of educational activity was lost at this time.
>
> (Grace 2004: 50)

In 'weakening its connection with the historical canon of sociology', the sociology of education has 'reduced its opportunities to take religions seriously in educational analysis'. Grace's analysis may apply to mainstream sociology of education but it cannot be supported when we find the prevalence of social science foundations for religious education. Indeed, within religious education we find such social scientific approaches, interpretations and methods not only in the origins of the modern field of religious education but in contemporary context proliferating.

The social sciences played a prominent early role in shaping the new thinking in mirrored in *Religious Education*. An early example was Greenwood Peabody's (1909) 'The Social Conscience and the Religious Life'. Amongst the most prominent was George A. Coe, a pioneer of religious education in America who, in 1922, in the aftermath of the First World War, contributed 'Religious Education and Political Conscience'. In 1932, Coe published a defining article on religious education and the social sciences, 'A Charter for the Social Sciences in the Schools'. This brought to religious educators' attention Charles Beard's (1932) report of the same title, *A Charter for the Social Sciences in Schools*. The latter underpinned the need for secular scholarship in the study of the religious:

> All forms of government, no less than the Constitution of the United States, all religions, all economic orders, all crafts and all arts, the noblest aspirations of humanity and the crimes of opinion and violence fall within the reach of their study and contemplation. Nature and natural

science in their manifold aspects are not alien to them, for mankind works with material instruments within geographical settings. A material scaffolding as well as accumulation of ideas accompanies the rise of civilization from primitive barbarism and cannot be ignored by those who would understand the past as it was and the present as it is foreshadowing always a future eternally in the process of becoming.

(Beard 1932: 6–7)

Coe's assessment of the report has all the optimism of Enlightenment, plainly read, that material advancement and social progress goes hand in hand with knowledge. With continued calls over intervening years – LeFevre's (1959) 'Religion and the Teaching of the Social Sciences' – half a century later, Wilhoit makes a more pessimistic assessment of the impact of the social sciences on religious education:

Throughout this century religious education has been admonished to ground itself on the social sciences. Tremendous benefits were to result; still little has occurred. Social scientists are frustrated because their work is either ignored or misused. Religious educators are frustrated because they are not supplied with answers to the questions they judge to be significant. So it is that educational ideologies, theology and 'commonsense' shape and inform religious education far more than rigorous empirical findings.

(Wilhoit 1984: 367)

Despite their claims to unify social science and religious education, Wilhoit criticizes Coe (for example, Coe 1917, 1932) – who 'gave us religious education without social science'; he 'simply told us [social science] was valuable'. He also condemned later advocates of social science for religious such as James Michael Lee (1973) 'who gave us social science without religious education', who had attacked 'nonscience based theories…without a comprehensive theory of religious education' (Wilhoit 1984: 367).

Three years later, Moore (1987) is *lauding* Coe and others – from Thomas Groome to Jack Seymour – for their contributions to the tradition. After Moore's paper, the tensions were highlighted once again in a profound and profoundly neglected paper in which Snelling (1989) examined not only the aims and objectives and respective methods of cross-fertilization of these between the social sciences and religious education but their respective *ultimate* ends. The interface has arguably been re-energized by a seeming resurgence of the social and political prominence of religion. Seymour (2012) in his *Religious Education* editorial – 'Theology, Education, and Social Science' – asks whether religious education is a theological, educational or social science discipline. Seymour argues that when we look at the theory and practice of religious education it is in effect all three, or at least contains elements of each.

However, social science approaches in religious education seem to be taking an ever more prominent role in international understandings of the subject, in terms of its aims, fundamental purposes and pedagogy. The increasing predominance of social science approaches in religious education have been greatly shaped of late by Robert Jackson's (1997) *Religious Education: An Interpretive Approach*, a seminal work which has had in a relatively short period of time, an immense international impact on educational thinking about the wider roles of religion, in schooling, education policy and research, across Europe and worldwide.

The interpretive approach was the method informing research and pedagogical thinking in the REDCo project. Drawing on methodological ideas from cultural anthropology, it recognizes the inner diversity, fuzzy edgedness and contested nature of religious traditions, as well as the complexity of cultural expression and the change from social and individual perspectives (Jackson and O'Grady 2007: 182).

As the critical realist sees the learner as a budding philosopher, the interpretive approach sees them as anthropologists and ethnographers. The interpretive approach aims to help children and young people to find their own positions within the key debates about religious plurality (Jackson 1997, 2004; Willaime 2007).

The origins of this approach lie in the founding socio-anthropological tradition just sketched. The most influential adaptation of sociocultural frameworks has been via the ethnographical work of anthropologist Clifford Geertz (1926–2006), particularly *The Interpretation of Cultures* (1973). Geertz was interested in 'thick' descriptions of particular cultures, to build up a sense of a culture through the minute detail of its lived realities. He undertook ethnographic fieldwork in Bali, Java and Morocco, collecting these into a theoretical framework in *The Interpretation of Cultures*. Towards the end of his life, for the 1999 Charles Homer Haskins Lecture, 'A Life of Learning', Geertz – a cultural anthropologist whose methods had wide influence beyond his own field, in the study of religion, as we shall see, in education and a general readership – modestly opens the lecture with the statement: 'It is a shaking business to stand up in public toward the end of an improvised life and call it learned' (Geertz 1999: 1). He was one whose 'speculative instruments' were applied as 'someone who saw human beings' as, paraphrasing Weber, 'suspended in webs of meaning they themselves have spun' (Geertz 1999: 14). He follows Durkheim, too, in looking at minutiae to understand the whole, not the whole to understand minutiae. What Durkheim wrote in *The Elementary Forms* might be said of Geertz, contrasting those 'formula[e] [which] attempt to express the nature of religion as a whole' and which proceed

> as if religion formed a kind of seamless entity, although in reality it is formed of parts ... Now the whole can de defined only in relation to the parts that comprise it, so it is more methodical to try and characterize

the elementary phenomenon that generate religion than to characterize the system they produce.

(Durkheim 2001: 35–6)

In the educational context, ethnographic studies in religious education have similarly focused on children in their own communities, what Arweck and Nesbitt (2010a) call 'plurality at close quarters' (see also Arweck and Nesbitt 2010b, 2010c). Ethnographic method thus forms the empirical and methodological basis for later curricula and pedagogical frameworks, establishing a 'close link between the activity of the ethnographic researcher, working on field research, and the activity of the learner in the classroom, attempting to understand religions in the contemporary world' (Jackson 2011b: 190; also Arweck 2009).

The interpretive approach, consciously attending to research and pedagogy, identifies three levels of operation: representation; interpretation; reflexivity.

> The interpretive approach is concerned with how religions are represented, for example, by practitioners, by the media and by resources for religious education. It takes a critical stance towards Western, post-Enlightenment models of representing world religions as homogeneous belief systems, whose essence is expressed through set structures and whose membership is seen in terms of necessary and sufficient conditions.
>
> (Jackson 2011b: 191)

Drawing on sociocultural models that assert the complexity of representation (ethnographers focus on *detail*), the approach is also critical of attempts to 'essentialise or stereotype religions' (Jackson 2011b: 191). A religious tradition is thus seen 'as a contested whole'. Religious traditions are researched and taught in all their 'complexity and internal diversity' (Jackson 2011b: 191).

The second feature of *interpretation* is also influenced by Geertz and is consciously distanced from theology: 'the interpretive approach is not derived from theology'. The approach, it is claimed, is not relativistic in relation to truth, acknowledging varying and often competing truth claims. Jackson contrasts this with the phenomenology of religion,

> in which researchers or learners are expected to leave their presuppositions to one side, the interpretive method requires a comparison and contrast between the religious symbols, concepts and experiences of those being studied and the nearest equivalent concepts, symbols and experiences of the researcher or learner (whether religious or not).
>
> (Jackson 2011b: 191)

Sensitivity to the perspective of the other is, however, a necessary condition of this approach, with the claim that 'genuine empathy' is 'possible once the concepts of the others' discourse have been understood'. A 'basic aim' for religious education is 'to develop a knowledge and understanding of the grammar, the language and wider symbolic patterns used by people within religious traditions, so one might understand better their beliefs, feelings and attitudes' (Jackson 2011b: 192).

Reflexivity is understood as 'the relationship between the experience of researchers/students and the experience of those whose way of life they are attempting to interpret'. Three aspects of reflexivity relate to religious education:

> Researchers/learners are encouraged to review their understanding of their own worldview in relation to what they have studied (edification). They are helped to make a constructive and informed critique of the material studied at a distance, and they are involved in reviewing their own methods of research/study.
>
> (Jackson 2011b: 192)

In the interpretive approach, 'the term edification is used to describe this form of learning'. In practice, 'such reflexive activity is not easily separable from the process of interpretation'. Interpretation 'might start from the other's language and experience, then move to that of the student, and then move between the two'. Thus, 'the process of understanding another's way of life is inseparable, practically, from considering issues and questions raised by it' (Jackson 2011b: 192–3).

The interpretive approach, in its use of ethnographic method, has increased our knowledge of the complexities of representation of religion, 'Edification need not only result from studying religions or cultures other than one's own. The study of one's own ancestral tradition, in religious or cultural terms, can also give new insights in re-examining one's sense of identity' (Jackson 2011b: 193). But the aims and purposes of edification seem, from my reading, to be directed primarily to towards meeting the challenges of such religious diversity, 'it builds upon a positive attitude towards diversity, recognising the encounter of people with different beliefs and cultural practices as enriching in principle', and so forth.

Nevertheless, in and through these sociocultural emphases, the ethnographic approach has been a key mover in the development of programmes of religion in education internationally, not least, as we shall see, because of its political applications.

Summary

Religion in education generally (see Cooling 2009) and religious education specifically (Arthur *et al.* 2010) have become a central part of long-contested historical and present-day debates around religion in the social sciences. These debates are refracted in and through discussions on the role of religion in education, in theory and practice. Each country worldwide has its own version of the story and ongoing attempts at – educational, legal, political – resolution (see Davis and Miroshnikova 2013). The prominence of religion in public and political life, as has been noted (Burleigh 2006, 2007; Casanova, 1994; Davis *et al.* 2005; Haynes 2008, 2009; Trigg 2007), undoubtedly accounts for the increased interest in religion in *education* (again, this is unarguable if we examine the contexts treated by Davis and Miroshnikova 2013). This international social and political profile for religion, and of religion in education, accounts for the prevalence of social scientific appropriations in religious education theory and practice. For the theoretical underpinning of the social sciences here provides a unity of social and political need (dealing with religious diversity and plurality) with pedagogical practice.

However, in closing this chapter, we might return to Seymour's (2012) *Religious Education* editorial, 'Theology, Education, and Social Science'. In asking whether religious education is a theological, educational or social science discipline, Seymour argued that when we look at the theory and practice of religious education it is in effect all three, or at least contains elements of each. Perhaps something more profound needs to be asked.

The really fundamental question here might be framed as: what is the extent to which each or all domains (theological, educational, social scientific) find not influence but priority in the field of religious education? The answer to that question, as Wilfred Cantwell Smith (1991) put it, depends upon the view taken of the meaning and end of religion itself. If religion is seen as (simply) an instrument of social progress or academic knowledge social scientific appropriations can be seen as entirely satisfactory, serving pedagogical as well as socio-political needs. Nevertheless, the answer will be very different if one holds that the core ends and purposes of religion are at root, in essence, of deeper (existential, salvific) significance than the (merely) social or political. A religious education in this latter, deeper sense would regard religion in education that acts (merely) as a servant of the social and the political as a limited and limiting educational goal, however profoundly insightful the social scientific theory and methods underpinning pedagogical practice.

5 Psychology, spirituality and religious education

Introduction

All psychology of religion ultimately reduces religious belief and practice to terms relevant to the mind, the psyche or psychological states. The terms 'reductionist' or 'functionalist' are traditionally applied in the study of religion to theories that seek to explain the underlying terms of religious belief and practice because (a) they *reduce* to a category outside of religion, or (b) theorize religion as a function of those reduced terms. Strands of psychology seeking more conciliatory paths admit the psychopathological possibilities of religion, while acknowledging aspects contributory to psychological health, from William James to analyses which regard religious experience as a 'natural' part of 'ordinary' cognitive processes (James 1985; Boyer 2001; and many other studies, see Inzlicht *et al.* 2011). Initially conflictual and then more conciliatory relations between psychology and religion would come to be reflected in religious education (Enger 1992).

Psychology and religion

Hall *et al.* assess the antiquity of psychological reflection in religion prior to the emergence of psychology as a discipline:

> Descriptive reflections on the relationship between faith and daily living can be found in writings now seen as the scriptures of the major world religions, and from St Augustine onwards the theological tradition has offered sophisticated accounts of the person. This trend is illustrated by the traditions of the medieval mystics, and the work of eighteenth and nineteenth century philosophers and theologians.
>
> (Hall *et al.* 2011: 260)

Psychology as a discipline, they argue, emerged from post-enlightenment roots 'in theology, as well as anthropology, physiology, education and philosophy'. These ancient and modern histories account for present-day preoccupations – tensions and accommodations – between 'psychology (as a

natural science of behaviour), the human spirit, theology, religious experience and practice' (Hall *et al.* 2011: 260–2). As the authors point out, the
religious and the psychological are not necessarily in tension but often
compete, illustrated by reference to the religious background of many seminal psychologists: Ivan Pavlov (1849–1936), in behavioural psychology
(Russian Orthodox background), Wilhelm Wundt (1832–1920), a founding
figure in experimental psychology (and Lutheran). Equally, we might cite the
Judaism of Sigmund Freud (1856–1939) in psychoanalysis; the Reformed
Protestantism of Carl Gustav Jung (1875–1961), analytical psychology and
psychotherapy or the Episcopalianism of William James (1842–1910),
amongst many fields, in philosophy but particularly the psychology of religion itself. There is often then an autobiographical influence on the manner
of resolution of relations between psychology and religion. But it always
involved some epistemological distancing between religious authority and
scientific finding. So, the 'stance of psychology of religion is one outside any
of the religious traditions, whose credal statements and theologies are not
treated as authoritative of themselves' (Hall *et al.* 2011: 262). The founding,
most influential writings on religion in modern psychology tended towards
the adversarial.

The psychological adversaries of religion

The earliest attempts to recognize in religion the underlying psychological or
psychic forces that account for the origin, development and persistence of
religion were influenced by the findings of social anthropology as much as by
psychology itself. As we saw in the last chapter, the origins of religion were
identified with primitive reflection on dreams, on the pro-scientific explanation and control of the world through ritual. Belief in spirits was
characterized as the defining feature of primitive belief as we have seen in
Tylor, Frazer and other pioneering anthropologists. Drawing on such socio-
anthropological insight, religious belief and practice became a model of the
neurosis, personal and collective.

Sigmund Freud (1856–1939) and psychoanalysis pioneered this interpretation. Freudian theory was in large measure drawn from a new form of
medical practice, talking with patients to elucidate conflicts between the
conscious mind and the repressed contents of the unconscious. Freud's
psychoanalytical method was derived from the idea that a rational, that is,
conscious understanding of the causes of such repression would help to
remove them. Since the sources of conscious or waking-state unhappiness
were often to be found repressed in unconscious mental states, psychoanalysis developed a particularly focus on dreams. *On the Interpretation of Dreams*
(1901) proposed dreams as the mechanism of release for repressed conscious
desires and fears. Sexual desire was the primary instinctual force (Freud
1991) and the family the most significant source of conflict for desires
prohibited; what Freud referred to as the Oedipus complex. In healthy

individuals, normal development led to resolution through maturity positive sublimation outlets for desire. In unhealthy, unhappy, individuals, this process of development was blocked and resulted in neurotic or psychotic states preventing normal development. The prime motive of psychoanalysis was the establishment of mental health; what Freud described as the alleviation of acute and chronic unhappiness, so patients could come to an acceptance of the normal unhappiness which is the human condition.

Only later did Freud see the potential of this theory of the unconscious for understanding culture more generally. Only in his final decades did Freud consistently focus on religion as the collective source of repressive tendencies in society at large. We see these ideas first applied to religion in systematic fashion in *Totem and Taboo* (Freud 1990), published within a year of Durkheim's (2001) *Elementary Forms of the Religious Life*. Here, Freud drew on anthropological studies to show the revered totem and the taboos surrounding it as displacements and repressions expressed in primal, sacred terms of the son's desire for the mother, repressed by the father, manifest through prohibitions on killing the totem (often an animal), a powerful desire which needed occasional release through the killing of the totem on ritual occasions. But in naming the Oedipus complex, as he did from Sophocles' drama, he had already intimated that these desires were to be found – likely unconscious – in cultural and particularly in religious form (Freud 1990).

In his later work, Freud more fully applied psychoanalytical theory of the individual unconscious to cultural and social contexts. The creative force of such sublimated desires accounts for the application of Freudian and psychological theories of the unconscious in their impact upon cultural theory (notably, Lacan 2007; Lévi-Strauss 1974, 1994, 2011; Ricoeur 1970). Freud had also drawn on many disciplines and recent work re-examines this (Kaplan and Parsons 2010).

For Freud, this was not merely a speculative but a therapeutic necessity. The signs of sexual and other forms of repression were individual but the sources were cultural, social and most often religious. If the causes of repressive mental states had their origin beyond the individual, the cause needed to be dealt with as well as the symptom. Early psychoanalytical theory and practice focused on conflictual relationships between conscious and unconscious. This developed into a more complex model of interaction between psychological and sociocultural factors. These were conceived as the interrelationship between primal unconscious desires (the id), the individual conscious self (ego) and those cultural and social mechanisms (super-ego), which perpetuated conflict between id and ego but which also found displaced ('narcissistic') satisfactions in cultural, especially religious forms. In *Civilization and Its Discontents* (1930), Freud (1985) recognized the positive contribution of repression to the development of culture. Freud saw in libidinous repression the transformation of such energies as the basis of civilization. Nevertheless, those forces that had helped to create were also capable of hampering the development of society as they were creating neurotic and psychotic states in individual lives.

Like Feuerbach, Freud saw religion as a projection of unfulfilled desires on an indifferent universe. Early psychoanalytical theory gave primacy to sexual desire as a key psychic force. Later, to account for the destructive inclinations of the psyche, Freud later conceived a competing aggressive force or 'death instinct' (Freud 1985). These instincts were real but the religious forms which human beings and civilizations gave them were illusory. Freud saw psychic expressions of the 'Oedipus complex' in cultural and especially in religious form, particularly in monotheistic traditions, which conceived of God as father or father-like, notably in terms of its origins and evolution in *Totem and Taboo* ([1912] Freud 2001). Without the self-censoring reserve of Tylor or Frazer, *Moses and Monotheism* (1939) with *Civilization and Its Discontents* (1930) identifies Judaism and Christianity as neuroses writ large. To achieve cultural as much as personal maturity, the sources of these displaced sexual desires needed to be recognized and transcended (Freud 1985, 1990, 2001).

It was in *Future of an Illusion* that Freud delivers his most openly hostile pronouncements against religion. 'Religious ideas,' he argues, 'are teachings and assertions about facts and conditions of external (or internal) reality which tell one something one has not discovered for oneself and which lay claim to one's belief'. They may be highly prized but they are delusional. Freud contrasts religious teaching with school subjects:

> Let us take geography. We are told that the town of Constance lies on the Bodensee. A student song adds: 'if you don't believe it, go and see.' I happen to have been there and can confirm the fact that that lovely town lies on the shore of a wide stretch of water which all those who live round it call the Bodensee; and I am now completely convinced of the correctness of this geographical assertion.
>
> (Freud 1985: 206)

'All teachings like these,' then, 'demand belief in their contents, but not without producing grounds for their claim'. Knowledge based on observation is provided for these the ideas, at least hypothetically. For instance, 'the Earth is shaped like a sphere' and 'the proofs adduced for this are Foucault's pendulum experiment, the behaviour of the horizon and the possibility of circumnavigating the Earth'. Although it is not necessary 'to send every schoolchild on a voyage round the world', we are 'satisfied with letting what is taught at school be taken on trust' while 'the path to acquiring a personal conviction remains open'. Of religious teaching, he makes a severe contrast:

> Let us try to apply the same test to the teachings of religion. When we ask on what their claim to be believed is founded, we are met with three answers, which harmonize remarkably badly with one another. Firstly,

these teachings deserve to be believed because they were already believed by our primal ancestors; secondly, we possess proofs which have been handed down to us from those same primeval times; and thirdly, it is forbidden to raise the question of their authentication at all. In former days anything so presumptuous was visited with the severest penalties, and even to-day society looks askance at any attempt to raise the question again.

(Freud 1985: 207)

[This] is bound to rouse our strongest suspicions . . . After all, a prohibition like this can only be for one reason – that society is very well aware of the insecurity of the claim it makes on behalf of its religious doctrines. Otherwise it would certainly be very ready to put the necessary data at the disposal of anyone who wanted to arrive at conviction.

(Freud 1985: 208)

It is no use appealing to ancestral or textual authority. The former were ignorant, the latter unreliable.

Special derision is applied to reliance on divine authority in religious texts:

It does not help much to have it asserted that their wording, or even their content only, originates from divine revelation; for this assertion is itself one of the doctrines whose authenticity is under examination, and no proposition can be a proof of itself. . . Thus we arrive at the singular conclusion that of all the information provided by our cultural assets it is precisely the elements which might be of the greatest importance to us and which have the task of solving the riddles of the universe and of reconciling us to the sufferings of life – it is precisely those elements that are the least well authenticated of any.

(Freud 1985: 209)

Why is it claimed that experience grounds belief? If religious belief is dependent on religious experience, Freud answers (as Kant had), how then might such experiences be verified? How are we to know their source? C. K. Vaihinger (1852–1933), a follower of Kant and admirer of Nietzsche, had proposed rather a philosophy of what came to be known as 'fictionalism'. In his book *Als Ob* (translated to English in 1924 as *The Philosophy of As If*) had proposed that, rather than give some sort of epistemological priority to reason (say) over religion, all forms of knowing the world were in a sense human constructions, including logic, and that these ways of thinking are simply useful ways of operating in the world. This was a radical notion. For Vaihinger, knowing the 'theoretical, practical and religious fictions of mankind', or knowing what we know is a fiction, a human construction, should not prevent us from living 'as if' such fictions were true, they are true in the sense that they are useful (Vaihinger 1935). Freud relates how he would tell his children fairy tales and when they asked if the stories were true and found they were not, they would 'turn away with a look of disdain'. So, if we live according to religious belief 'as if' it were true, then what is the difference between this and living according to a fairy tale: 'We may expect that people will soon behave in the same way towards the fairy tales of religion, in spite of the advocacy of "As if"' (Freud 1985: 201–11). 'It would be very nice', Freud acknowledges,

> if there were a God who created the world and was a benevolent Providence, and if there were a moral order in the universe and an afterlife; but it is a very striking fact that all this is exactly as we are bound to wish it to be.
>
> (Freud 1985: 215)

His reason, however, tells him that religion is no more than, following Feuerbach, a wish fulfilment.

We need an 'education to reality', one that rids us of religious illusion. Religion and education are contradictory. Science is neither illusory nor contradictory. Modern-day critiques of Freud most often relate to the lack of scientific rigour in the wider applications of his psychoanalytical theories to areas of social and cultural life far beyond individual psychoses. Where Freud's scientific rigour was questioned, this opened the way for his framework to applications in philosophy, in the humanities, especially in art and literature, which had often been used by Freud as exemplars and also formed the basis for whole fields of enquiry in feminist theory, sociolinguistics and social anthropology. But Freud did not share the Enlightenment optimism about some sudden transformation of the social and political order. Since religion emerged from deep psychic needs and desires, any holistic substitutes – and here Freud is talking of political as well as psychological states – would need 'another system of doctrines' and 'such a system would from the outset take over all the psychological characteristics of religion – the same sanctity, rigidity and intolerance, the same prohibition of thought – for its own defence' (Freud 1985: 235).

The atheistic outlook of the founder of psychoanalysis and his Jewish heritage are factors outlined by Gay (1989) in *A Godless Jew: Freud, Atheism, and the Making of Psychoanalysis*. One of the claims made of Freud, notably by Rieff (2006) in *Triumph of the Therapeutic* was that psychoanalysis had itself had become a belief system, with its own view of the human condition. The psychoanalyst in this framework replaced the priest. Indeed, in 1912, Freud formed a self-designated 'secret committee', an inner sanctum of believers, to protect the core truths of psychoanalysis. Barrett (2012) treating of this 'secret committee', argues that it was a mistake which separated psychoanalysis from still wider influence, not simply to heal patients but also society.

The social influence of Freud's psychological theories was, however, considerable. In a visit (29 August to 21 September 1909), Freud visited the

United States, giving five lectures at Clark University in Worcester, Massachusetts. Freud had predicted that America would be the future of psychoanalysis. In *After Freud Left: A Century of Psychoanalysis in America*, Burnham (2012) shows how profoundly Freud's influence has been felt there since that one short visit.

But the influence has extended far beyond America. Rieff's (1979) *Freud: The Mind of the Moralist* showed Freud's influence manifest in the emergence of psychoanalysis' own morality. The sexual liberation it preached would have far-reaching moral consequences in sexual attitudes and practice across the Western world. The sociological analysis of this is indirectly attested to, especially in its secularizing impact, in Brown's (2009) *The Death of Christian Britain* (also Brown 2000). Brown argues that the real effect of secularization was in moral attitudes and behaviour, especially the sexual liberation of the 1960s counter-culture. The sexual liberation that Freud saw as psychological health had its secularising effects. In social psychology, the once influential Erich Fromm (1900–1980) identifies these changing sexual attitudes not only with social and political but existential freedom (Fromm 1957, 1994, 2001). All individual freedom is in part a struggle with constraint, for Fromm a perennial tension between the restraints any community places upon individual freedom – the more extreme the community, the more restrictive the freedom. Religion is naturally restraining but it is at the time (for some) liberating. In his 1957 Terry lectures (Jung had delivered these in 1937), Fromm chose to discuss the importance of the relationship between *Psychoanalysis and Religion* (Fromm 1959). Psychoanalysis and religion can work together to enhance freedom, for Fromm only through the realisation of this freedom is it possible to realize the potentiality of human being.

Black (2006) contests too the antagonistic frame between religion and psychoanalysis. From the origins of psychoanalysis, this antagonism was not universally shared. This we see demonstrated in Fromm's interests in religion, positively *framed* but an interpretation which sees religion also *reframed* in the image of psychoanalytical theory and practice.

The psychological advocates of religion

The psychological advocates of religion pioneered the description and classification of psychological aspects of religious phenomena without unduly pejorative judgement, understanding religion as a *psychological* reality, potentially, but not necessarily, harmful and in many respects potentially conducive to mental health. Two trends epitomize this more conciliatory relationship between psychology and religion: first, the analytical psychology of Carl Jung and, more widely, the positive psychological traditions of psychotherapy and some branches of psychiatry; second, descriptive–naturalistic approaches to understanding, without necessarily pejorative judgement of religion, which emerge from the descriptive psychological treatments of Williams James, and a diverse range of similarly naturalistic explanations of religion, which seek to explain religion as part of cognitive function.

First, then, we can sketch the analytical psychology of Carl Gustav Jung (1875–1961), the implications for a psychology of religion and its impact on psychotherapy. Even as Freud's major works on religion were being published, Jung was systematically re-evaluating the relationship between psychology and religion. Both Freud and Jung saw signs of the repression of individual and collective instinctual forces but conceived of them differently. The differences arise in how the unconscious is modelled. For Freud, if civilization was to progress, humanity needed to be increasingly rational, recognizing but triumphing over and thus transforming instinctual forces. To this extent, Freud recognized the need if humanity was to develop a psychologically balanced compromise between the id, the ego and super-ego. Not all desires can and should be satisfied. This would result in anarchy, disorder and, ultimately, the destruction of civilization. Reason not instinct should therefore rule. As we have noted, for Freud, there was no court higher than the court of reason.

Differences between Freud and Jung, however, centred initially around understandings of the unconscious which subsequently provided new interpretations of religion. *Jung's Map of the Soul*, Stein's (1998) survey of Jungian analysis – Jungian analysis was thus differentiated from Freudian psychoanalysis – indicates profound difference between the two approaches. Jung took a deep understanding and more sympathetic view of those manifestations of the psyche that are found in material expression in human cultures worldwide. He postulated a collective unconscious in which certain prevalent *archetypes* – the shadow, the anima and the animus, respectively the 'dark', the 'female' and the 'male' – were common elements in all human consciousness. His ideas, spanning six decades on this topic, are collected in *The Archetypes and the Collective Unconscious* (Jung 1981). These were inherited psychological structures from evolutionary history, which, as with Freud, manifest in dreams. In *Memories, Dreams, Reflections*, Jung ([1962] 1989) shows how his understanding of the unconscious differed from Freud's, providing a radical new interpretive frame for understanding how the psychic effects become a manifest cultural form, an idea which Jung saw as a means of widening the public appeal of his ideas (Jung 1968). For Jung, the unconscious was a vast reservoir of psychic material inherited from a primeval past. Only through unification of these unconscious elements of the psyche with conscious processes could the mind achieve psychological harmony. Jungian analysis was not a battle for supremacy of conscious reason over unconscious irrationality but a process of integration of conscious and unconscious, which Jung termed 'individuation'. Individuation is the central task of Jungian analysis. It was pointless simply to use the rational mind to understand the unconscious without somehow integrating one with the other. The irrational unconscious was as much a part of what it was to be human as the rational conscious. Simply to assert the supremacy of reason over unreason or instinct was to Jung precisely the problem of modern man in the first place. The overemphasis on the rational had led to a complete dissociation of the mind from its unconscious self. The result was evident in individual neuroses and psychoses but also in a psychically divided world. In his later years, for example, Jung saw the Berlin Wall and the Iron Curtain division between East and West as symbolic of psychological disaggregation of conscious and unconscious, psychic disharmony manifest as a destructive political divide.

Jung's last major work, *The Undiscovered Self* ([1957] 2010), was a piece of self-analysis, giving insights into the mind of analyst himself. The volume spans autobiography, personal and professional, including formative years with Freud, the break with psychoanalysis, Jung's innovative thinking on culture and the collective unconscious, reflections on religion and psychology, specific discussions of Christianity, the existence of God and personal reflections on death, as his own approached. Of all modern figures in psychology, Jung represents the most significant rapprochement with religion, one which Freud regarded as a personal as well professional betrayal of the principles of psychoanalysis and a regressive step for psychiatry. Disagreements over religion were as central a source of disagreement as their respective understandings of the unconscious, evident from correspondence between Freud and Jung onwards (McGuire 1974; Palmer 1997).

The idea that religion can be a means whereby human beings unify the conscious and unconscious opened entire new avenues for psychotherapeutic models of healing as much as did for the interpretation of religion. In fact, interpreting the unconscious mind as manifest in the symbols of religion and culture more generally could be part of a healing not only of persons but societies.

Such rehabilitation between psychology and religion is demonstrable in psychotherapeutic and psychiatric practice (for example, Koenig *et al.* 2001). The residual scepticism towards religion and spirituality persists but the perceived therapeutic usefulness of religious belief and practice is becoming a more acceptable aspect of treatment in the mental health profession (Black 2006; Pargament 1999; Miller 2012). The British Psychiatric Association opens: 'Spirituality and psychiatry – on the face of it, they do not seem to have much in common. But we are becoming increasingly aware of ways in which some aspects of spirituality can offer real benefits for mental health'. The guidance it provides is for patients and anyone with a general interest in spiritual and mental health but the undercurrent of potential resistance is apparent in the suggestion that the material is also for 'professionals who may not be sure about how to explore spiritual issues with their clients/patients'. Its focus is threefold, examining: 'how spirituality, mental health and mental healthcare can connect; how to make a place for spiritual needs within a mental health service'; and 'how spirituality can help mental health'.

This is part of a well-documented tendency to describe themselves as 'spiritual-but-not-religious' (Collicutt 2011), including those who claim to be atheists but at the same time 'spiritual' (Streib *et al.* 2009). This inclusivity means minimal or no dogmatic or doctrinal requirements: 'You don't need to hold a formal religious belief, to take part in religious practices, or belong to an established faith tradition ... to experience spirituality'. Spirituality is defined as involving 'experiences' relating to: 'a deep-seated sense of meaning and purpose in life; a sense of belonging'; a sense of connection of 'the deeply personal with the universal; acceptance, integration and a sense of wholeness'. These experiences 'are part of being human'. Spirituality, thus interpreted, 'often becomes more important in times of distress, emotional stress, physical and mental illness, loss, bereavement and the approach of death'. Thus, while '[a]ll health care tries to relieve pain and to cure ... good health care tries to do more': 'Spirituality emphasises the healing of the person, not just the disease. It views life as a journey where good and bad experiences can help you to learn, develop and mature'.

Prevalent in such approaches is a distinction between 'spirituality' and 'religion':

> Religious traditions certainly include individual spirituality, which is universal. But each religion has its own distinct community-based worship, beliefs, sacred texts and traditions. Spirituality is not tied to any particular religious belief or tradition. Although culture and beliefs can play a part in spirituality, every person has their own unique experience of spirituality – it can be a personal experience for anyone, with or without a religious belief. It's there for anyone. Spirituality also highlights how connected we are to the world and other people.
>
> (RCPSYCH 2013)

People with mental health problems have said that they want:

- meaningful activity such as creative art, work or enjoying nature
- to feel safe and secure
- to be treated with dignity and respect
- to feel that they belong, are valued and trusted
- time to express feelings to members of staff
- the chance to make sense of their life – including illness and loss
- permission/support to develop their relationship with God or the Absolute.

Someone with a religious belief may need:

- a time, a place and privacy in which to pray and worship
- the chance to explore spiritual (and sometimes religious) matters
- to be reassured that the psychiatrist will not try to undermine their faith
- encouragement to deepen their faith
- to feel universally connected
- sometimes – the need for forgiveness.

The guidance offers parameters for 'religious/spiritual' assessment:

> A helpful way to begin can be to ask 'Would you say you are spiritual or religious in any way? Please tell me how.' Another useful question is, 'What sustains you?' or 'What keeps you going in difficult times?' The answer to this will usually reveal a person's main spiritual concerns and practices.
>
> (RCPSYCH 2013)

A 'gentle, unhurried approach works best – at its best, exploring spiritual issues can be therapeutic in itself'. Life reflection – the 'past', 'present' and 'future' – are integrated into a 'setting the scene', asking, for example: 'What is your life all about? Is there anything that gives you a sense of meaning or purpose?' The extent of the rapprochement shows the level of integration of religion with psychiatric practice: 'A spiritual assessment should be part of every mental health assessment'. Mental health professionals 'also need to be able to distinguish between a spiritual crisis and a mental illness, particularly when these overlap'. 'Spiritual practices' themselves may 'span a wide range, from the religious to secular – which may not be obviously spiritual', include the following rather diverse psychotherapeutic directions:

- belong to a faith tradition and take part in services or other activities with other people
- take part in rituals, symbolic practices and other forms of worship
- go on pilgrimage and retreats
- spend time in meditation and prayer
- read scripture
- listen to singing and/or playing sacred music, including songs, hymns, psalms and devotional chants
- spend time enjoying nature
- appreciate the arts
- be creative - in painting, sculpture, cookery, gardening, etc.
- join in team sports or other activities that involve cooperation and trust.

(RCPSYCH 2013)

Such guidance is directed to practitioners as well as potential patients. It is evidence based and justified on the needs of patients:

> Medicine, once fully bound up with religion, retains a sacred dimension for many. Differing religious beliefs and practices can be divisive. Spirituality, however, links the deeply personal with the universal and is essentially unifying. Without boundaries, it is difficult to define, but its impact can be measured. This is important because, although attendance in churches is low and falling, people increasingly... admit to spiritual and religious experiences.
>
> (Culliford 2002: 1434)

Psychiatric practice may thus be more sophisticated than the generalities presented by the Royal College of Psychiatry guide to the issues for a general readership (see for example, Anandarajah and Hight 2001; Culliford 2002, 2007; Cook *et al.* 2009) but a psychotherapeutic principle becomes apparent – that religion does not have to be true to be useful.

These and other developments – the British Psychological Association, the Spirituality and Psychiatry Special Interest Group (SPSIG) of the Royal College of Psychiatrists, and so forth – demonstrate how far mental health practice has incorporated the spiritual and how far this position has shifted from antagonism in the origins within psychoanalysis. These reconciliations of psychology and religion recognize positive benefits in encouraging religious belief and practice. These psychotherapeutic approaches also tend though to favour the use of the term spirituality rather than religion. This might be seen as these approaches distilling spiritual practice (prayer, meditation, mindfulness) without the requirements of doctrine. For this reason, psychotherapeutic approaches will also tend to be more favourable to those traditions which themselves depend less on the acceptance of doctrine on the basis of religious authority and encourage the individual search and testing of experience. Here, there is little separation between psychological and 'spiritual' health. Yet, even if religious practice is encouraged, evidence shows persistently low levels of religious belief amongst academic and psychotherapeutic professionals themselves (see Ecklund and Scheitle 2007; Ecklund *et al.* 2011).

Thus, many (for example, Heelas *et al.* 2004) identify this as a 'revolution' in spirituality where 'spiritual life' is no longer solely associated with religious traditions, 'belief beyond religion' (Lynch 2007), even a failure of organized religion, allowing a new 'sociology of spirituality' (Flanagan and Jupp 2009). Widely aligned to personal wellbeing, such forms of spirituality even being associated with the future of religion, few such analyses take into account the contemporary persistence of the very historical forms of spirituality that such alternative models have supposedly subsumed (cf. Sheldrake 1996).

The second trend in the reconciliation of psychology and religion are descriptive–naturalistic approaches. In America, Edwin Starbuck's *The Psychology of Religion* (Starbuck 1911, with a preface by William James), was followed a quarter of a century later in Britain with Robert Henry Thouless's (1971) 1920s text, *Introduction to the Psychology of Religion*. The naturalistic premise here is that religion is an aspect of psychological state and function. William James's (1985) *Varieties of Religious Experience* is a pre-eminent example. Except in dealing with neurotic and psychotic states, much contemporary cognitive scientific interest in religion is also in this category, seeking less to judge the religious life as delusory and seeking to understand the psychological effects of religion on the religious actor and believer. James took a phenomenological–pragmatic stance. Before Freud developed his sexual interpretation of religion, James was anticipating a rejection of it. James nevertheless does frame religion in terms of human psychology and this he is able to do by focusing specifically upon religious *experience*. James's 1902 Gifford lectures in Edinburgh, *The Varieties of Religious Experience* (James 1985) is a foundational text in the psychology of religion. Recognizing the difficulty of defining religion – it 'cannot stand for any single principle or essence, but is rather a collective name' – and oversimplified understanding being 'the root of all that absolutism and one-sided dogmatism by which both philosophy and religion have been infested', James is pragmatic: let us not descend into a one-sided view but rather say 'freely at the outset that we may very likely find no one essence, but many characters which may alternately be equally important to religion' (James 1985: 26).

It is religious experience (the 'religious sentiment'), itself diverse in object and interpretation – allied to 'the feeling of dependence' or 'a derivative from fear' or 'sexual life' or a 'feeling of the infinite' – that interests James. As concrete states of mind, made up of a feeling *plus* a specific sort of object, religious emotions, of course, are psychic entities distinguishable from other concrete emotions but there is no ground for assuming that a simple abstract 'religious emotion' exists as a distinct elementary mental affection by itself, present in every religious experience without exception (James 1985: 27). There is 'no one elementary religious emotion' but rather 'a common storehouse of emotions upon which religious objects may draw'.

One way to mark it out easily 'is to say what aspects of the subject we leave out'. At the outset, he states,

> we are struck by one great partition which divides the religious field. On the one side of it lies institutional, on the other personal religion . . . one branch of religion keeps the divinity, another keeps man most in view . . . in these lectures I propose to ignore the institutional branch entirely, to say nothing of the ecclesiastical organization, to consider as little as possible the systematic theology and the ideas about the gods themselves, and to confine myself as far as I can to personal religion pure and simple.
>
> (James 1985)

He addresses the question that the 'religion' should

> be reserved for the fully organized system of feeling, thought, and institution, for the Church, in short, of which this personal religion, so called, is but a fractional element . . . But if you say this, it will only show the more plainly how much the question of definition tends to become a dispute about names. Rather than prolong such a dispute, I am willing to accept almost any name for the personal religion of which I propose to treat. Call it conscience or morality, if you yourselves prefer, and not religion – under either name it will be equally worthy of our study.
>
> (James 1985: 29–30)

Religion in James's study shall 'mean for us *the feelings, acts, and experiences of individual men in their solitude, so far as they apprehend themselves to stand in relation to whatever they may consider the divine*' (James 1985: 27).

James's account remains a critical foundation to modern discussions on religious experience. James influenced to some degree all subsequent psychology and much philosophy of religion. In the third lecture on the 'reality of the unseen', we see strands of the thinking of Rudolf Otto's (1950) *The Idea of the Holy* and Mircea Eliade's (1957) *The Sacred and the Profane*. The psychotherapy of religious experience remains still indebted to James's analysis of the 'religion of healthy-mindedness' (lectures IV and V) and the 'sick soul' (lectures VI and VI). Prefacing the work of Carl Jung is James's chapter (lecture IX) on 'The Divided Self, and the Process of its Unification'. James gives considerable attention to 'saintliness' (lectures XIV, XV, XVI and XVII) and mysticism. Philosophy itself is given relatively short shrift, identifying, as the preceding chapters intimate, 'Primacy of feeling in religion, philosophy being a secondary function'.

Naturalistic approaches to psychology and religion grounded by James were no match for the influence of the adversarial approaches of Freudian psychoanalysis or Jungian or related psychotherapeutic models. Along Jamesean lines Michael Argyle was a leading mid-twentieth century psychologist responsible for a revival of interest in naturalistic approaches to psychology of religion, in works such as *Religious Behaviour* (1958) *The Psychology of Happiness* (1987), *The Psychology of Religious Behaviour, Belief and Experience* (Argyle and Beit-Hallahmi 1997), *Psychology and Religion* (Argyle 2000). Argyle (2002), summarizing a lifetime of work, conceptualized religious faith as attitude with cognitive, behavioural and emotional components, with self-evident social–psychological importance:

> Religion presents a range of phenomena falling outside what is usually studied by psychologists, and for which there often appears to be no psychological explanation. Religious experiences are reported by one third of the population, sacrifice is practised in most religions, sudden adolescent conversion is common for religious attitudes, and some religious beliefs are remarkably non-rational. We need to understand these things.
>
> (Argyle 2002: 22)

Developments divided into those which provided a renewed interest in the empirical study of religious experience, particularly the Alister Hardy Research Centre for Religious Experience, by the zoologist Alister Hardy and subsequently by theorists such as David Hay (1987; Hay and Nye 2006) and the pastoral role of psychology in religious communities. Hall *et al.* (2011) identify resurgent interest in psychology and religion as attributable to 'the emergence of a number of individuals who are both psychologically and theologically trained and who have sustained innovative research and educational programmes' (see Watts 2007). Groups of psychologists of faith have established bodies such as the British Association of Christians in Psychology. There are many instances of psychological investigation supporting not only the ordained but individual church members, through spiritual counselling and at a collective level conflict resolution within congregations (see Watts *et al.* 2002; Savage and Boyd-Macmillan 2008). Psychology becomes a means to 'enable people to acquire beliefs and values on which to base their lives', to psychologically construct, as Csikszentmihalyi and Csikszentmihalyi (2006) put it, 'a life worth living'. Academic psychologists and ordained theologians have sought accommodations between psychology and religion through 'empirical theology'. Leslie Francis identified five priorities: conceptual clarification of relations between psychology and theology: applying psychological theory to biblical hermeneutics; the uses of psychology in ministries and congregations; exploration of divergent attitudes, beliefs and values between clergy, churchgoers and 'church-leavers'; and examination of religious attitudes among young people (Francis 2005; also de Souza *et al.* 2009; Francis *et al.* 2005).

In 'Divine Therapy', Sayers writes:

> Like many psychologists I do not believe in God. But I am intrigued by religious and mystical experience. I am also happy to credit the healing effects of the revelatory experience of feeling oneself at one with nature, or with God.
>
> (Sayers 2003a)

Like other cognitive psychologists, she is interested in what psychology can tell us about 'the hard-wiring of such experience in the brain'. Distinguishing the 'A-region' of consciousness and the 'B-region' of the unconscious, the latter she intimates is the source not only of dreams but of mystical experience. The B-region, however, might as easily mediate 'not mediate God, but disturbing sexual drives?' For Sayers, following Bion, expression is dependent on cultural stimuli (Bion 1992; cf. Bion 1955, 1962; Sayers 2003b). Other cognitive psychologists similarly relate brain activity in dreaming to mystical and religious experience (Hood 1995; Hood *et al.* 1996; Hood *et al.* 2009). While rejecting religion's 'stultifying', 'cruel', 'antiscientific dogma', Sayers accepts psychoanalytical and neuropsychological evidence shows religion 'might well be therapeutic, restorative, enlivening' (Sayers 2003a: 466–7).

James' naturalistic approach to religion has been adopted by empirical and especially cognitive psychology (Hood 1995; Hood *et al.* 1996; Hood *et al.* 2009). Finding a natural receptiveness to religious concepts, these, if finding wide acceptance, lead to the embedding of these beliefs as key factors in social and cultural life. In a later study, Barrett (2011) asks how far this natural predisposition to religious belief extends across societies. *Cognitive Science, Religion and Theology* (Barrett 2011) accounts for the development of complex beliefs – about God, the afterlife – in international and cross-cultural context. Barrett (2011) confirms a natural propensity to religious belief. The same propensity, it is claimed, underlies all the world's religions, uniting them under the cognitive 'instinct for religion'. Barrett (2012) finds that we are 'born believers' (cf. Schroeder 2009, 2010).

Just as classical psychology recognized that the contents and impulses of the mind also shaped society, so modern psychologists of religion are also interested in how religious belief and practice have sociocultural impact. In the field of social psychology, Riis and Woodhead (2012), in their *A Sociology of Religious Emotion* show that the relationship between the psychological and the social sciences remains strong; that the 'affective' as much as the 'rational' dimension is a factor which still shapes social motivation as well as social structures. With certain types of politically driven religious 'fundamentalism' having achieved some degree of prominence, social psychological attention has also been drawn to such phenomena. The psychologist Robert Altemeyer had long been interested in the psychological bases of political authoritarianism – from *Right-wing Authoritarianism* (Altemeyer 1981) through *Enemies of Freedom* (Altemeyer 1988) to *The Authoritarian Specter* (Altemeyer 1996) – and developed a scale to measure 'militant conservative belief', to examine the relationships between authoritarianism and religious fundamentalism. The 'religious fundamentalism' scale for example, shows 'religious ethnocentrism' conceived an 'us' and 'them' mentality, with fundamentalists conceiving a small 'us' and a large 'them' (Altemeyer and Hunsberger 1992). Altemeyer and Hunsberger (2004) have maintained its usefulness but refined the scale, using responses to the following 12 statements – a shortened version of an original list of 20 – to measure 'authoritarian' inclinations:

1. God has given humanity a complete, unfailing guide to happiness and salvation, which must be totally followed.
2. No single book of religious teachings contains all the intrinsic, fundamental truths about life.
3. The basic cause of evil in this world is Satan, who is still constantly and ferociously fighting against God.
4. It is more important to be a good person than to believe in God and the right religion.
5. There is a particular set of religious teachings in this world that are so true, you can't go any 'deeper' because they are the basic, bedrock message that God has given humanity.
6. When you get right down to it, there are basically only two kinds of people in the world: the Righteous, who will be rewarded by God; and the rest, who will not.
7. Scriptures may contain general truths, but they should NOT be considered completely, literally true from beginning to end.
8. To lead the best, most meaningful life, one must belong to the one, fundamentally true religion.

9. "Satan" is just the name people give to their own bad impulses. There really is *no such thing* as a diabolical 'Prince of Darkness' who tempts us.
10. Whenever science and sacred scripture conflict, *science* is probably right.
11. The fundamentals of God's religion should never be tampered with, or compromised with others' beliefs.
12. *All* of the religions in the world have flaws and wrong teachings. There is *no* perfectly true.

(Altemeyer and Hunsberger 2004: 47–8)

Social psychological studies at the interface of fundamentalism and terrorism have now proliferated (see, for example, Bushman et al. 2007; Canetti-Nisim 2004;.Ginges *et al.* 2009; Kruglanski *et al.* 2008; Jones 2012; Mavor *et al.* 2011). As we shall see, the appropriations of psychology in religious education manifest not dissimilar applications of the psychological and the religious to the political.

Psychology and religious education

Early interest in the psychological aspects of religious education included what can be learned for the study of religion from psychiatry. In the decade of Freud's *Future of an Illusion*, the journal *Religious Education* published Boisen's (1928) 'The Psychiatric Approach to the Study of Religion', the following year Staebuck's (1929) 'Religious Psychology and Research Methods'. The potential of psychiatric insights persisted to the 1940s (Reid Martin 1943) and 1950s (Houston Clark 1959). William James's studies had surprisingly less direct impact, perhaps because his approach was more concerned with descriptive analysis than application, although Crump Miller (1991) made an attempt at a retrospective and revival on the educational implications of James for religion in education. Carl Jung, too, made surprisingly little direct impact on the field of religious education until the 1960s and early 1970s (Kelsey 1970) and then significantly for moral education (cf. Drumheller 1968). Psychology of religion in general, however, had clearly made a general impact long before, relating religious education and counselling (Hiltner 1956) and what was on occasion referred to a 'mental hygiene' (Milo and Whittaker 1932; Hiltner 1943; for a review, see Hiltner and Rogers 1962). Such approaches have helped to make therapeutic approaches to religious education, as for example contributing to 'wellbeing', a commonplace (for example, de Souza *et al.* 2009).

Recently, much attention has been given to the cognitive science of religion and its application to religious education (see, for example, Brelsford 2005; Blevins 2011; Seymour 2011b). Yet, in the century or so from which I am dating the history of modern religious education, it is, in that retrospective, versions of developmental psychology which have over that century dominated models of religious education (see Dowling and Scarlett 2005; Francis *et al.* 2005). Here, the Enlightenment idea of a forwards movement of history, of social and political progress, aided by science, found psychological expression. Here, Jean Piaget (1896–1980) exerted a profound influence.

Influenced by the rise of psychology and psychiatry as sciences in his own time (Vidal 1994), Piaget provided a specific psychology of children's development which would offer less a psychotherapeutic model than an influential framework for thinking about how children learn. After initial interest in psychoanalysis developed at the University of Zürich, he left to work in France at the École de la rue de la Grange-aux-Belles. It was here, working with Alfred Binet and De Simon, he was influenced by their work on intelligence. Returning to Switzerland in 1921, Piaget became director of studies at Geneva's Jean-Jacques Rousseau Institute. In 1923, he married Valentine Châtenay. The marriage of a prominent scientist would not usually factor in the narrative of his or her scientific career. For Piaget it would. The couple's three children – Jacqueline, Lucienne and Laurent – became the family laboratory and Piaget studied the development of his children from infancy. It was from these studies that he derived much of the theory of children's development for which he is known. His developmental psychology 'had one unique goal: how does knowledge grow'? His answer is that the growth of knowledge is a progressive construction of logically embedded structures superseding one another by a process of inclusion of lower, less powerful, logical means into higher and more powerful ones up to adulthood. Therefore, children's logic and modes of thinking are initially entirely different from those of adults (Smith 1997).

Piaget's development psychology proposed five stages in children's cognitive or intellectual development, in which the child adjusts his or her thinking according to a series of schemas that involve both mental and physical responses to the processes of knowing and understanding the world (for example, Piaget 1928, 1953, 1957). By relating knowledge acquisition and conceptual understanding, Piaget sees epistemological capacity as related to psychological development. A process of constant adjustment to knowledge and understanding of the world involves the assimilation of new information, the accommodation of this new knowledge into prior understanding and the process of equilibration where the child cognitively adjusts with new assimilations and accommodations and allows interstage transition. While mental development may not proceed according to the 'normal' expected pattern (for Freud this was the source of neurosis and psychosis), Piaget identified five age-related stage of development in children's mental development: from birth to two years (the child knows the world through sensation, that they can affect the world by their demands); the preoperational, up the age of seven (the child begins to think symbolically and learns the power of language, pictorial or linguistic, but thinks in concrete terms); in the concrete operational stage, from seven years to 11, Piaget identifies as the beginning of logic and reasoning capacity; in the formal operational stage, from 12 years onwards, the adolescent and the young adult begins to develop the capacity for abstract thought (Beilin 1992; Mussen 1983; Smith 1993).

The developmental model dominated the psychology of education and shaped education as a field of enquiry (Furlong and Lawn 2010). Piaget's influence was facilitated throughout his career as an educational professional as well as a psychological practitioner (Bringuier 1980; Evans 1973; Piaget 1952). Most prominently, in addition to his numerous chairs spanning psychology and education, he held roles more or less concurrently as Director of the International Bureau of Education, Geneva, and Director of the Institute of Educational Sciences, University of Geneva. His international reputation and influence was further facilitated through his work with the United Nations Educational, Scientific and Cultural Organisation (UNESCO), as Co-Director of its Department of Education.

Religious education and the appropriation of psychology

If Piaget's theories of children's development shaped psychology of education, such frameworks of children's development were later significant to particular theories of *moral* development, notably by Lawrence Kohlberg (1927–1987). Kohlberg's stages of moral development bear the unmistakable influence of Piaget (Kohlberg 1981; see Crain 1985; Munsey 1980). Three levels divide the six stages: level 1 (the preconventional), focused on the child learning from parental obedience, punishment and reward (stages 1 and 2); level 2 (conventional), where moral choice is determined by social norms and legal constraints, in personal and interpersonal relations (stages 3 and 4); and level 3 (postconventional) where moral decision-making and choice is informed by but is to some degree selfless and autonomous from societal norms and pressures, the individual thinks of society's good as much as his or her own. Variations on a Piagetian/Kohlbergian theme include Robert Coles' (1986, 1992) 'moral archaeology of childhood' and the spiritual life of children and Fritz K. Oser's (1994) stages of 'religious judgement' (Oser and Gmünder 1991; Oser 1994).

Rooted in understandings of faith as meaning making – especially influenced by the thinking of Reinhold Niebuhr (1892–1971; for example Niebuhr 1960) and Wilfred Cantwell Smith (1916–2000; for example Smith 1993) – where differences between religions are considered more as variants in cultural expression than essential differences, the most influential faith development theorist using such an interpretation of religion has been James Fowler. Fowler (1981) applied psychological/moral developmental thinking to a seven-stage schema of 'faith development'. Fowler's schema included: *primal faith* (stage 0) in infancy, faith as trust in parents; *intuitive–projection* (stage 1) associated with the acquisition of language and the development of imaginative as well as (but less developed) cognitive capacity; *mythical–literal* (stage 2) with enhanced logical thought, sources of faith move beyond parental to other figures of authority; *synthetic–conventional* (stage 3) marked in adolescent capacity for abstract conceptual thought, confirming or rejecting of culturally and socially religious influences; *individua-tive–reflective* (stage 4), occurring with increasing moral and intellectual autonomy in adulthood is characterized by a review of faith stances; *conjunc-tive* (stage 5) is marked by heightened autonomy and internalization of faith perspectives, personal ownership of belief, relinquishing the need for external authority; *universalising* (stage 6) is a height reached only by rare individuals, for Fowler manifest in figures such as Gandhi, Mother Theresa and Martin Luther King (Fowler 1981; also Coyle 2011; Reich 2005). Fowler subsequently refined his theory of faith development 'as a system of types, in contrast to a sequence of stages' (Fowler 2001: 159, 2004; also Gottlieb 2006; Heywood 2008; Streib 2001a). Streib (2005) attempted to 'account not only for structural diversity, but also for narrative and content diversity' in faith development theory.

Greer (1984a, 1984b) reported on 50 years of influence of the psychology of religion on religious education – the first five decades of the *British Journal of Religious Education*. In religious education, we see that the psychology of education developed in close conjunction with the psychology of education and, in this regard, had a strong impact on the subject, as noted above, through the work of Colin Alves (1966a, 1966b), Edwin Cox (1967, 1971, 1983), Ronald Goldman (1964, 1969), Kenneth Hyde (1984, 1990) and Harold Loukes (1961, 1963). The effect of such studies, small scale as they were, was dramatic. Arguing that their findings in the psychological development of children showed a marked unreadiness for religion in its formal institutional guises, religious education increasingly began to focus on those forms of religion for which they *were* ready. The result was often an emphasis placed upon ethical and moral questions and decision making and facilitating children's search for meaning in their lives, informed but not governed by religious authority and tradition.

The correlations between psychology and religion in education were thus reflected in appropriations of child development that shifted away from specific traditions to generic and universal stages, which, although expressed differently across cultures and religious traditions, were invariant across them. The thinking which undergirded these may have been psychological – from Piaget through Kohlberg to Oser and Fowler – but they also presupposed a particular understanding of religion. The conception of faith development as universal, transcending in deep structures its cultural expression, religious tradition was understood as a cultural vehicle for that development. Theorists of religion, such as Müller, had early facilitated a path that would be followed by guided by Eliade and Otto, Niebuhr and Wilfred Cantwell Smith and, later, as noted, Ninian Smart and John Hick (2004). Those who favoured psychological and developmental models allowed for the individual appropriation of cultural expressions of the traditions which formed them. But, since all development was *invariant* across cultures, the *variant* expressions were superficial and not reflective of deeper psychological structures. Where public or state education systems were pre-empted from favouring particular traditions, this developmental model appeared therefore ideally inclusive.

In discussing the relationship between the social sciences and religion and its appropriations within religious education, we noted supposed revolutions which favoured spirituality over religion (for example, Heelas *et al.* 2004). Since the language of *faith* development was associated with formal religion, even though it argued that faith was universal across cultural difference, *faith* development seemed to hold to many of the old associations. After all, faith implies, surely, faith in something, as for example with Oser, the Ultimate Being. Psychological models of faith development theory would thus give way to the language of *spirituality*. The notion of development was retained but more loosely, even as we have seen by Fowler. The religious education literature thus began to reflect less the language of *faith* than *spiritual* development.

The reasons might be as sociological as they were psychological but the shift is apparent. Where spirituality had as a matter of course been associated with the religious life and a progression in holiness, more scientifically based interpretations were conjoined with them (Dowling and Scarlett 2005). These were not only seen to be more psychologically grounded but in their pluralistic understandings of spirituality they also came to be seen as transcending their different cultural expressions. A special issue of *Religious Education* dedicated to such issues from the late 1970s thus considered 'Spirituality, World Religions and Education' (Arnett Dixon 1978) and the 'Dilemma of the New Spirituality' (Hargrove 1978). The trend has continued, with leading sociologists of religion favouring new inclusive spiritual terminology (Wuthnow 2000). The language of spiritual development is seen as building bridges between and not divisions across religions (Yust *et al.* 2006).

The benefits of understanding religion as spiritual and or psychological experience has been seen as liberating in both philosophical as well as political terms. Philosophically, spiritual development understood in psychological ways – psychotherapeutic and as individual meaning-making (Hyde 2008a) – has been both celebrated as a liberating postmodern deconstruction of spiritual knowledge and experience (Erricker 2001; Neiman 1999) and, for the same reasons, attacked as conceptually incoherent and epistemologically vacuous (Wright 2003a). Politically, since such models of spirituality did not worry overly about doctrinal difference – or doctrine at all (as we have seen in psychotherapeutic and psychiatric practice today) – the approach has also seen as being a model for religious education which does not infringe constitutional proscription (Yob 1995; Revell 2008), a framework for facilitating a 'spirituality of dialogue' (Ratliff 2010), a 'spiritual questing' (Hyde 2008b) apt for 'a troubling world' (Moore and Wright 2008; also Csinos 2009). If these were the themes, they also generated pedagogical methods which syncretistically blended religious traditions, psychotherapeutic thinking and humanistic psychology in *New Methods in Religious Education*, subtitled 'an experiential approach' (Hammond *et al.* 1990). In the early 1990s, the book and the approach provoked some high-profile debate in the *British Journal of Religious Education*.

Thatcher's (1991) 'Critique of Inwardness in Religious Education' specifically targeted Hammond, Hay and colleagues for a philosophical naïvety based on a simplistic notion of the inner and outer person, a dualism which Thatcher suggested the modern philosophy of language undermined: we think inner thoughts only through the language that we have been given by our culture; there is, as the later Wittgenstein (2009) put, no possibility of a private language. Given that one of the contributors to this volume had argued the case for the 'removal of theology from religious education' (Netto 1989), Hammond and Hay (1992) responded with (given the psychotherapeutic presuppositions a peculiarly) a theological defence, apparent in the title of their reply, '"When You Pray, Go To Your Private Room" A Reply to Adrian Thatcher'. Their defence was that the pursuit of inward reflection was rooted in Biblical tradition but it was also mirrored in all the world's religions and, critical to Hammond *et al.*'s (1990) argument, supported by modern psychotherapeutic practice. Yet, if spirituality was so diffuse and all-encompassing, giving validity to all spiritual paths, as Rebecca Nye (1996) put it, 'How Do You Start Without a Starting Point?' Like those psychologists who had argued that the psychological development and thus learning begins with the child, *this* was the starting point, the child.

It is where Coles' (1986, 1992) pioneering studies had also begun. This thinking had its originating impulse in the forming by Clive and Jane Erricker with Catha Ota of *The International Journal of Children's Spirituality* (Erricker *et al.* 2001). But neither the debates nor the focus for spirituality in education ended there. Spiritual education debates, which began as a means of uniting psychological and religious development across cultural differences, soon began to consider the frontiers of those very cultural, religious and social differences (Erricker *et al.* 2001). They subsequently extended (given the links between Kohlberg's moral development and Fowler's faith development) to the ethics of spirituality (Alexander 2003, 2004). The domain of ethics was not restricted, however, to personal morality but to public and political considerations; what I had once characterized as a 'spirituality of dissent' (Gearon 2001).

While debates over spirituality in the *British Journal of Religious Education* were short-lived – the social and the political have in recent times taken centre stage – the critique of spiritual education on various philosophical, especially epistemological grounds became central. Carr's (1996) early indication of philosophical interest in marked in 'Rival Conceptions of Spiritual Education' argued that the spiritual found most conceptual coherence within religious traditions, although it was becoming particularly prevalent beyond them, especially in the arts. Carr and Haldane's (2003) collection *Philosophy, Spirituality and Education* brings together a range of philosophical analyses to consider the possibilities for a spiritual dimension in education. Attempting to 'bring to this subject a depth of scholarly and philosophical sophistication that was previously missing' the collective efforts of their contributors focus on the conceptual underpinnings of the spiritual and its philosophical analysis. The volume considers subjects as diverse as the meaning of the spiritual, spiritual values, spirituality and virtue, spirituality and morality, and even spirituality and science.

Carr and Alexander (2005) subsequently suggest there are four key, philosophical questions: 'What can it possibly mean to educate in spirituality? Does it make sense to construe spirituality as an innate quality that develops naturally in human beings? How is education in spirituality possible given the demand for rational autonomy or substantive choice in open, liberal societies? And in what institutional settings is spiritual education possible or desirable?' (Carr and Alexander 2005: 73). The problem of definition is fundamental to all others. It is not simply that spirituality is difficult to define because of 'deep ambiguities of everyday usage' but that these definitional ambiguities have themselves encouraged 'educational theorists, policy makers, and practitioners to pursue diverse social, cultural, and political aims, agendas and outcomes in the name of spiritual education'. At a deeper level, however, they recognize that 'resistance to defining spirituality is symptomatic of fundamental, ontological uncertainty over the very nature, objects, or referents of spiritual discourse' (Carr and Alexander 2005: 74). Carr and Alexander (2005) thereby demonstrate that a term once rooted in religious tradition has become assimilated into secular educational contexts.

The historical process of the secular appropriation of the terms of 'spirituality' had been demonstrated by Copley (2000) in *Spiritual Development in the State School.* Crawford and Rossiter (1996) this called the 'secular spirituality of youth'. For them, it necessitated a positive accommodation to secular influence, a religious education which was less bound by the strictures of religious tradition. One way would to see spirituality as less aligned to religious tradition than a kind of aesthetic. This identification of the spiritual and the aesthetic has its own and deeper philosophical origins which, as I show in Chapter 8, is also characterized by a separation of religious education from the religious life.

Summary

That psychology of education has had a major impact on modern education is as undeniable as is the impact of psychological, especially development theories on religious education. These have drawn from particular, pluralistic interpretations of religion, which show that development in faith or spirituality is invariant across variant cultural and religious expression. The ground has shifted dramatically. Where once spirituality meant *de facto* an association of religious education the religious life is now abandoned; for, as Carr and Alexander (2005) show, the emphasis upon autonomy and individual choice proscribes such an association; and, if spirituality were to be identified with religious tradition, in a liberal democratic context each has their own legitimacy (Alexander, 2003). Perhaps nowhere more than here, in the complex of relations between psychology and religion and psychological–spiritual models of religious education, has an Enlightenment emphasis upon individual choice and rational autonomy been more apparent. Indeed, it is this very emphasis upon the individual autonomy which provides psychological–spiritual approaches their appeal in modern religious education.

Since it is psychological and faith development theories which provided a validation of all spiritual quests – all religions are in essence different cultural manifestations of one essence – the choice of which tradition does not really matter. An amalgam of world religions provides here in equal measure an appropriate resource for religious education. This underpins the phenomenological approach, considered in the next chapter (Chapter 6). As I will subsequently show (in Chapter 7), an epistemological ground becomes a political justification, yet one less concerned with the truth of religion (as knowledge) than with the political usefulness of religious education.

6 Phenomenology and religious education

Introduction

Phenomenology was once an influential 'science', which impacted on mainstream philosophy and psychology and now resides on their margins. Sharpe's (2009) study of the history of comparative religion shows how phenomenology was thrown a lifeline by the exploitation of its possibilities in the most contested of studies, religion. It is here that phenomenology found its enduring legacy, in the study of religion, in van der Leeuw's (1933) *Phenomenology of Religion*, Kristensen's (1960) *The Meaning of Religion: Lectures in the phenomenology of religion* and across many of the works of Smart (1969, 1973, 1996, 1998, 1999).

It is from Smart's attempts to show phenomenology as a unifying tool in religious studies that its effects have been most pronounced. His efforts to use phenomenology as a tool to synthesize other disciplines in the study of religion were profound, particularly in demonstrating, not least in the Department of Religious Studies he established at the University of Lancaster (for his personal reflections, see Smart 1967; also Roberts 2001; Veitch 2001). Here he pioneered an approach which facilitated how disparate arts, humanities and (at least social and psychological) sciences could be utilized in the study of religion. Smart extended significantly beyond the Academy, since he recognized the importance of taking developments in the academic study of religious into school religious education.

Phenomenology and religion

Phenomenology is not outwardly directly antagonistic of religion. Indeed, of all the new sciences, phenomenology – although little concerned with religion in its foundation *as* an independent science – would inadvertently provide the grounds for a 'neutral' study of religion. In this supposed neutrality, phenomenology has become perceived as a highly suitable approach for those sociopolitical and educational contexts which directly confront religious plurality. The connection between phenomenology and religion were by no means at all evident from the formative years of the discipline. Edmund Husserl is credited with the development of phenomenology as a system whose originating terms are from Kant.

The phenomenological adversaries of religion

Kant's (1999a) assertions in *The Critique of Pure Reason* concerning 'the Ground of the Division of all Objects into Phenomena and Noumena' would become the founding distinction of phenomenology. Kant distinguished the phenomenal and the noumenal to identify those domains we could know and those of which we could have no direct knowledge. Much post-Kantian philosophy, would thereby exclude metaphysics, theology and revelation (God revealing the transcendent through and in the phenomenal world). Edmund Husserl (1859–1938) began his researches on logic and mathematics but would stray to those areas Kant which argued were beyond knowledge. Phenomenology would follow and transgress the Kantian demarcation: phenomenology's defining problem was to know things in themselves, what would become a theory of consciousness. By this route, Husserl re-entered epistemological territory that Kant had foreclosed and, in so doing, he would, if indirectly, become an important strand in the study of religion as a phenomena. Phenomenology's influence would be overshadowed by intellectual histories of his time, particularly the ascendancy of philosophy of language and psychology, its most profound influence would be on existentialism (see Dreyfus and Wrathall 2009) and, in ways which would have surprised Husserl, religion and, even more surprisingly, religious education.

Husserl's academic background, as noted, was in mathematics and philosophy, undertaking under Franz Brentano a dissertation *On the Concept of Number* (1887), followed, on the basis of this work, by *Philosophy of Arithmetic* (1891). Husserl's youthful self-confidence (an ambitious attempt to unite philosophy, mathematics and logic) was dented when the renowned logician Gottlob Frege (1848–1925) accused Husserl's work of 'psychologism'. This was a category error of identifying non-psychological with psychological entities. This may seem arcane but it is central both to the development and decline of phenomenology marked above all by the rise of psychology itself. 'Psychologism' entered the English language as a translation of the German word *Psychologismus* through the Hegelian J. E. Erdmann. The word was coined to synthesize those approaches in philosophy that made logical laws psychological ones. Human psychological laws and logic are not comparable. Are numbers dependent on the human consciousness of number? Erdmann concluded not. The laws of the mind are not the laws of mathematics. This seemingly arcane distinction is then far from a mere technical point but was one which transformed philosophy of mind, gave rise to the modern field of philosophy of language and the philosophy of mathematics, and substantially weakened the premises of phenomenology even before it was fully formed (Dreyfus and Wrathall 2009; Sawicki 2011; Smith and Woodruff Smith 1995).

Phenomenology thus became embroiled in theories of consciousness and the emergent science of psychology. While there are variants of phenomenology, it can be defined as an attempt to uncover the laws of consciousness itself; if we can know only the phenomenal world and not the noumenal, how is possible to know even phenomena, the things in themselves? To identify logical laws, including mathematics, with psychological processes is thus regarded as 'psychologism'. It was a criticism applied to an emergent phenomenology by philosophers. Indirectly, such criticisms were also a critique of the new science of psychology. Psychologism can also be used in a neutral descriptive sense, simply that is as a description of psychological states and it was self-evidently what psychology was concerned with. Psychologism is used approvingly when applied to problems of philosophy and, particularly, of epistemology, which attempt to describe the world as known as the world conceived or perceived in consciousness. The tools by which we perceive the world are the means of its conception.

Husserl's first 'phenomenological' work was *Logical Investigations*. Not insignificantly, it is also a forceful attack against psychologism. He distinguishes between the 'descriptive–psychological' and the 'epistemological', formally separating on the one hand descriptions of psychological states (consciousness) and the formal, logical basis for knowing (how we know consciousness as reality). In this position, Husserl argues that what we know is mediated by many factors, including language, meaning, and intention. We cannot know the world as it is because how it is known through other factors. Husserl developed these ideas in Göttingen between 1901 and 1916. He obtained a post there thanks to *Logical Investigations* and the respect that this work had garnered from Wilhelm Dilthey (1833–1911). Husserl's international reputation was at its height in the 1920s, marked for example by *Phenomenological Method and Phenomenological Philosophy*, lectures given at University College London in 1922.

In 1927, Husserl wrote an entry 'Phenomenology' for *Encyclopaedia Britannica*, summarizing the accumulated the complexities of his work:

> The term 'phenomenology' designates two things: a new kind of descriptive method which made a breakthrough in philosophy at the turn of the century, and an a priori science derived from it; a science which is intended to supply the basic instrument ... for a rigorously scientific philosophy and in its consequent application, to make possible a methodical reform of all the sciences.
>
> (Husserl 1927: 1)

The phenomenal–noumenal distinction was thus foundational to phenomenology. So, too, was the distinctions of *a priori* and *a posteriori*:

> Together with this philosophical phenomenology, but not yet separated from it, however, there also came into being a new psychological

discipline parallel to it in method and content: the a priori pure or 'phenomenological' psychology, which raises the reformational claim to being the basic methodological foundation on which alone a scientifi-cally rigorous empirical psychology can be established.

(Husserl 1927: 1)

'An outline of this psychological phenomenology,' he states, 'standing nearer to our natural thinking, is well suited to serve as a preliminary step that will lead up to an understanding of philosophical phenomenology'.

Since phenomenology is a philosophy of consciousness, it is upon the then new field of psychology which Husserl sees phenomenology having its most immediate impact:

Modern psychology is the science dealing with the 'psychical' in the concrete context of spatio-temporal realities, being in some way so to speak what occurs in nature as egoical [sic], with all that inseparably belongs to it as psychical processes like experiencing, thinking, feeling, willing, as capacity, and as habitus. Experience presents the psychical as merely a stra-tum of human and animal being. Accordingly, psychology is seen as a branch of the more concrete science of anthropology, or rather zoology.

(Husserl 1927: 1)

He recognizes that consciousness itself has a physical or neurological basis, the operation of physical minds. Thus: 'Animal realities are first of all, at a basic level, physical realities'. The problem of knowing *these* belong to 'the closed nexus of relationships in physical nature', to 'pure natural science; that is to say, an objective science of nature' (Husserl 1927).

Husserl's concern therefore is with the 'purely psychical in self-experience and community experience'; that is, human psychic realities. This is the realm of the

universal description of intentional experiences...To establish and unfold this guiding idea, the first thing that is necessary is a clarification of what is peculiar to experience, and especially to the pure experience of the psychical and specifically the purely psychical that experience reveals, which is to become the theme of a pure psychology.

(Husserl 1927: 1)

When engaged in 'conscious activity' persons 'focus exclusively on the specific thing, thoughts, values, goals or means involved but not on the psychical experience as such, in which these things are known as such'. Our consciousness of these things reveals this by directional goals (intentions, their 'intentionality'). Phenomenology, however, enables us to understand the 'corresponding subjective experiences', as they become 'conscious', as they 'appear':

> For this reason, they are called 'phenomena,' and their most general essential character is to exist as the 'consciousness-of' or 'appearance-of' the specific things, thoughts (judged states of affairs, grounds, conclusions), plans, decisions, hopes, and so forth.
>
> (Husserl 1927: 2)

These phenomena are the 'field for a pure psychological discipline related exclusively to phenomena, we can understand the designation of it as phenomenological psychology'.

Here, however, Husserl recognized a problem. It was arguably an irresolvable variant of the original charge of psychologism made by Frege 40 years earlier:

> To what extent does the unity of the field of phenomenological experience assure the possibility of a psychology exclusively based on it, thus a pure phenomenological psychology? It does not automatically assure an empirically pure science of facts from which everything psychophysical is abstracted. But this situation is quite different with an a priori science.
>
> (Husserl 1927: 4)

This is where Husserl defines but does not fully resolve the problem of 'eidetic reduction' or therefore achieve his goal of 'phenomenological psychology as eidetic science'. By eidetic science in this context, Husserl means the search essences, the essential nature of 'the things themselves'. Husserl believed that one could move from the world of observed facts (the *a posteriori*) to the essence (the *a priori*). Thus, 'every self-enclosed field of possible experience permits *eo ipso* the all-embracing transition from the factual to the essential form, the eidos'. Therefore:

> If the phenomenological actual fact as such becomes irrelevant; if, rather, it serves only as an example and as the foundation for a free but intuitive variation of the factual mind and communities of minds into the a priori possible (thinkable) ones; and if now the theoretical eye directs itself to the necessarily enduring invariant in the variation, then there will arise with this systematic way of proceeding a realm of its own, of the a priori.
>
> (Husserl 1927: 4)

This *eidos*, 'the essence, the things in themselves' 'must manifest itself throughout all the potential forms of psychical being in particular cases' if it is to be 'thinkable', that is, 'intuitively conceivable'. Phenomenological psychology is 'eidetic phenomenology'; it is 'exclusively directed toward the invariant essential forms'.

The method which Husserl sought career-long refinements was phenomenological *epoché*. This is most commonly translated as 'bracketing'. It is a restraining of but sharpening of assumptions which allowed to see the things in themselves. This cornerstone phenomenological method was critical to searching out of essences. It is a methodological concern from *Logical Investigations* onwards, especially *Ideas for a Pure Phenomenology and Phenomenological Philosophy* (1913).

This latter work is not only of methodological but wider disciplinary importance for understanding phenomenology's substantive interests. It is not only concerned with the objective fact about the world – sense and experience – but also those data beyond sense and experience; that is, to the complex of relations between sense and experience, as noted above, 'thoughts (judged states of affairs, grounds, conclusions), plans, decisions, hopes' as they are lived and even 'things' known intuitively.

Husserl retired from the University of Freiburg in 1928. Martin Heidegger took Husserl's chair, a post which warranted by Heidegger's publication of the year before, *Being and Time* (Heidegger 1978). The last years of Husserl's life (he died in 1938) were marked by desolation at the political climate in Hitler's Germany. This was compounded by disappointment at seeing much of his phenomenological work undone by a new, more fluid, metaphorical, even anti-logical mode of philosophy epitomized by his successor Heidegger.

Husserl had tried to maintain a link to the formalities of logic while extending its interests. He had sought to establish phenomenology as a rigorous science. The new continental philosophy was marked by a wider methodological breach with 'Anglo-Saxon' (much of English and American) analytical philosophy. Heidegger's philosophical method did not look like philosophical method at all.

In the quest for an understanding of the ground of Being itself and of the consciousness of beings in time, Heideggerian thought impacted French existentialism – notably Albert Camus (1913–1960) and Jean-Paul Sartre (1905–1980) (2003; Couzens Hoy 2009).Through literary influences in particular philosophy would become looser, less disciplined but seen too as more accessible, philosophy became the here and now for everyone; in Camus and Sartre, literature became an important means of doing philosophy (Camus 2000a, 2000b, 2005). Heightened emphasis on the philosophy of language would also undermine the possibility of Husserl's central task, to seek the essence of things. Derrida's later influence on the philosophy of language would mean that not only would things in themselves be impossible to determine but they would also be impossible precisely to express.

Heidegger was appointed Rector of Freiburg in 1933 as a Nazi appointment (see Farias *et al.* 1991). In a first speech as Rector, he enthusiastically supported the work of Adolf Hitler, part of an association with Nazism that Heidegger was never able to or perhaps even interested in removing (Sheehan 2013). Husserl's last work, based on lectures delivered in Prague in 1935, was *The Crisis of European Sciences and Transcendental Phenomenology* ([1938] 1970). This last work reflects Husserl's obvious personal desolation and professional disappointment.

The phenomenological advocates of religion

Husserl's method, in all, is an attempt at a studied neutrality of consciousness, an epistemological undertaking to know things as they are in themselves. However, phenomenology's attempt to ground all phenomena, including religion as phenomena, was reductive in impact if not in intention. By reducing phenomena, including religious phenomena, to essences, Husserl's approach would open the way to a relativism that he had not intended. Nor was this apparent in the foundational and enthusiastic applications of phenomenology to the study of religion. Yet it is unclear, given the broadly sceptical premises of Husserlian phenomenology, how it came to be applied so directly and prevalently to the study of religion at all.

Phenomenology of religion arguably owes in fact less to Husserl than to Hegel. Hegel's systematic idealist philosophy in *The Phenomenology of Spirit* presents an obvious link. Although Hegel's transcendental philosophy took the form here of a universal narrative of Spirit, his concern with reason moving toward 'absolute knowledge' put consciousness of the transcendent to the fore and this is a 'spiritual reality':

> Consciousness . . . must have taken up a relation to the object in all its aspects and phases, and have grasped its meaning from the point of view of each of them. This totality of its determinate characteristics makes the object *per se* or inherently a spiritual reality; and it becomes so in truth for consciousness, when the latter apprehends every individual one of them as self, i.e. when it takes up towards them the spiritual relationship just spoken of.
>
> (Hegel 1910: 801)

In the move towards absolute knowledge, Hegel had first to understand how it was known in limited ways; first, in the progression to a final state of knowledge, an epistemology was also a teleology. Phenomenology of religion would remove Hegel's teleology but would retain his interest in the centrality of religion and spirituality to phenomenology and combine these preoccupations with the methods of Husserl.

As James L. Cox's (2006) first-rate guide to the key figures and influences of phenomenology of religion shows, phenomenology provided the main theoretical framework, the guiding principles, for religious studies as an academic discipline, particularly in Europe and North America. Although Cox argues that the phenomenology of religion was a means to distinguish it from theology, the case for its separation from the social and psychological sciences and philosophy is less strong. For, as can be demonstrated, the leading figures of phenomenology of religion (van der Leeuw, Kristensen, Smart) justify a field of study but continuously draw from a range of other disciplines. The phenomenology of religion defined a field by its object but, as a discipline, it became increasingly defined by hybridity. But the more fundamental preoccupation with religion among such scholars would have astounded and shocked the thinker most associated with its emergence as a distinctive field of enquiry, Edmund Husserl, whose basic categories are derived from Kant.

Religious education and phenomenology

As we have noted, Sharpe's (2009) study of the history of comparative religion shows how phenomenology was appropriated by religious studies and where it found its legacy (van der Leeuw 1963; Kristensen 1960; Smart 1969, 1973). It is Smart's efforts to show phenomenology as a unifying tool in religious studies which made the bridge between the academic study of religions to school religious education. Smart (1969) described the essence of religion as consisting of six 'dimensions': the doctrinal; the mythological (or narrative); the ethical; the ritual; the experiential; and the social. Later (Smart 1998, 1999), he added a seventh material dimension, religious aesthetics. Smart took a complex discussion from philosophy, as it had filtered through 'phenomenology' and applied it very loosely to the understanding of religion as a *phenomenon*.

Smart thus comments that to 'religionists' (those who study religion) 'it means the use of epoché or suspension of belief, together with the use of empathy in entering the experiences and intentions of religious participants'. This implies that 'in describing the ways people behave, we do not use, as far as we can avoid them, alien categories to evoke the nature of their act and to understand those acts' (Smart 1996: 2). It was, however, Gerardus van der Leeuw ([1933 trans. 1938] 1963) in *Religion in Essence and Manifestation* who is acknowledged (by Smart, Eliade and others) as having applied this largely notional 'phenomenology' to the study of religion. Disliking the implied essentialism of van der Leeuw – 'essence' implies 'definition' and also the conceptualization of 'worldviews' (considered 'too cerebral') – Smart is more concerned with 'the attitude of informed empathy' which 'tries to bring out what religious acts mean to religious actors'. Smart's approach therefore presents 'a functional delineation of religion in lieu of a strict definition'.

However, methods of detached observation in 'the science of religion' were keen to differentiate their field precisely from others who, in other fields, had studied religion, especially socio-anthropologists. That accepted, Smart also openly acknowledges his debt and the debt of the 'science of religion' not only to the social sciences but psychology and psychoanalysis, explicitly and technically in *The Science of Religion and the Sociology of Knowledge: Some Methodological Questions* (Smart 1973). In *Dimensions of the Sacred* (Smart 1996), he explicitly contextualizes this study by relating the seven dimension to the disciplines which had helped to shape religious studies: textual and philological studies; anthropology and sociology; psychology and psychoanalysis.

Smart also identified adjunct problems with which the subject is wrestling today; for example, which religions to teach, how much coverage is to be given and how to represent them, and by whose account:

> Thus, in an important sense, the study of a religion involves *presenting* that faith, and so the exercise frequently involves considerable powers of sensitivity and imagination. But, it will be objected, only the member of a faith can effectively perform the presentation.
>
> (Smart 1969: 27)

Smart disagrees. His principle of advocating understanding, seeing the faith as an insider might, done well means that even an outsider to a tradition can make a faithful representation of it. Given that Smart was himself presenting an account of the world's religions, he would have to hold to this position. The phenomenological position (van der Leeuw, Smart, and so forth) attempts to differ from reductionist accounts by this faithful representation of religious tradition. There will also be tensions here: Smart had encouraged a multidisciplinary approach to the study of religion, as we have noted, and many of these were reductive in approach. Smart nevertheless exerted an immense influence on the study of religion. *The Religious Experience of Mankind* (Smart 1969) was an attempt to argue systematically the case for the non-confessional approach to the study of religion. In other words, to understand religious belief you did not have to be a believer. The neutrality is a contested premise of phenomenological neutrality has been the most widely critiqued aspect of all its assumptions, most vehemently from the philosophical perspectives. Its appropriation in religious education terms was to provide a rationale for a subject which had been subject to critiques from a range of natural, social and psychological sciences, some as we have seen more favourable to religion than others.

Religious education and the appropriation of phenomenology

By the time that phenomenology had begun to be appropriated by scholars of religion (van der Leeuw, for example, in the 1930s), phenomenology was almost a spent intellectual force, long overtaken in influence by psychology. Smart appropriated phenomenology not simply for the academic study of religion in university but also for school religious education, which gave phenomenology an epistemological lifeline.

By 1972, Smart was integral to the new phenomenological spirit of religious education, writing in that year a guest editorial for the *British Journal of Religious Education*, then called *Learning for Living* (Smart 1972; after an earlier contribution to the journal, Smart 1970; and later, Smart 1974). In the mid-1970s, Eric F. Sharpe defined the parameters of university study of religion for schools in 'The Phenomenology of Religion' (Sharpe 1975). One year later, John Marvell had, it seems, correctly anticipated that phenomenology was inseparable from the future of religious education (Marvell 1976). By the early 1980s, his 'dimensional account of religion' was widely accepted as a method (Sealey 1982). Smart and the phenomenology of religion were, as Bent Smidt Hansen (1983) put it 'A Bridge between the Scholarly Study of Religion and Religious Education'.

Phenomenology – the approach which became forever associated with Smart – was, in a world ever more conscious of religious plurality, a central part of moving religious education away from the teaching of Christianity in Britain in particular (Bates 1996). Even before his renowned article in *Religious Education* (Smart 1969), he had already considered – and in *Learning for Living* – the question of the study of religion in Western educational context as one of 'The Christian and other religions' (Smart 1962). In a keynote address in the United States to the Religious Education Association, Hull, from a British perspective, made this plain as a welcome development, outlining the move 'From Christian Nurture to Religious Education' (Hull 1978). Phenomenology as a method therefore met part of its success in its seeming ability to deal with religious difference and diversity and was lauded in official reports (Swann 1985).

By the late 1980s, scholars were beginning to take 'Another Look at Phenomenology and Religious Education' (Leech 1989). In the first decade of the 1990s, the real clash came from the 'experiential' and the phenomenological: did not the latter overemphasis surface facts about religion and lead precisely to the sorts of disengagement which psychological interpretations had found? Hammond *et al.* (1990) made such a charge explicit in their *New Methods*, experiential approach. But a decade earlier, Kenneth Surin had already asked, 'Can the Experiential and the Phenomenological Approaches be Reconciled?' (Surin, 1980).

By the early 1990s, the limits of phenomenology were beginning to be recognized: how open could one be (Arthur 1985; see also Gardner 1993)? How open in particular to the religious perspectives of others could one be without undermining a personal faith commitment and could phenomenology actually be damaging to this? How far could one walk in 'other people's moccasins'? (Haussmann 1993).

Although the philosophical problems of phenomenology were inherent in its founding Husserlian forms, they had begun to be anticipated early if sporadically, Reno (1979) identifying problems in the notion of (epistemological, perspectival) 'Distance in the Study of Religion'. The most systematic assault came from (as would not surprise Husserl) a philosophical perspective (Barnes 2000, 2001a). Strenski (2001) had recognized a fault line in phenomenology of religion/religious education which was inherent in Husserl's work, writing of the 'role of Ninian Smart and the overcoming of philosophy'. The argument against phenomenology was that what amounted to a comparative study of religion relativized truth. In an early paper in *Learning for Living*, Smart (1970) had anticipated the question, what is truth in RE? But his rhetoric left the question for many unanswered. The critical realist religious educators such as Barnes and Wright (2006) took on the mantle over a dispute which continues today. Barnes (2001b) asked, 'What is Wrong With the Phenomenological Approach to Religious Education?', prompting Lovat's (2001) defence. Phenomenology had also to be defended from the critical realists (O'Grady 2005, also Barnes 2007a). Smart had become a 'disputed legacy' (Barnes 2000, 2001a, 2001b, 2006, 2007a).

Undeniably though Smart left for religious education, as well as religious studies worldwide, an extraordinary legacy, however much contested. Apart from his work in the study of religion within universities, Smart was, and in many direct and indirect ways continues to be, influential in advocating the practice of the study of world religions in school religious education. No other scholar of religion has prompted such a diverse range of tributes in recognition of his achievement, as might be indicated by articles of academic reminiscence – from allies and opponents – and fond personal remembrance which were prompted by his death (a sample includes Larson 2001; Siegler 2001; Neusner 2001; Erricker 2001; Cunningham 2001; Saltzman 2001; Sharma 2001; Wiebe 2001; Deutsch 2001; Hinnells 2001; Clayton 2001; Hackett 2001; Pearson 2001; Corless 2001; Morris 2001; Lamb 2001; Barnes 2001a). Shepherd (2005) details the establishment of the Ninian Smart Archive and Bibliography. A disputed and deeply contested legacy has been a profound one.

Summary

There is no pure phenomenology of religious education as, today, there is no pure phenomenology of religion. The philosophical and related challenges to phenomenology have made this virtually impossible, at the very least epistemologically uncertain ground. Religious education has faced a plethora of influences, many of which the subject has shown extraordinary virtuosity in being able to incorporate within its subject boundaries. But these boundaries are inevitably strained by the sheer range and diversity not of only religions to be taught but also the startling range of modes of interpretation and epistemological challenge, not simply in the natural, social, psychological sciences but also in the political domain. It is this latter political domain where the facts of sociopolitical life have been used to ground the subject most recently. Smart had the foresight to recognize the importance of school religious education for the future health of university religious studies. He also recognized the perennial and likely continuing future political importance of phenomenology in and for a religiously plural world. Smart had the foresight to see that the political would be one of the lasting justifications for the study of religion. The last chapter of *Dimensions of the Sacred* directly addresses therefore, the 'political effects of religion'. And it is religion and politics, and the politics of religious education, to which I now turn.

7   The politics of religious education

Introduction

The Enlightenment was not simply a reorientation of the foundations of knowledge but a restructuring of political power. This is why the political dimension of religion remains so important. For political structures either facilitate or deny those forms of knowledge which are sympathetic rather than antipathetic to its maintenance (for example, on the construction of knowledge in the social sciences, see Foucault 1994). Only by a radical rupture between ecclesiastical authority and political power – in the East, the Orthodox and the Byzantine; in the West, the Reformation – could the influence of forms of knowledge challenging of Christianity take root.

That the Eastern Orthodox churches were less affected by the Enlightenment is a case in point. In the East, particularly in Russia, were the 'Enlightened despots' (Oppenheim 1990) who sought intellectual accommodations to Enlightenment while retaining autocratic powers, leaving the Orthodox churches intact until the 1917 Revolution, which simultaneously removed theological with political hegemony.

A quest for the grounds of political legitimacy in the absence of religious authority thus became the engine driving both modern liberal democracy as much as the political extremes of totalitarianism. In political moderation and political extremes, then, religion has been separated from political power as well as repressed by it. This is why John Gray (2008: 1) claims that 'Modern politics is a chapter in the history of religions'. The ground of theological certainty was progressively replaced by epistemological uncertainties but was facilitated by political change. Education in religion has now become an integral part of these processes. Those historical and contemporary circumstances which initiated and which continue to maintain the momentum of ruptured, repaired and revised relationships between religion and politics have emerged in a new worldwide politics of religious education.

Religion and politics

In *Reflections on the Revolution in France*, Edmund Burke (1729–1797) reminds us, 'the spirit of liberty in action' is 'a strong principle at work'

(Burke 2009). But, he writes, 'I must be tolerably sure, before I venture publicly to congratulate men [sic] upon a blessing, that they have really received one'. Flattery being corrupting of giver and receiver and adulation 'not of more service to the people than to kings', Burke writes that he should therefore suspend his 'congratulations on the new liberty of France until I was informed how it had been combined with government'. He asks how the new liberty will be combined with civil peace and public order, fiscal policy, 'an effective and well-distributed revenue', 'the solidity of property', and with 'morality and religion':

> All these (in their way) are good things, too, and without them liberty is not a benefit whilst it lasts, and is not likely to continue long. The effect of liberty to individuals is that they may do what they please; we ought to see what it will please them to do, before we risk congratulations.
>
> (Burke 2009: 8–9)

On religion, Burke noted that the revolution had begun 'to wage war with heaven itself'. *Rights of Man* (published in 1791) was a personal as much as a political response by Thomas Paine. Paine upbraids Burke's lack of empathy for those subject to tyranny:

> Mr. Burke might have been in the Bastille his whole life, as well under Louis XVI as Louis XIV, and neither the one nor the other have known that such a man as Burke existed. The despotic principles of the government were the same in both reigns, though the dispositions of the men were as remote as tyranny and benevolence.
>
> (Paine 1984: 48–9)

Paine's tract becomes both a defence for one revolution and a blueprint for future others:

> In casting our eyes over the world, it is extremely easy to distinguish the governments which have arisen out of society, or out of the social compact, from those which have not; but to place this in a clearer light than what a single glance may afford, it will be proper to take a review of the several sources from which governments have arisen and on which they have been founded... They may be all comprehended under three heads. First, Superstition. Secondly, Power. Thirdly, The common interest of society and the common rights of man. The first was a government of priestcraft, the second of conquerors, and the third of reason.
>
> (Paine 1984: 69)

When 'a set of artful men pretended, through the medium of oracles, to hold intercourse with the Deity, as familiarly as they now march up the back-stairs in European courts, the world was completely under the government of superstition'. The oracles consulted 'whatever they were made to say became the law; and this sort of government lasted as long as this sort of superstition lasted' (Paine 1984: 69–70; see also Paine 1995). That modern politics is founded on a replacement of ecclesiastical authority by political power Paine makes clear. That modern politics is reconceptualized secular theology is further articulated with the 1922 publication of Schmitt's *Political Theology*.

In Schmitt's (2005) *Political Theology*, a critical historicity allowed him to claim that 'All significant concepts of the modern theory of the state are secularized theological concepts' (Schmitt 2005: 36). This shift of power of long-held ecclesiastical authority to the secular state took in modern form political religion, state religion and civil religion, expressed by the framing, one century after Schmitt, a still-forming political theology. This notion – that 'all significant concepts of the modern theory of the state are secularized theological concepts' – is the case:

> not only because of their historic development – in which they were transferred from theology to the theory of the state, whereby, for example, the omnipotent God became the omnipotent lawgiver – but also because of their systematic structure . . . The idea of the modern constitutional state triumphed with deism [over] a theology and metaphysics.
>
> (Schmitt 2005)

Schmitt, above all theorists, thus demonstrates how the political becomes 'theological' or, as in Eric Voegelin's (1999) description, 'political religions' (Maier 2004, 2007; Maier and Schafer 2007).

The theological has been transposed into the political:

> not only because of their historic development – in which they were transferred from theology to the theory of the state, whereby, for example, the omnipotent God became the omnipotent lawgiver – but also because of their systematic structure . . . The idea of the modern constitutional state triumphed together with deism, a theology and metaphysics that banished the miracle from the world.
>
> (Schmitt 2005: 36)

In post-Enlightenment political structures, Schmitt sees 'reminiscences of theology' but used with polemical intent, for:

> In a positivistic age it is easy to reproach an intellectual opponent with the charge of indulging in theology or metaphysics. If the reproach were intended as more than mere insult, at least the following question could suggest itself: what is the source of this inclination for such theological and metaphysical derailments?
>
> (Schmitt 2005: 38–9)

The foundations of this derailment are in the seeking of a new foundation or ground for politics and ethics. Schmitt sees here a distinction between the order that is apparent in the natural world and the moral disorder apparent in sociopolitical relations; modern polity an attempt to shape the disorder of the latter in the order of the former: 'At the foundation of [the] state and legal order rests a metaphysics that identifies the lawfulness of nature and normative lawfulness. This pattern of thinking is characteristic of the natural sciences' (Schmitt 2005: 38–9). As we have noted, the formation of the social sciences followed this pattern, the social sciences attempting to uncover laws in society in imitation of the natural sciences. In this context too, politics and the construction of utopian societies became the practical application of such laws.

So, 'The metaphysical image that a definite epoch forges of the world has the same structure as what the world immediately understands to be appropriate as a form of its political organisation'; for Descartes, 'It is God who established these laws in nature just as a king establishes laws in his kingdom' (ibid: 47). This idea dominated seventeenth and eighteenth century political thought. The idea that the universe was, following Isaac Newton, determinable by universal laws must surely mean that society was also so determined. So it is not unnatural for John Locke (1632–1704) to make referential tribute to Isaac Newton in *The Second Treatise of Government* (1690) alongside the idea of God as a lawmaker (Locke 1988). We see the lawgiver personalized in dictatorial form in the political theory of Thomas Hobbes (1588–1679), notably in *Leviathan* (1651). So Schmitt comments:

> The seventeenth and eighteenth centuries were dominated by this idea of the sole sovereign, which is one of the reasons why... Hobbes remained personalistic and postulated an ultimate concrete deciding instance, and why he also heightened his state, the *Leviathan*, into an immense person and thus point-blank straight into mythology.
>
> (Schmitt 2005: 47; cf. Hobbes 1996, 1998)

As Schmitt comments, throughout the Enlightenment, until the French Revolution, the law and the sovereign were one, the sole 'architect of world and state was called the legislator'. A dramatic shift occurs when the Sovereign is identified not with the One but the many, the people, and the Will of the people, 'when not one person but the people became the arbiter'. The rule of the people fused with the rule of science. Now the sovereign, 'who is in the deistic view of the world, even if conceived as residing outside the world, had remained the engineer of the great machine, has been radically pushed aside'. 'The machine', Schmitt says, 'now runs by itself' (Schmitt 2005: 48).

This is the state as living machine, organic, self-sustaining, not only consciously separated from but denying the ground that had previously determined all social, political, moral relations. The transcendent ground now abandoned, all becomes immanent. Here, 'Conceptions of transcendence will no longer be credible to most educated people' who display an 'indifference to any metaphysics'. In so far as any notion of the transcendent is retained, 'the immanence philosophy, which found its greatest systematic architect in Hegel, draws God into the world...But among the most extreme radicals, a consequent atheism began to prevail' (Schmitt 2005: 50).

This pattern of development having being shown in other chapters, any contemporary interpretation of religion is, even for negative reasons, incomplete without an account of its political role and the wider aetiology of the latter's practical application of philosophical and scientific ideas. To demonstrate the ways the latter have increasingly taken, as Schmitt assumed they would, we look to those extremes of political thought and organization where such patterns demonstrated most profoundly.

Thus, Maier's (2007) analysis of 'Political religion – state religion – civil religion – political theology' unmasks the key terms critical to these debates. Beginning with the first of these terms he states:

> By political religion, we mean a kind of religion that is rooted in a political community – to the extent that it could not exist without this political foundation. The best known example is the city and state cult as it developed in the Greek polis and republican and ancient Rome. All examples taken from the ancient world and the elementary forms of the religious life as practised in simple societies are characterized by a greater or lesser proximity to political structures. Under such circumstances, religion is an abbreviation of the society.
>
> (Maier 2007: 197)

As Maier points out, this is also integral to the sociological analysis of the cohesive role of the sacred as symbolically representative of society itself or, as Maier puts it, following Durkheim, religion is nothing less (and to many thinkers nothing more than) the 'concentrated expression of the entire collective life'.

The flourishing of the gods, Maier reminds us, was dependent upon the thriving of the political community: 'State and religion are thought to exist in an elementary symbiosis'. The emergence of philosophical critique, Maier points out, was an aspect of the maturing of religious thought, the emergence of theology, but also a beginning of the separation of the political from its original unity with the religious:

> The naive unity of cult and politics first became problematic in light of the philosophical question concerning religion...No longer contenting itself with the mere presence of the gods in the public cult, the philosophical question is aimed at the essence of the gods, their nature. Whereas the Platonic critique of the Homeric tales of the gods already anticipates the Greek 'Enlightenment', the tension only intensifies in the

Christian era: the god beyond the world resists integration into the cult of the political community. From this point on, the city (state) is no longer simply the 'church of its religion.

(Maier 2007: 197–8)

On the term 'state religion', Maier comments that 'the privileging of Christianity by Constantine' itself gave rise to the idea of the state religion: 'This religion is characterised by the fundamental independence, even the supremacy of religion over the state'. This 'age of the Christian state religion', which 'lasts well into modernity', with the post-Reformation fracturing of ecclesiastical authority, placed the religious legitimacy of the state and religious authority into 'a crisis of identity'. The consequences of this, Maier points out would be profound: 'The supremacy of the Church over the state weakens to the point where the system ultimately reverts into its opposite form: the superiority of the state over the Church' (Maier 2007: 197).

Rousseau, 'the earliest theoretician of civil religion' requires in this time of identity crisis 'a confession that is made by all citizens' (Maier 2007: 198). 'The relationship of Christianity,' suggests Maier, 'in the ecclesiastical sense remains open'. Yet any reading of the penultimate chapter of *The Social Contract* shows that the position of Christianity is for Rousseau far from open. Indeed, the 'civil religion' is the zenith of the social contract, the crowning achievement of the general will and the will of the people replaces the will of God. Christianity is unfit to govern, its concerns are too other-worldly to be a future pattern for governance or social organization (Maier 2007: 197).

The fourth term that Maier addresses is political theology:

The concept of political theology (*theologia civilis*) arises from Graeco-Roman antiquity. Understood in a Christian sense, it means the illicit 'theologization' (or, as the Patristics would say, the idolization) of these entities in the sense of an intermingling of the earthly and divine, of the cult and politics. For the ancient human being, such intermingling seems entirely natural as a pattern of thought and perception. The ancient lives, after all, in a world for which state and gods belong together in a constitutive sense, one for which there neither is nor can be a godless state or stateless divinity. In the ancient conception, *polis* and *civitas* are religious concepts. Both have divine qualities. It is Christianity, with its world-transcending concept of God, which first breaks through the connection of an immanence that is both theological and political. Accordingly, a critique of political theology first emerges during the Christian period.

(Maier 2007: 199)

Thus, loose applications of political theology fail to recognize the very distinctions that were its foundation. Augustine's *City of God* is not thus the origins of the political theology but a theology which proscribes it

(Augustine 1998, 2001, 2003). It is precisely this justification of theology in political life that is seen by many as the means of re-legitimizing theology's lost influence in the public sphere. But the reverse is true. That the political justification of theology is but one means of further de-legitimizing its transcendent claims.

This was also the source of providing politics itself with transcendent claims, most vividly realized in totalitarianism understood as political religions (for example, Voegelin 1999). Rousseau was influential, if for no other reason than *The Social Contract* played in shaping the French Revolution and the latter for being the a blueprint for subsequent revolutions. As Hobsbawm remarks 'The French Revolution is a landmark in all countries' (Hobsbawm 1994: 75), including the Communism which arose across Europe in the following century.

These latter revolution take the French 'template' further. For *The Communist Manifesto* dismisses 'charges against Communism made from a religious, a philosophical and, generally, from an ideological standpoint, are not deserving of serious examination'. What of the objection that 'religious, moral, philosophical, and juridical ideas have been modified in the course of historical development' and that 'religion, morality, philosophy, political science, and law, constantly survived this change'? No, for, 'Communism abolishes eternal truths, it abolishes all religion, and all morality, instead of constituting them on a new basis; it therefore acts in contradiction to all past historical experience', the 'most radical rupture with traditional ideas' (Marx and Engels 2002: 242; also Marx 1994, 1996; for the collected works, see Marx and Engels 1975–2005; on the reception of the Communist Manifesto, see Stedman Jones 2002). Communism becomes the transcendent claim. As Feuerbach again made plain 'what is regarded as atheism today will be religion tomorrow'.

National Socialism and State Communism have both been characterized by a persistent use of religious metaphors, rituals, images and symbols, by eschatological thought and revolutionary messianism. These histories, in short, would 'be indescribable without an analysis of religious undercurrents' (Rohrwasser 2004: 336). They become salvific, they promise 'total salvation' (ibid.: 336). Where previously 'political thought had regarded the questions concerning the political freedom of the individual and the legal and institutional structures' the terms of political assessment: 'Now, the potentizing concept of the totalitarian arched above such older concepts of the theory of rule as tyranny, absolutism and dictatorship to become the sign of this new experience of reality' (Petersen 2004: 2). The political becomes epistemological.

Totalitarianism is *totalizing* then in attempting to assert an absolute transcendent in the immanent political realm (Friedrich and Brzezinski 1967; Gleason 1997; Isaac 2003; Power 2007; Roberts 2006). As with Talmon (1961), 'dictatorial democracy' becomes 'political messianism'. The 'age of revolution') would over the next centuries lead to the modern 'age of extremes' (Hobsbawm 1995).

But, for critics of modern liberal states – seen as heavily militarized, technologized, and surveillance – seemingly open societies can also replicate totalitarian features (Aron 1957; Popper 2011; Wolin 2008; Zizek 2011). Just as Arendt (2004) and Bauman (1989) recognized totalitarianism and Holocaust outcomes of Enlightenment, the political religions of totalitarianism are for Voegelin (1999) 'modernity without restraint'.

The political advocates of religion

If modern politics reconceptualized secular theology, articulated with Schmitt's *Political Theology*, such transformations have not ended there. Although Schmitt and *Political Theology* were, for many decades, regarded as tainted by Nazism, both are now not only rehabilitated but dominate *political* discourse on *religion* and the *religious* discourse on the *political* (de Vries and Sullivan 2006; Scott and Cavanaugh 2003). Schmitt's notion of political theology has therefore become adapted to a range of geopolitical contexts. The interdependence comes from the calls for religion to have a voice in contemporary politics and the manufacturing of contemporary politics to allow for these diverse and plural voices without allowing them to ground political discourse.

The founding years of the United Nations manifested the first stirring of this in international political context. The Holocaust as the defining aspect of Nazi policies meant that the founding ideals of the UN were based on the universality of political ideals which could accommodate the particularities of cultural, ethnic and religious as well as political difference. In the light of such events, the UN's Universal Declaration of Human Rights (UN 1948) was an attempt to prevent for future generations 'the barbarous acts' of totalitarianism. To do so, the Declaration emphasized what diverse cultures shared rather than what divided them – what was 'universal'. Education was seen as contributing to legal and political frameworks from the UN's inception, especially through the the the forming of UNESCO.

Neither the Cold War – which saw the persistence not only of massed totalitarian regimes but the proliferation of dictatorships, the decline of European colonialism and the rise of the non-aligned nations – nor the post-Cold War were ideal political milieus to engender such universal ideals. Although 'the forty-five years from the dropping of the atom bombs to the end of the Soviet Union do not form a single homogenous period in world history' (Hobsbawm 1994: 225), one of the marks of this period's heterogeneity has been the diverse ways in which religion has both accommodated to the ideals of political liberalism and reacted violently against them.

The post-Cold War triumphalism of Western political liberalism was thus short-lived. Indeed, to present this in simple oppositional terms, the 'end of history' history thesis (Fukuyama 2006) was met fairly immediately by the 'clash of civilizations' counter-thesis. The usefulness of this analogy is that it frames what has been a perennial opposition of the polarities of politics on the one hand and religion on the other. As Maier outlined, this polarity has been never been successfully or permanently established but lives in continual, invariably messy conceptual and empirical circumstances which find expression in terms which define and attempt to resolve the problem; in phrases such as political religion, state religion, civil religion and most recently (or revived most recently) the terms of political theology.

If political theology is the framing discourse which now finds voice more often from theology than it does politics, political liberalism is the framework of accommodation between politics and religion to which both political theorists and theologians work for a voice in the public square accede. John Rawls frames it thus:

> Political liberalism addresses two fundamental questions. The first question is: what is the most appropriate conception of justice for specifying the fair terms of social cooperation between citizens regarded as free and equal? ... The second question is: what are the grounds of toleration understood in a general way, given the fact of reasonable pluralism as the inevitable result of the powers of human reason at work within enduring free institutions? Combining these two questions into one we have: how is it possible for there to exist over time a just and stable society of free and equal citizens who still remain profoundly divided by religious, philosophical, and moral doctrines?
>
> (Rawls 2005: 3–4)

As Ratzinger and Habermas (2007) state, this is part of the 'dialectics of secularization' framed, in the West, as an ongoing tension between secular traditions which seek to ground human life in rational epistemologies and rationally ground moralities (doctrines of human rights, and legal framework which uphold them – from antiquity to Enlightenment) and the Judaeo-Christian tradition which draws on these latter traditions but ultimately grounds epistemology and morality in religious faith. For Habermas, this still leaves the problem of what positive role religion can play in public life, a critical aspect of much debate (see Audi and Wolterstorff 1997; Audi 2005), not 'liberal premises *per se*, but against an overly narrow, supposedly secularist definition of the political role of religion in the liberal frame', or 'what line gets drawn to claims that reach beyond a liberal constitution'. Here, Habermas contends, 'Arguments for a more generously dimensioned political role for religion that are incompatible with the secular nature of the state should not be confused with justifiable objections to a secularist understanding of democracy and the rule of law' (Habermas 2006: 6). The foundational principle of such contexts is that the

> principle of separation of church and state demands that the institution of the state operate with strict impartiality vis-a-vis religious communities; parliaments, courts, and the administration must not violate the prescription not to privilege one side at the cost of another.
>
> (Habermas 2006: 9)

For Habermas:

> Irrespective of how the interests are weighted in the relationship between the state and religious organizations, a state cannot encumber its citizens, whom it guarantees freedom of religious expression, with duties that are incompatible with pursuing a devout life – it cannot expect something impossible of them.
>
> (Habermas 2006: 7)

This is part of a growing focus on religion in the works of Habermas (2008; see also Calhoun *et al.* 2013). The accommodating views of religion took form in UN international human rights standards (see Lerner 2002; Donnelly 2002) which, in this context, are means of adjudicating when such circumstances are encountered, when those 'pursuing a devout life' are expected to do 'something impossible'.

Stepan (2000) takes the same problem framed as 'twin tolerations'. This position may be defined as follows: open plural democracies need the dual legitimacy of support by religious leaders of government and government to allow religious not simply private worship but participation in the public sphere. Cold War history was a politically moderating response to the extremes of totalitarianism in its suppression of cultural, ethnic and religious difference. Post-Cold War history has become a politically moderating response to the extremes of precisely the same cultural, ethnic and religiously difference. What had once been perceived as needing protection by the international community is now perceived as something from which the international community needs protecting. It has meant that the United Nations system has increasingly sought not only accommodation but moulding of religion in the light of its founding ideals; that is, the insistence on the conformity of religion to the political frameworks agreed by the international community, citizenship, democracy, human rights.

Formed in the early 1990s, in the aftermath of the Cold War, the Special Rapporteur on freedom of religion or belief is an independent expert appointed by the UN Human Rights Council and has, since then, played an important role in monitoring infringement of religious freedom around the world. The mandate holder is to 'identify existing and emerging obstacles to the enjoyment of the right to freedom of religion or belief and present recommendations on ways and means to overcome such obstacles' (UN 2010). In 2000, the Commission on Human Rights widened the original mandate related to freedom of religion to 'freedom of religion or belief'. The Special Rapporteur has been mandated through the Human Rights Council to promote the adoption of measures at the national, regional and international levels to ensure the promotion and protection of the right to freedom of religion or belief (UN 2010). At an early stage this included references to the uses of religion in education (Amor 2001).

The Human Rights Council concluded its nineteenth main session of 23

March 2012, adopting 41 texts or resolutions on a wide range of issues, including 'Resolutions of Particular Relevance to Freedom of Religion or Belief' (UN 2012). The text of A/HRC/19/L.23 recalls the Resolution 36/55 of the UN General Assembly of 25 November 1981, the Declaration against Discrimination on the basis of religion or belief (UN 1981). What is new in the March 2012 commentary is 'the inclusion of an element of education to promote', through the educational system and other means, mutual understanding, tolerance, non-discrimination and respect in all matters relating to freedom of religion or belief by encouraging, in society at large, a wider knowledge of different religions and beliefs and of the history, traditions, languages and cultures of the various religious minorities existing within their jurisdiction' (UN 2012; see also the Association of Religion Data Archives: www.thearda.com).

Resistance to this religiously advocated model of political liberalism appears in the public domain in local, national and international dimensions. What happens then with theological and other religious frameworks refuse the accommodation given to it by modern liberal democracy? This is a question posed by Rawls (1999) in *The Law of Peoples*. There seems to be growing consensus in the international community that religious education is the model by which such political problems.

Thus the Special Rapporteur Heiner Bielefeldt (2012) outlines the ways in which education plays a role in the international promotion of freedom of religion or belief:

> The more we experience pluralism and diversity on a daily basis and perhaps even within our immediate neighbourhoods or families, the more we may see the necessity of learning at least to civilize the concomitant disagreements by according one another a basic respect that should guide the way in which we cope with on-going disagreements, competitions and conflicts.
>
> (Bielefeldt 2012: 3)

Grounded in a fundamental and inalienable notion of human dignity, the 'daily experience of pluralism itself' thus 'ultimately helps to find a new common ground on which we can normatively organize our coexistence'(Bielefeldt 2012: 3). For Bielefeldt, this indicates that the concept of human dignity 'at least in the context of international human rights, must remain open for a wide diversity of religious or philosophical readings' (Bielefeldt 2012: 4), In Bielefeldt's terms, 'based on such an understanding, religious or belief pluralism can only unfold within a predefined set of permissible options', a freedom limited by law. Although 'at times . . . interpreted in very restrictive or ideological ways clearly at variance with respect for freedom of religion or belief' (Bielefeldt 2012: 11), only the secular state provides both the conceptual coherence and pragmatic means to ensure freedom of religion or belief. If such considerations are apparent in the early decades of a modern religious education (Brickner 1938; Smith Leiper 1938; Mathews 1937), now such political thinking does not merely, dimly, inform, it *permeates* the discourse of religious education as it does the discourse of religion in public life (although, for a nuanced review of the role of religion in mainstream educational research, see Nelson 2010).

The politics of religious education

Rousseau's *Emile or On Education* was published in 1762, the same year as *The Social Contract*. The banning of these works by those public authorities amongst whom he was much celebrated prompted Rousseau's self-exile. It was arguably this secular martyrdom, with a European tour in which he met the renowned figures of his age, which enhanced an already great reputation in France abroad.

The controversy of *Emile* showed a negative role of religion in Enlightenment philosophy of education. In the *Profession of Faith of the Savoyard Vicar*, Rousseau interposes a derision of which by design and default would therefore remove religion from education. Emile's tutor, the narrator, tells of a young man who had been forced into exile. The young man meets a priest who had himself encountered scandal and been dismissed from the priesthood. Rousseau writes from the young man's perspective as he recalls the Savoyard Vicar's story (a literary device which provides authorial distance from controversial views). The priest tells the young man how, doubting all prior religious beliefs, by deep conviction he knows himself to be a free being, a free will in a physical body. The priest sees religious truth not in dogma but in civil and social duty. He sees no harm in the practice of any religion so long as it conforms to such non-dogmatic claims. The search for religious truth is self-evident futility: 'Are you desirous of gaining information from books? What a fund of erudition will not this require! How many languages must you learn! How many libraries must you turn over!' (Rousseau 1914: para. 189). Rather,

> [to] form a proper judgment of any religion, we are not to deduce its tenets from the books of its professors; we must go and learn it among the people. Each sect have their peculiar traditions, – their customs, prejudices, and modes of acceptation, which constitute the peculiar mode of their faith. This should all be taken into consideration when we form a judgment of their religion.
>
> (Rousseau 1914: para. 189)

Yet, then,

> if there be in the world but one true religion, and if everyone is obliged to adopt it under pain of damnation, it is necessary to spend our lives in the study of all religions – to visit the countries where they have been

established, and examine and compare them with each other. No man is exempted from the principal duty of his species, and no one has a right to confide in the judgment of another.

(Rousseau 1914: para. 190)

In which case, Rousseau then argues, we must 'bid adieu to the arts and sciences, to trade, and to all the civil occupations of life. Every other study must give place to that of religion'. Rousseau presumes however that,

> while the man who should enjoy the greatest share of health and strength, and make the best use of his time and reason for the longest term of years allotted to human life, would, in his extreme old age, be still perplexed and undecided.

(Rousseau 1914: para. 215)

He adds, 'and it would be indeed wonderful if, after all his researches, he should be able to learn before his death what religion he ought to have believed and practiced during his life'.

Like Dewey's (1916) *Democracy and Education*, which acknowledges a debt to Rousseau, both authors and their works show how the critical works of Enlightenment educational philosophy are integrally related to their respective political theory. The theory of education reflects, in other words, a theory of the state and the role of the citizen in it. Dewey implicitly sees the work of dismissing religion's contribution to education as accomplished. This is why he looks to democratic theories of education first in the classical, especially Greek, contexts and moves from there directly to the eighteenth century. Both Rousseau and Dewey's positive educational agendas stress drawing out each child's innate aptitudes, interests and moral qualities, rather than rigidly imposing an authoritarian body of knowledge. Mirroring political notions of liberty, equality and fraternity, the pedagogical approach of his dictum: 'The source of whatever is dead, mechanical, and formal in schools is found precisely in the subordination of the life and experience of the child to the curriculum'. Never dissociated from a political context, these ideas are found in *Experience and Education* (Dewey [1938] 1997). This excluded religion, except insofar as it was 'a common faith', like Rousseau's secular civil religion. It is not for no reason that the two great pedagogical exponents of this method come respectively from France (Rousseau) and America (Dewey), two countries whose Revolutions exerted such powerful political aftershocks and whose educational systems to this day remove religious education from the curriculum.

The appropriation of politics in religious education

Willaime (2007) notes, of religious education in European context, that: 'School instruction about religious faith is a strong indicator of the way church–state and school–religion relations are constructed inside a given national framework'. This is a battle unresolved in either European (see Arthur and Holdsworth 2012; Hunter-Henin 2011) or American courts and classrooms (Strassner 2011). *The Routledge International Handbook of Religious Education* (Davis and Miroshnikova 2013) shows indeed how *worldwide* – from Argentina to Vietnam – religious education has been and how it continues to be impacted by legal and political context. Durham writes in the introduction: 'Few areas of social and political life attract such profound concern and intense attention as the religious education of each successive rising generation', making religious education a major issue for both religious and political communities (Durham 2012: 7). The educational conditions in which religious education is either disavowed or encouraged is invariably a reflection of state attitudes to religion itself. Thus, 'the structuring of religious education systems reflects in profound ways the extent to which religion is restricted to the private sector or is recognized as having a legitimate role to play in the public order of a society'. This always mirrors historical and political antecedence, whether religion has been 'seen as a threat in the educational process' or reflecting 'concerns about reinforcing predominant religions' or 'worries about respecting the rights of smaller groups' (Durham 2012: 2).

Ferrari (2012a) suggests three models of religious education which are reflective of the European situation:

> 1) disallowing religious education within the formal curriculum in schools opened by the state (e.g. France, with the exception of Alsace-Moselle); 2) providing non-denominational teaching about religions; and 3) providing denominational teaching of religion for prevailing religion(s) within the country.
>
> (Ferrari 2012a: 100–3)

In Europe, too, by way of reminder, Willaime (2007) identified three models of religious education in Europe: (1) 'no religious instruction in schools'; (2) 'confessional religious instruction'; (3) 'non-confessional religious education' (Willaime 2007: 60). Although legal and policy issues arise in regard to these three situations at a national level, Durham suggests 'these appear to be the major options not only in Europe, but worldwide' (Durham 2013: 2).

Countries where the historical antagonisms to religion have been maintained through revolutionary principles antipathetic to religion are diminishing in number but prominent amongst them is China (Zhou 2013: 76–83). But France (Dericquebourg 2013) and the United States of America (Clark 2013) retain their formal exclusion of religious education from the public schools for well-known reasons which date to their respective revolutions, both of which were founded on the basis of very different attitudes to religion (for a more detailed examination of the historical, legal and political interface of religion in education, see Strassner 2011).

The advocates' position is represented in the United Nations era as a resolution then of a deep-seated conflict which has different national (legal, policy and political) nuances in each country's history (AoC 2013; UN 2010, 2012; USCIRF 1999), with an increasingly educational dimension facilitating political management of religious diversity and plurality (CoE 2008a, 2008b; UNESCO 2006, 2011).

What Willaime identifies as a 'double constraint' shows the extent to which models of religious education today are often compelled to comply with universal standards of democratic citizenship and human rights initiated in the same era of the United Nations:

> a *sociological* one, in that the religious and philosophical pluralisation of European societies obliges them to include ever more alternative religions and non-religious positions into their curricula, and . . . a *legal* one, through the importance of the principle of non-discrimination on religious or philosophical grounds (as well as others such as gender or race) in international law, especially in the European Convention on Human Rights.
>
> (Willaime 2007: 65, emphasis in original)

The instances of inclusion or reinclusion of religious education where especially Marxist-inspired revolutions prohibited them are numerous. In the former Soviet bloc, these countries include Azerbaijan (Ibadov 2013); Estonia (Kiviorg 2013); Hungary (Schanda 2013); Kazakhstan (Podoprigora 2013); Latvia (Balodis 2013); Lithuania (Alisauskiene 2013); Poland (Zielinska and Zwierzdzynski 2013); Romania (Pavel Tavala 2013); Slovakia (Moracikova 2013); Slovenia (Cepar 2013), Ukraine (Fylypovych and Gavrilova 2013) and, of course, Russia herself (Gennadievna Romanova 2013).

Spain (Garcimartin Montero 2013), under the reign of Francisco Franco, and Portugal (Gouveia 2013), under António de Oliveira Salazar, are interesting exceptions in the Cold War and post-Nazi era, where the revolutionary policies of the right had maintained Catholic denominational religious education and yet are now subject to the same legal and sociological constraints which in many respects their regimes stood in opposition. Ireland (O'Mahony 2013) and Italy (Ferrari 2013b), two predominantly Catholic heritage countries, had similarly strongly Catholic denominational religious education.

In Greece (Maghioros 2013), too, while religious education was hardly the concern of the coup d'état Lieutenant Colonel Kostas Aslanides (the rule of the 'colonels', 1967–1974) the Orthodox Church has maintained a consistent role in contributing to religious education and remains important, just as the Orthodox churches have emerged in a post-Communist context as integral to national identity through education across the former Soviet bloc.

The liberal models of European religious education which allow a diversity of public school and denominational provision (see Ferrari 2013a), with considerable diversity in specific legal and policy contexts nationally, are: Austria (Konigsberger and Kubarth 2013) Belgium (Martin and Fautre 2013); Canada (Young 2013); Finland (Kotiranta 2013); Norway (Thorson Plesner 2013); Scotland (Lyall 2013); Sweden (Friedner 2013); Switzerland (Pahud de Martanges and Suess 2013). The United Kingdom, although Newcombe (2013) does not make this case, is also in this European list. It is an exception, since it has to some large degree pioneered, especially through the work of Smart, those models that can loosely be called phenomenological worldwide.

Post-Second World War countries where this adaptation of liberal models of inclusion for differing forms of religious education were integrally related to complex political–educational programmes of de-Nazification or similar programmes were of course Germany (Schmalzle 2013) and to some lesser extent, Austria (Konigsberger and Kubarth 2013).

Amongst Latin American countries (Navarro Floria 2013), where Marxist revolutionary struggle has as an almost equally old history as it has in Europe, here, above all other countries in the region, it was Mexico's 1917 revolutionary constitution which, if only a matter of months before the Russian revolution, represented the deepest antagonism to religious education by constitutionally forbidding it within schools (Gonzalez 2013). The region mirrored a Cold War struggle that was evident in conflicts which religious education found itself between prior to, during and after the Cold War: in Argentina (Padilla 2013); Brazil (Xavier Gomes 2013); Colombia (Prieto 2013); Peru (Santana 2013); and Uruguay (Pereira 2013).

In the Far East, Japan (Takahata 2013) makes a particularly interesting study of the tensions between what was an essentially forced democratization and the survival of Japanese imperial order.

Australia (Babie and Mylius 2013) is distinct in the Asia-Pacific region. Although historically identified with Britain rather than with America and Europe, it has experienced an increasing diversity in its population but its models of plural religious education provision remain closer to the European model.

Across Asia (Mahmood 2013a), those formerly non-aligned, 'developing' countries are distinguished by a postcolonial struggle and with resolving their own national and cultural identities through religious education, which only to more limited degrees than for example in Europe gives credence to issues of religious plurality and difference: in Bangladesh (Alam *et al.* 2013); India (Mahmood 2013b); Indonesia (Abdillah 2013); Malaysia (Hashim 2013); Nepal (Thapa and Mukhia 2013); Pakistan (Khan and Javed Mian 2013) and Vietnam (Thi Minh Ngoc 2013).

Senegal (Camara and Seck 2013), South Africa (du Plessis 2013) and Sudan (D'Angelo 2013) represent the only African nations in Davis and Miroshnikova's (2013) study. The Middle East is sparsely represented as well but two critical players in the region represent some of the immense complexities of the religious and political settlement of the region: in Israel (Maoz 2013) and in Syria (el-Hakim 2013). These countries, above all others, suggest that ancient rather than simply longstanding conflicts of a political, religious and territorial nature will not be resolved through a particular model of religious education in the school curriculum.

Many European political institutions have in the past decade developed policy initiatives on religion in education, underscoring the importance of teaching and learning about religion as a means of encouraging understanding of and between religions in Europe (Jackson 2009, 2011a; Weisse 2009, 2011). Amongst the most influential of these initiatives, in terms of growing global impact, is the Organization for Security and Cooperation in Europe (OSCE). Closing aligned with NATO and the Council of Europe throughout the Cold War to counter the Soviet threat, one of the OSCE's post-Cold War and post-9/11 interests is how culture and religion can be harnessed for harmony rather than for conflict (on the contemporary security aspects of religion in global governance see Schmid 2011; Seiple *et al.* 2011). The teaching of some form of religious education in this context is now regarded as a priority and is most evident in the *Toledo Guiding Principles on Teaching about Religions and Beliefs in Public Schools* (OSCE 2007; see also Gearon 2013a), accentuated by the growth of global terrorism (Gearon 2013c; Miller 2013; Moulin 2012).

The OSCE's Office for Democratic Institutions and Human Rights (ODIHR) and the Advisory Council of its Panel of Experts on Freedom of Religion or Belief thus developed the *Toledo Guiding Principles* look to historical models for contemporary co-existence where it is

> important for young people to acquire a better understanding of the role that religions play in today's pluralistic world...The need for such education will continue to grow as different cultures and identities interact with each other through travel, commerce, media or migration. Although a deeper understanding of religions will not automatically lead to greater tolerance and respect, ignorance increases the likelihood of misunderstanding, stereotyping, and conflict.
>
> (OSCE 2007: 9)

In short, the *Toledo Guiding Principles* were 'prepared in order to contribute to an improved understanding of the world's increasing religious diversity and the growing presence of religion in the public sphere'. Their primary purpose is thus 'to assist OSCE participating states whenever they choose to promote the study and knowledge about religions and beliefs in schools' (OSCE 2007: 11–12).

It is this educational and *legal* consensus which means that the *Toledo Guiding Principles* laid 'should be taken into consideration *by all OSCE participating States when devising schemes for teaching about religions and beliefs'* (OSCE 2007, emphases added). A human rights justification becomes important here, confirming not only the importance of social cohesiveness through the teaching of religion but legal–political emphases on the voice of the child, exemplified by the 1989 Convention on the Rights of the Child. In religious education terms, this Convention framed the rights of children within religious education. Here, the learning of 'civilizations' and religions other than their own are regarded as pedagogically foundational (AoC 2013; Commonwealth 2007; Jawoniyi 2012).

The growing worldwide impetus for teaching religious education is by the nature of its influence *political* but it is also and of absolute necessity *historical*. One of the problems in implementation was that we have the politics without the history: the acceptance of (and clearly many European students have) accepted liberal democratic values as the core rationale for religious education. Religious education here risks however limiting religion to its public and political face.

Political liberalism, though, makes on the surface no claim to judge between truth claims. It holds, within the bounds of law, the need for religious plurality to be respected. It is what, to remind us, Willaime calls the double constraint of law and sociology: under the law religions are equal and, given the sociological circumstances of all societies, are religiously plural. In this context, one religion, it is deemed, cannot have social or political priority over any other religion. Although far from the political realities in many countries, where freedom of religion is negligible or severely restricted, as an educational ideal it has its appeal. Given the close relationship between politics and pedagogy, it should be no surprise that a problem in modern-day democratic politics is presented for liberal education to solve.

The philosophical–theological counterpart of political liberalism in regard to religion is a theological notion of religious pluralism, in which all religions represent cultural variations of one ultimate reality (Hick 2004). There cannot logically, Hick argues, be more than one ultimate reality; for there to be more than one ultimate reality or ultimate truth would be a contradiction. This position was espoused, as we have seen, by many theorists who have formed post-Enlightenment attitudes to religion, the frames of knowledge used to understand it and, through these, to make use of it in education. The trend toward integrating religious education and its political ends is clear and the link between pedagogy and a new, revisionist model for religious education often made explicit, as socially, politically 'integrative religious education' (Alberts 2010; Loobuyck and Franken 2011), addressing social and community cohesion (Grimmitt 2010; Jackson 2012) or initiatives which align religious education and peace education, evident in a special issue of the *British Journal of Religious Education* dedicated to the theme (for example, Jackson and Fujiwara 2007; cf. King 2007; Schweitzer 2005). Along similar lines, 'what children need' is defined in terms of 'cooperative religious education' (Schweitzer and Boschki 2004); a model that originated, like the Enlightenment itself, in Europe (for example Hunter-Henin 2011;

Jackson *et al.* 2007; Schreiner 2008) is now attaining a global reach (UN 2010, 2012; UNESCO 2011).

The assumption that religious education should confirm to democratic and liberal principles remains not only a commonplace but is an increasingly default justification, where political context justifies some form of religious education. Davis and Miroshnikova (2013) provide, as we have seen, some international overviews of the context of the diverse ways in which this is true. Legal-political-pedagogical contexts today thus provide manifold opportunities to confirm a social and political relevance for religious education which dates to its modern origins, in part through alignment with the social sciences (Coe 1922, 1932; Lee 1973) but also in having something to contribute to changing political milieu. Thus, in regard to Soviet Russia, Fisher (1936) wrote of 'The Place of Religious Education in the Social Revolution'. In the pre-Second World War period, with particular focus on Nazism, Silcox (1937) wrote on 'The Significance of Religious Freedom in the Modern World' (also Hubben 1937, on the 'totalitarian mind'), Yarros (1937) on 'Religion and the Totalitarian State' or Bernstein *et al.* (1940) on the relationship between religion and democracy (again, see Harner 1950). Historically reviewing the same mid-twentieth century period, Freathy (2008) has showed a preoccupation at the time with religious education serving political goals.

In 2008 a special issue of *The British Journal of Religious Education* showed this developing convergence in goals between of religious, citizenship and human rights education in the UK (Gearon 2008; also Gearon 2002; Mason 2003, Watson 2004) and worldwide (Tan 2008; Leirvik 2008; Miedema and Bertram-Troost 2008; Sztokman 2008). In a subsequent issue, Guyette (2009) usefully highlights a shift in relations between human rights education and religious education as a move 'from mutual suspicion to elective affinity': once antagonistic relations between the religious and the political have, in short, moved into closer alignment. But, Mark A. Pike (2008) asks if this convergence is an expediency which requires a new 'faith in citizenship' involving 'teaching children to believe in liberal democracy'. Hull, once editor of the *British Journal of Religious Education*, by contrast, has lauded the 'blessings of secularity' (Hull 2003) as facilitating a religious education as socially and politically encounter with religious difference (Bates *et al.* 2005; Gates 2011). To this extent, the political justification of religious education is now commonplace (Alexander and Agbaria 2012; Parker *et al.* 2012), a politicized 'cooperative religious education' (Schweitzer and Boschki 2004), which is 'integrative' (Alberts 2010) and which, through emphases on dialogue, is a pedagogical model for conflict resolution (ter Avest *et al.* 2008). A special issue of the *British Journal of Religious Education* on the REDCo Project illustrates the international reach of such political justifications for religious education across Europe (Everington *et al.* 2011) or in critically reflective methodological terms (Bertram-Troost 2011; Jackson 2011; Weisse 2011).

Similar debates across the Atlantic are reflected in *Religious Education*. As in philosophy for children, Enlightenment reason meets Enlightenment politics (for example, Shabani 2011). Taking Jürgen Habermas's positive reappraisal of religion in the context of public reason, Shabani distinguishes this 'over the classic *liberal proviso*', which has three dimensions: '(1) it releases religious citizens from an undue cognitive burden; (2) it distributes the cognitive burden of justification symmetrically across the citizenry; and (3) it offers a multidimensional concept of reason that becomes self-critically aware of its boundaries'. Emphasis is placed here upon religious education and the study of religion as a point of critical dialogue, the classroom mirroring in microcosm the macrocosmic context of society (Engebretson *et al.* 2010). The perceived resurgence of religion in public and political life is seen in some religious education quarters, as we have noted, as evidence of counter-secularization (Weisse 2011) or post-secularity (Bowie *et al.* 2012) and that this justifies the place of religious education as an essential critical pedagogical adjunct of a political context.

Summary

There is, then, unarguably much modern-day international political interest in the *uses* of religion in education. This is often perceived as a *means* of establishing understanding between cultures and religions. Interest in religion in education extends even to those countries where religion is not part of the school curriculum in state schools.

The problems of secular liberal religious educators here are (at least) twofold: one, the confinement of religious education to limited (liberal democratic) political and pedagogical goals (pedagogy serving political purpose) risks limiting religion as much as religious education to the political and public profile and purposes of both; two, even if it could be shown to be political useful, is political justification sufficient as epistemological ground for religious education?

In 'Post-Secularism, Religious Knowledge and Religious Education', David Carr (2012) elaborates the argument that 'post-secularism' like other 'postal' perspectives – 'post-structuralism, postmodernism, post-empiricism, post-positivism, post-analytical philosophy, post-foundationalism' – is part of a 'questioning or repudiating what it takes to be the epistemic assumptions of modernism'. Here, post-secularism is preoccupied 'with one particular assumed implication of modernism – namely that there can be no epistemic warrant for religious faith or belief'. Carr, sympathetic to this attempt to rehabilitate religion, considers three philosophical critiques 'for the justification or dismissal of religious belief' – the pre-modern, modernism and a range of 'postal' perspectives. Finding these lacking, Carr opts instead of a political–philosophical justification for religion and, thus religious education, in 'a narrative account of religious meaning and understanding…On this view, religious texts, stories and myths – like other non-scientific narratives of wider literary and artistic culture – are crucial to the spiritual and moral cultivation of practical wisdom'. It is appropriate, then, that we move from the political–philosophical to the aesthetic justification of religious education.

8   The aesthetics of religious education

Introduction

The history of art is also a history of religion. Since the relationship between religion and art has been so connected in the history of both, often to the extent that the history of one is the history of the other, we should not be surprised that aesthetic theory shifted as attitudes to religion changed. Aesthetics is therefore often defined through its relationship with religion. Enlightenment aesthetics would arise in a century that was revolutionary in other ways and would be a cultural measure of a philosophical and political process seeking new non-religious grounds for human experience.

The arts can here be defined as the material expression of meaning shaped by cultural context. The broad definition is justified by the range of what is defined as art today. For the most part, I shall draw exemplars from the visual and literary arts. These were as affected by the Enlightenment as any other aspect of social, scientific or political life. The arts were not passive recipients of those changes in knowledge which mark modernity. The arts *re-present* those changes in the history of ideas in aesthetic form.

The visual arts provide the most graphic form of this representation. If we examine any major collection of art, we can read in visual form a dramatic story of religion's removal from the canvas. The Sainsbury Wing of the National Gallery, for instance, houses medieval art from the period 1250–1400. It is exclusively religious. The art embodies religion in pictorial form. The paintings are, as much as any written document, a visual window to medieval religious life, showing how these people perceived and placed into perspective a short earthly life. The galleries *beyond* the 1500s, the beginnings of the modern world, show a parallel with the individual finding his or her own sense of world. Kant's Enlightenment motto – 'Have courage to use your own understanding!' – is transmuted into aesthetic form: have courage to express yourself. Above all, this is evidenced with what is essentially a modern view of the artist as individual genius.

The Reformation would, however, mark the greatest shift in aesthetics, for theological as well as artistic reasons. Medieval Catholic art was regarded as both unscriptural (the communion of saints, purgatory) but pictorial representation (especially of God) was regarded by Reformers as idolatrous. European art, as a result, suffered an unprecedented destruction of an irreplaceable cultural heritage. Artists used to undertaking such devotional work were neither needed nor wanted. Some fled to Catholic countries. Others remained in their native lands. In these latter instances, the portrayals of religious life disappear. What emerges are more allegorical portrayals of the same existential context – for example, in the form of the 'vanitas', visual representations of the fleeting nature of human life and its everyday preoccupations, shown in allegorical form. The Reformation thus had a profound effect not only on European theology but also on European art. As society changed and conceptions of the person in society changed (subjects to citizens), so was art transformed.

Religion and the arts

Rousseau, who did so much to shape this politics, unlike his Enlightenment contemporaries, thought little of art or artists. The young Rousseau, indeed, found fame with his submission to the Academy of Dijon for an essay which would win first prize – *Discourse on the Sciences and Arts*. For Rousseau, art contributed not to the moral vibrancy of society but rather to a narcissism that was its inverse. In this idea, we can see the emergence of an important tension in aesthetics contested across subsequent centuries, whether art was primarily a means of self-expression or serving the needs of society.

The idea that art should have a political role shows the emergence of a parallel notion which sees the social and the political replacing the religious and the theological. Religion had once been the meaning, form and expression of art; now, the social and political should be. This understanding of art is a secularized interpretation of the role of religion in art. It is the aesthetic dimension of Schmitt's notion that all modern political concepts are secularized theological concepts. It was thus in the eighteenth century Enlightenment that aesthetic theory confronted the political. As Jacques Morizot puts it:

> The birth of aesthetics as a field lies at the junction between Enlightenment ideals and the teachings of taste: reason is no longer seen as a truth system but increasingly as a faculty of testing and evaluating, and accordingly it cannot put aside as irrelevant the lessons of sentiment and individuality. Art becomes a powerful stimulant of human social activities and an inexhaustible subject for philosophical inquiry.
>
> (Morizot 2011)

The singular point of resistance to the notion that art should be political was thus found in another Enlightenment idea, that individuals should be autonomous and free.

The aesthetic adversaries of religion

In 1735, Alexander Baumgarten (1714–1762) called for an *aestheticae*, a science of perception which would impact on, indeed prompt the aesthetics of Hume and Kant (see Guyer 2003, 2005). As they relate fundamentally to the senses – *are* the senses represented in material form – Leibniz had argued that the arts are a type of cognition, although only poorly related to reason (see, for instance, Kukla 2011). Baumgarten, seeing aesthetics as concerned with the beautiful, related this the same impetus as reason, to the creation of harmony, in philosophy through ideas, in art through representation. Baumgarten suggested that the judgements involved in considering beauty, aesthetic judgements, were *qualitatively* different and not necessarily inferior to reason. (Descartes' scepticism played an important role here: if we cannot be certain of the world through our senses, the arts, as an expression of them, are hardly a source of rational certainty.) Baumgarten can be seen as the foundational figure who gave thinking about the arts a philosophical credence. Integrally related to this was what counted as art, what should be the subject of this *aestheticae*? If Baumgarten's call for a science of aesthetics were valid, were all the arts of equal stature? Charles Batteux's (1713–1780) *Les Beaux Arts Reduits à un Même Principe* (1746) sought a series of laws for the arts, that which would define good taste, most critically in high art or what Batteux seminally called the fine arts. Batteux's (1747) *Principes de la Littérature* extended the procedure to the literary arts.

The distinction between practical, mechanical, technical crafts and the fine arts built on Baumgarten to shape an idea which was immediately influential. In his *Discourses on Art*, the renowned English painter Joshua Reynolds (1723–1792) would espouse Batteux's views. Baumgarten is known today almost solely because of his influence on Kant. As Kant comments in a footnote of the *Critique of Pure Reason*, 'The Germans are the only people who at present use this word to indicate what others call the critique of taste'. Kant writes of the 'disappointed hope', which 'the eminent analyst, Baumgarten, conceived, of subjecting the criticism of the beautiful to principles of reason, and so of elevating its rules into a science' but whose 'endeavours were vain'. Kant had followed Hume in assuming that aesthetics were beyond systematization. This view we see here is still maintained in the first *Critique*.

David Hume's (1757) 'Of the Standard of Taste' was an aesthetic theory not only of art but also of the artist, the characteristics of those who produce art to the highest degree, the genius. It was a work which influenced the Kant's (1981, 2003) pre-critical aesthetics in *Observations on the Feeling of the Beautiful and the Sublime*, a work he published, inspired by Hume, in 1764. To Kant, the Enlightenment idea of human progress and perfectibility suggested a hierarchy of the arts. Since the arts were often debated in terms of how they represented nature, Kant also framed discussion of the arts in these terms. The high or fine arts imitate nature, the mechanical arts or crafts simply utilize it. *Genius* in high or fine art is not merely the imitation of nature but its transformation, showing nature as more perfect than itself. Through art and artistic genius, we see things in nature as a wholeness not apparent to those not possessed of such rare abilities. (Aristotle, in the *Poetics*, had stressed *unity* as one of the determining feature of literature, so the ideas are not new; in the Enlightenment they were newly formed.)

Enlightenment preoccupation with genius would itself be transformative. The Enlightenment would come, as a result, to reflect changing perceptions of both art and of the role of the artist but also the Enlightenment stress in political and philosophical terms of the autonomy, liberty of, the individual. (The focus on the *individual* genius would have been unthinkable for theological reasons during the medieval period.) The eighteenth-century Enlightenment, so famed for its revolutions in politics and philosophy, would thus also see a unique flowering in all the creative arts. The age of reason was also the age of high art, of Wordsworth, Coleridge, Austen, Fielding, Goethe, and in music of Haydn, Mozart and Beethoven. It is perhaps curious that a period so preoccupied with genius should produce so many of them.

Many analyses of the Romantic movement are often portrayed as the antithesis of the rationality that was the cornerstone of the Enlightenment and this view has its validity. However, we can see that the most sceptical of rational philosophers did most to raise art not simply to representation but as a fundamental impulse of the human spirit, if not equal then complementary to reason.

Kant had not always felt like this. If Kant's *Critique of Pure Reason* removed metaphysics and theology as legitimate concerns of philosophy, the *Critique of Practical Reason* ([1781] 1909) had the moral sense within him and above him the wonder of the starry heavens as new measures of the sublime. Kant (1764) had once made plain that art was not the proper subject of philosophy, a view reversed in his *Critique of Judgement* ([1790] 2007).

Art – for Kant fine art – is not practical but 'contemplative'. Kant's aesthetic theory is rooted in those two works noted: the pre-critical, where art is not the subject of philosophy but is now (in the *Critique of Judgement*) the *culmination* of the critical. In the early phase, Kant is one in seeing art as a matter of morally informed taste; in his more mature work he sees it as concerned with disinterested observation of the true and the beautiful. It is in the *Critique of Judgement* where these ideas crystallize. In removing religion and, notably, God from rational judgement (*The Critique of Practical Reason*), he finds place for God in morality (*The Critique of Practical Reason*), in *The Critique of Judgement* we read almost a yearning for the aesthetic to fill the void that Kant had himself done so much to create. The space vacated by the sacred is taken by the sublime.

Kant's emphasis upon 'contemplation' of the sublime, re-roots, or re-routes, our contemplation of God to the natural world:

> Might is a power which is superior to great hindrances. It is termed dominion if it is also superior to the resistance of that which itself possesses might. Nature, considered in an aesthetic judgement as might that has no dominion over us, is dynamically sublime.
>
> (Kant 2007: 83)

The emotions it inspires are similar to those which Otto, a century later, would ascribe to the holy:

> If we are to estimate nature as dynamically sublime, it must be represented as a source of fear (though the converse, that every object that is a source of fear, in our aesthetic judgement, sublime, does not hold). For in forming an aesthetic estimate (no concept being present) the superiority to hindrances can only be estimated according to the greatness of the resistance. Now that which we strive to resist is an evil, and, if we do not find our powers commensurate to the task, an object of fear. Hence the aesthetic judgement can only deem nature a might, and so dynamically sublime, in so far as it is looked upon as an object of fear
>
> (Kant 2007: 83)

The sense of the sublime once contained, however, becomes the source of the aesthetic not the religious sense. Thus,

> we may look upon an object as fearful, and yet not be afraid of it, if, that is, our estimate takes the form of our simply picturing to ourselves the case of our wishing to offer some resistance to it and recognizing that all such resistance would be quite futile.
>
> (Kant 2007: 83)

Here, Kant draws an analogy with religious experience:

> So the righteous man fears God without being afraid of Him, because he regards the case of his wishing to resist God and His commandments as one which need cause him no anxiety. But in every such case, regarded by him as not intrinsically impossible, he cognizes Him as One to be feared.
>
> (Kant 2007: 83)

Kant argues, however, that where there is fear there can be no room for judgement: 'One who is in a state of fear can no more play the part of a judge of the sublime of nature than one captivated by inclination and appetite can of the beautiful.' In fear, a person flees the object of dread. The ending of the dread is the beginning of joy and wonder at the object of awe. This is the recognition of the sublime:

Bold, overhanging, and, as it were, threatening rocks, thunderclouds piled up the vault of heaven, borne along with flashes and peals, volcanoes in all their violence of destruction, hurricanes leaving desolation in their track, the boundless ocean rising with rebellious force, the high waterfall of some mighty river, and the like, make our power of resistance of trifling moment in comparison with their might. But, provided our own position is secure, their aspect is all the more attractive for its fearfulness; and we readily call these objects sublime, because they raise the forces of the soul above the height of vulgar commonplace, and discover within us a power of resistance of quite another kind, which gives us courage to be able to measure ourselves against the seeming omnipotence of nature.

(Kant 2007: 75)

We note in this passage, too, that, although part of nature, there is something out of the ordinary about the experience and yet part of it: 'In the immeasurableness of nature and the incompetence of our faculty for adopting a standard proportionate to the aesthetic estimation of the magnitude of its realm, we found our own limitation'. The human response to nature finds something though which is 'above' it, the discovery in 'our rational faculty another non-sensuous standard' and 'one which has that infinity itself under it as a unit, and in comparison with which everything in nature is small, and so found in our minds a pre-eminence over nature even in it immeasurability' Kant 2007: 75).

Art is here not simply a physical, mechanical or practical representation of this sublime, much less the crafts which enable us to use the goods of nature to serve our material needs, nor is it concerned with a moral state or sense, although it may lead to it. Rather, for Kant, the high arts are those productions which represent disinterestedly those forces of sublimity in nature in material form – in literature, music and the visual arts. These aesthetic judgements are disinterested, *universal, necessary* and purposive without (practical, determinable) purpose. How are such judgements possible?

The critical disagreement in aesthetic theory was the extent to which assertion that beautiful objects and our responses to them were essentially involved in sense or feeling. Kant asserted the basic distinction between intuitive or sensible presentations on the one hand and the conceptual or rational on the other. Kant was led to speculate that the operation of judgment might be organized and directed by a fundamental *a priori* principle that is unique to it. The third *Critique* sets out to explore the validity and implications of such a hypothesis (see Burnham 2000).

As we have seen in the *Critique of Pure Reason*, freedom is that capacity to transcend, not to be limited by nature, which is determined. If all were determined, there would be no room for morality, in the sense of a freedom to act in a moral way. So, too, for Kant's aesthetics, the genius is a means of that freedom through the expression of aesthetic acts. So 'genius is a talent for producing that for which no definite rule can be given' (Kant 2007: 113): 'Genius is the talent (or natural gift) which gives the rule to art' (Kant 2007: 112). Yet, since talent, as the innate gift, belongs to nature but is also related to nature, genius is also 'that innate mental disposition through which nature gives the rule to art'. Such art, the opposite to imitation, therefore both represents and transcends, wherein lies the association of art to freedom in Kant's aesthetics. For Kant, too, though, this freedom is shared in the appreciation of the arts:

> If someone reads me his poem or takes me to a play that in the end fails to please my taste, then he can adduce Batteux or Lessing, or even older and more famous critics of taste, and adduce all the rules they established as proofs that his poem is beautiful ... I will stop my ears, listen to no reasons and arguments, and would rather believe that those rules of the critics are false ... than allow that my judgment should be determined by means of *a priori* grounds of proof, since it is supposed to be a judgment of taste and not of the understanding of reason.
>
> (Kant 2007: 94)

Artistic genius and aesthetic judgement are ends in themselves. Neither genius nor aesthetic judgement, even at lower levels of aesthetic judgement, can be determined by proximate goals. Hence, the fine arts can be distinguished from the practical, from crafts, design, technology. For Kant, art, notably in its association with freedom, is its own justification. All the arts contain the technical means to achieve aesthetic goals but art that attains to the sublime cannot be reduced to them: 'For there neither is, nor can be, a science of the beautiful, and the judgement of taste is not determinable by principles' (Kant 2007: 151).

The *Critique of Judgement*, with all its talk of the sublime, reads almost as if Kant were nostalgic for that which he had once labelled 'pernicious and disgraceful'. For he writes with a passion for the sublime which has every bit as much fervour as Otto wrote of the holy, as much admiration for nature and its raw power as any Romantic poet or composer or artist. One is almost regretful to place Kant here in the role of the adversary. Where his sneering comments in *Religion within the Boundaries of Reason* do not easily endear, in the third *Critique* we read rapturous passages that might have been written by Coleridge or Keats. But Kant's *Critique of Judgement* provided more than an aesthetic in the limited sense (a way to understand or appreciate the arts); he provided the means for seeing how the arts could serve as an emotionally powerful surrogate for the lost consolation of religion, a rule-less intuitive book, a lesson on how to possess the sublime without the sacred.

The aesthetic advocacy of religion

Hegel's aesthetic re-established the integral link between art and religion, although giving it his own peculiar form, as part of that movement towards Absolute Knowledge and Absolute Spirit. Kant wrote in powerful terms of the arts as an almost mysterious expression of the sublime, in abstract terms; for Hegel, the abstract in manifest as an evolutionary process towards ever greater consciousness:

> At the earlier stage it is instinctive in its operation; its operation is steeped in existence, works its way out of existence and works right into the existent; it does not find its substance in the free life of an ethical order, and hence, too, as regards the self operating does not exercise free spiritual activity.
>
> (Hegel 1910: 771)

For Hegel, the abstractions of art are integral to the life of the spirit:

> Spirit has raised the shape in which it is object for its own consciousness into the form of consciousness itself; and spirit produces such a shape for itself. The artificer has given up the synthesizing activity, that blending of the heterogeneous forms of thought and nature. When the shape has gained the form of self-conscious activity, the artificer has become a spiritual workman.
>
> (Hegel 1910: 725)

Phenomenology of Mind/Spirit, as we have seen, presents the Hegelian system: the certainty of truth (consciousness in relation to sense experience; perception and deception; consciousness in nature; 1–3); the forms of consciousness in history (4); truth and reason as the realization of consciousness, Spirit (5); 'self-estrangement' amidst 'the discipline of culture and civilization', the birth of higher consciousness (6); religion in the evolutionary progress of Spirit (7) towards 'Absolute Knowledge' (8).

Being is ultimately thought, consciousness and philosophy the realization, the moving toward that knowledge of Absolute Being. Even if institutional forms of religion are regarded by Hegel as a stage in this development, they are an important one. Understanding the contemporary relationship between religion and aesthetics in a positive sense cannot be undertaken without regard to Hegel's *Phenomenology*. Particularly relelvant is the chapter (7) which examines 'Religion in General' under three headings: 'natural religion'; 'religion as art'; and 'revealed religion'.

In natural religion, Hegel's theory of consciousness and of spirit sees in religion the development of both. Through 'the Religion of Art',

> spirit has passed from the form of substance into that of Subject; for art brings out its shape and form, and imbues it with the nature of action, or establishes in it the self-consciousness which merely disappears in the awesome substance and in the attitude of simple trust does not itself comprehend itself.
>
> (Hegel 1910: 759–60)

In revealed religion, which Hegel in a footnote denotes as 'Christianity':

> That Absolute Spirit has taken on the shape of self-consciousness inher-
> ently, and therefore also consciously to itself – this appears now as the
> belief of the world, the belief that spirit exists *in fact* as a definite self-
> consciousness, i.e. as an actual human being; that spirit is an object for
> immediate experience; that the believing mind *sees, feels, and hears* this
> divinity. Taken thus it is not imagination, not a fancy; it is actual in the
> believer. Consciousness in that case does not set out from its own inner
> life, does not start from thought, and in itself combine the thought of
> God with existence; rather it sets out from immediate present existence,
> and recognizes God in it.
>
> (Hegel 1910: 759–60)

If Hegel's logic is related to a philosophy of consciousness and consciousness
in nature, Hegel's philosophy of religion and his aesthetics all form part of a
whole, including a philosophical-theological view of the unity of history
(Hegel 1981, 1991, 1999; also Beiser 1993, 2008; Hodgson 2012), as is
early evident from the *Phenomenology*. As Wicks comments: '[he] tacitly
assumed that his readers would view his aesthetic theory as part of this
greater metaphysical symphony – as a reflection and extension of his conception of a dynamic but essentially rational and harmonious universe' (Wicks
1993: 348). Yet, given the way that Hegel conceived his system, Pippin
argues, however, that:

> Hegel does not offer, anywhere in his discussions of fine art, a recogniz-
> able theory of aesthetic judgment . . . He does not even work out a well
> defined account of aesthetic experience…largely due to the complexity of
> the concept of art itself as Hegel invokes it. For Hegel's treatment is
> famously historical; the account of the nature of art is narrative rather
> than analytic.
>
> (Pippin 2008: 394–5)

Indeed, art eventually, like religion, will transcend itself: 'Later on, spirit goes
beyond art in order to gain its higher manifestation, viz. that of being not
merely the substance born and produced out of the self, but of being'
(Pippin 2008: 394–5).

The idea of art as freedom had equivalence in critical philosophy's notions
of rational autonomy: both would have existential as well as political conno-
tations. For John Stuart Mill (1806–1873), freedom of expression was the
very cornerstone of political liberty (Mill 2003). The aesthetic emerging
from the Enlightenment is integrally related to expression of freedom, as the
aesthetic expression of personal as well as political autonomy. In the social
and political contexts of this aesthetic, it will undo divides between craft and
high art, through a democratization of the arts and, in totalitarian form,

through other forms of revolution. Freedom of expression in its aesthetic expression (in literature, music, the visual arts) is thus always limited and defined by its historical and political contexts (Gearon 2006).

Through art as expression of the human spirit, freedom of expression becomes the high watermark of human being itself. It includes all movements which place art and the life of the artist as the highest form of human being: from the long list of representatives of late eighteenth and early nineteenth century 'Romanticism' through to the late nineteenth and early twentieth century 'Modernists' through the mid-twentieth century countercultures to present-day mass media 'popular culture'. Such movements are associated not only with a form of expression but a form of living. This response to the arts also contained an existential aesthetic that rejected the Enlightenment political ideals. In the literature of existentialism, the literary, the aesthetic becomes philosophy. Sartre's (1970) *Nausea* or Camus' (2000) *The Outsider* laid bare the absurdity and bad faith of the former faiths, religious, political, legal and moral. Art, here, was not mere self-expression but a way of being.

Where the aesthetic recovered a pragmatic or social purpose – the sort of art of which the young Rousseau *would* have approved – we see this manifest in the arts and crafts movement, where William Morris and others broke down the old distinctions between fine art and practical craft. But art was also, and particularly in the nineteenth century, beginning to take the role as a bastion against forces which unravel civilization, as Matthew Arnold famously explored in *Culture and Anarchy* (Arnold 1993).

This aesthetic took more extreme pragmatic forms when art became integral to and or expressive of historical purpose. Art again is freedom but is differently conceived. We have seen the relationship between beauty and freedom in Kant, in Hegel animated by an idealist philosophy. A mere few decades later, Marx would retain the Hegelian conception of progress and give it a materialistic interpretation (see, for example, Wood 1993); a century later and State Communism would give a materialistic interpretation political and aesthetic form. The idea of art as expressive of ideology was not limited to Communism and can be seen, for instance, in the roles that art played under Fascist and Nazism regimes. Art serves the aims of the State (in Fascism and Nazism) and (in State Communism) the dictatorship of the proletariat. There can be no toleration of art, just as there can be toleration of ideals not oriented towards the proper ends. The first spontaneous act of Nazi Germany was, after all, the burning of books, of that art as well as philosophy and the sciences seen as antipathetic to Nazism.

But, as expression of *ideals*, totalitarian states gave high honour to artists. In Soviet Russia, the repression of religion was coterminous with the elevation of the arts to revolutionary honour: in the literature, this was evident in the formation of the Union of Soviet Writers. Such 'totalitarian' aesthetics were perpetuated by education. The Soviet organization of education and the arts is what Sheila Fitzpatrick (2002) called the 'Commissariat of

Enlightenment'. Resistance to this political aesthetic manifested itself in calls for the instatement of freedom of expression and democracy.

In democratic form, Dewey's (1980) aesthetic, notable in *Art as Experience*, similarly collapses distinction of practical and fine art. The museum for Dewey, 'high' art, separates not only art from experience but people from artistic experience.

Yet, across the arts, such a political aesthetic has become a nexus of cultural-theological-political conflict. Such clashes between religious author-ity and the arts are thus part of a political–philosophical movement which were the wellsprings of an aesthetic movement.

One notable exemplar must suffice. The cause celebre of Salman Rushdie's *The Satanic Verses* is an extreme example that illustrates the princi-pal points of conflict where the arts replace the sacred and do not avoid conflict with it. In his 1990 Herbert Reade lecture, published shortly after the *fatwa*, Salman Rushdie posed the question,

> Is nothing sacred?
>
> Until recently, however, it was a question to which I thought I knew the answer: 'The answer was No.
>
> No, nothing is sacred in and of itself, I would have said. Ideas, texts, even people can be made sacred – the word is from the Latin *sacrare*, 'to set apart as holy' – but even though such entities, once their sacredness is established, seek to proclaim and to preserve their own absoluteness, their inviolability, the act of making sacred is in truth an event in history.
>
> (Rushdie 1990)

It is contingent, subject to questioning, deconstruction, 'even to declarations of their obsolescence . . . To revere the sacred unquestioningly is to be para-lyzed by it'. The 'idea of the sacred' is 'one of the most conservative notions in any culture, because it seeks to turn other ideas – Uncertainty, Progress, Change – into crimes'. Rushdie considers himself 'living in the aftermath of the death of god . . . It has always been clear to me that god is unlike human beings in that it can die, so to speak, in parts'. His 'sense of god ceased to exist long ago, and as a result I was drawn toward the great creative possi-bilities offered by surrealism, modernism and their successors'. 'It did not seem to me', he writes, 'that my ungodliness, or rather my post-godliness, need necessarily bring me into conflict with belief'. The sacred, what he describes as the miraculous and the mundane became avenues for (in his case) exploration in fiction. The sacred is, in this view of course, itself a fiction. 'Now, however', he writes, 'I find my entire world-picture under fire'. 'Do I,' he asks, 'perhaps, find something sacred after all? Am I prepared to set aside as holy the idea of the absolute freedom of the imagination?' Is this, he reflects a 'secular fundamentalism?'. He closes with the rhetorical: 'must I accept that this "secular fundamentalism" is as likely to lead to excesses, abuses and oppressions as the canons of religious faith?'.

These conflicts have themselves become the subject of literary treatments. Tate and Bradley's (2010) *The New Atheist Novel* shows post-9/11 literary responses, including Ian McEwan, Martin Amis, Salman Rushdie and Philip Pullman, whose literary antagonism to 'religious fundamentalism' is somewhat contrived, since each were religiously antagonistic long before 9/11 (see also Versluys 2009; Gray 2011). Roy (2010) identifies points of dissociation between religious and secular culture. If, since antiquity, religion and the arts have swung between alliance and antipathy, between the expression of the sacred and sacrilege, often framed as blasphemy (Dacey 2012; Nash 2010), for Roy, secularization has not freed the world of religion, just encouraged a 'holy ignorance', anti-intellectualism, emotionalism, feelings towards modern arts and culture which seem anathema to the sacred, when art insults the holy.

The arts and religious education

The arts in religious education are often seen as a neutral space for the exploration of meaning, expressly religious or in a-religious terms, but the foregoing analysis, placing the arts in a post-Enlightenment context, presents a far more nuanced, multi-levelled complexity. Certainly, the picture is more than might be presupposed from analyses that oppose Enlightenment with Romanticism or see the arts (visual and literary in particular) as a means of bypassing difficult truth claims in religious education. Reviewing this history of aesthetics as a complex philosophical and political history shows how appropriations of the arts in religious education are not the solution to the problem they appear, in the main because they limited in understanding where the arts fit in a broader history of ideas.

The appropriation of the arts in religious education

Amongst the first uses of the arts as a vehicle for religious education was Albert Edward Bailey (1871). In *The Use of Art in Religious Education*, Bailey adopts, as Hegel, the idea that the history of religion is also a history of art, beginning his study with consideration of the art of the ancient world as the religion of art. Bailey's primary consideration, however, was to show the means by which this history could be a thematic point of entry for teaching and learning in religious education.

Links between religion and art are now commonly regarded as an uncontentious aspect of religious education. Art galleries have education departments which cater for the treatment of religion in art. Initiatives for learning outside the classroom now strongly feature art galleries and museums as a source of enrichment. What is often lacking in these approaches is a linking of aesthetic theory and religious understanding. Art galleries and museums are often seen as the province of the art and not of the religious educator; what is often missed is the treatment of the ways in which religion is not only formally expressed in these material arts but is an explanation of how and why religion disappeared to a great extent from these expressive forms.

This mode of advocacy seeks not to change art in religion but sees art as a means whereby we can understand not simply religious art but religion through its art. First published in Dutch in 1932, van der Leeuw's (2006) *Sacred And Profane Beauty: The Holy in Art* provided a foundational theology of aesthetics. Its agenda is positive, showing across literature, music, the performance and visual, arts how the expression of beauty is integral to the search for the sacred. The holy in art, as van der Leeuw conceives it, is a means of transportation to and not simply a representation of the holy. His broadly phenomenological approach to religion provides obvious bridges to the study of material culture in social anthropology and, not least, for the ways in which the division between the sacred and profane are demarcated in religious cultures as they would be later dissolved in secular cultures.

Given this, it is perhaps surprising that Smart's phenomenological model had originally included six dimensions and only latterly, in works such as *The Anatomy of the Sacred*, did he add a seventh, material dimension. This aesthetic dimension is, however, inextricably a material expression of other dimensions – the physicality of scripture, narrative or the materiality of ritual. The 'artefact' in religious education, as much as art and architecture, is part of an aesthetic of religious education.

The use of art in religious education has become, however, not simply a part of the representation of the holy but its generation, not simply a theme but a method. The simple way to understand the distinction between van der Leeuw and Smart is in one key difference in their approaches: the material dimension in Smart rests, as does his phenomenological theory generally, on a breaking down of the distinction between the sacred and the secular, whereas van der Leeuw's approach (like Eliade and Durkheim) maintains it. For Weber, the loss of the distinction between sacred and profane was through the processes of instrumentalization and rationalization, the means by which the modern world became a disenchanted one.

In the United States, contemporaneous educational parallels are found in Durka and Smith's (1979) *Aesthetic Dimensions in Religious Education* or Harris's (1987b) *Teaching and Religious Imagination*; in the United Kingdom, it can be found in collections such as in Starkings' (1993) *Religion and the Arts*.

The established root by which art theory and spirituality is usually derived in modern times is Wassily Kandinsky's (1911) *Concerning the Spiritual in Art*. Kandinsky made self-conscious the relationship between religion and art as spiritual quest. It is Michael T. H. Sadler, Kandinsky's translator, as much as Kandinsky himself, who cements the link between the moderns, whose work is defined as spiritual without being explicitly religious, and medieval art dominated by religious themes but not necessarily 'spiritual'. As Sadler comments, 'religious painters need not paint Madonnas'. Sadler makes a comparison here between the post-impressionists and impressionists:

Picasso and Kandinsky make an interesting parallel, in that they have developed the art respectively of Cézanne and Gauguin, in a similar direction. On the decision of Picasso's failure or success rests the distinction between Cézanne and Gauguin, the realist and the symbolist, the painter of externals and the painter of religious feeling. Unless a spiritual value is accorded to Cézanne's work, unless he is believed to be a religious painter (and religious painters need not paint Madonnas), unless in fact he is paralleled closely with Gauguin, his follower Picasso cannot claim to stand, with Kandinsky, as a prophet of an art of spiritual harmony.

(Sadler 1914: xxv)

For Sadler, Kandinsky stands for a wider movement within modern art, of art not simply as freedom of expression but a lived aesthetic metaphor for freedom itself, the artist becomes 'a champion of the freedom of art' (Sadler, 1914: xxv).

Teaching religion in and through the arts has become an integral part of religious education but, underneath, there is something of the latter aesthetic, which I have shown emerges from eighteenth- and early nineteenth-century aesthetics, notably Hegel. The teaching of the arts in religious education becomes through 'self-expression' a means towards other goals, the cultural, or as a contribution to spirituality. The two often elide consciously or unconsciously one into the other. The presumption becomes that because the arts in religion are a means of expressing the sacred and the spiritual, the arts and 'creativity' in religious education become the means of not simply learning about religion in art but stimulating through the arts and creative activity an awakening of the 'spiritual'. This view permeates many studies of religion and the arts in education (Starkings 1993; Watson 1993). These religious educators perceive legitimacy in seeing artistic and religious forms of this expression as emerging from the same imaginative impulse. The justification for such a move is strong, as it is also made in the philosophical and theological literature (see Apostolos-Cappadona 2006). Daniel Gold (2004) argues, for example:

Because historians of religion often seem to share little else than a fascination with the human depth of the material they study, the aesthetics of their writing may be more central to the institutional coherence of their field than many of them realize. What most of all engages their attention as a group are products of religious imagination - rituals and myths, human histories and historical dramas – all of which demand perceptive interpretation to be appreciated beyond specialist fields. Appraising one another's interpretations, further, they give due value to clarity in argument but find arguments *perceptive* to the extent that they appear to penetrate the imaginative depth of religious worlds. Like artists, then, writers whose aim is to interpret religious traditions are likely to find professional success to the extent that they make the depth they see in their material visible to others.

(Gold 2004: 1–2; also Gold 2003)

In theology, Mary Warnock's (1990) 'Imagination – Aesthetic and Religious' outlines a similar parallel. In the aesthetics of religious education, a similar correspondence is evident. Religious educators move between 'The Arts as a Dimension of Religion' (Watson 1993) to the arts as a means of countering rational approaches to religious education; here, using the arts as a means of facilitating the spiritual in the classroom. The association also provides bridges – thematic and methodological – between religious education and the spiritual via the psychological interpretation of religion. These approaches emphasize the aesthetic in other words in content – drama, poetry, story, the visual arts. Through religious form the aesthetic is in itself a form of pedagogy that sees in creative activity itself a means of accessing 'the spiritual in the curriculum' (Priestley 1985, 1996), as a means of enabling a sensitivity to spirituality beyond it (Watson 2008). This approach, we saw, found expression in *New Methods in Religious Education* (Hammond *et al.* 1990). Maria Harris's (1978) 'Model of Aesthetic Education' becomes a justification of 'fantasy' as an 'entrance into inwardness' (Harris 1978a) and a means of 'exploring inner space' (Hay 1987).

The aesthetic in religious education is not simply a means of teaching about religions but also of contributing to spiritual development. These approaches align religious education with the arts themselves and with creativity. Here, there is evident antagonism to 'organized' or institutional religion, a preference for spirituality over religion. The aesthetic of religious education sees the arts as an expression of the human spirit.

Religious education, in addition to a more generalized aesthetic association (Watson 1993), is closely aligned to 'story' (for example, Priestley 1981), 'fantasy' (Hall 1987; Huber 1988) and 'imagination' (Webster and Tickner 1982). The language of metaphor itself invades religious education, authors themselves becoming self-consciously 'poetic': Lealman's (1982a) 'The Ignorant Eye: Perception and Religious Education', or Lealman's (1982b) 'Blue Wind and Broken Image' or her (Lealman 1993) 'Drum, Whalebone and Dominant X' 'model for creativity'. In the pinnacle of popularity for such approaches, in the aftermath of publication of *New Methods*, Nicola Slee's (1992), 'Heaven in Ordinarie' thus assumes the connection between 'imagination, spirituality and the arts in religious education'. For Priestley (1982) it is even 'teaching transcendence'.

While such approaches persist (see de Souza *et al.* 2007, for example), they have also diversified into other media, notably film, as in Goldburg (2004). There remains however an abiding interest in art's classical visual forms (see Hayward 2012). Miller (2003) provides a useful critical evaluation of how these approaches persist in the visual arts, presenting a four-fold schema:

1. the use of the arts to promote awareness and exploration of mystery and the transcendent in pupils;
2. phenomenological approaches to religious education in which the arts enable pupils to enter empathetically into religious experience and practice;
3. the promotion of pupils' spiritual development through imagination and reflection on the arts;
4. creativity as a means of expressing and deepening the understanding and religious awareness of students and their teachers.

(Miller 2003: 200)

In her conclusion she restates her intentions,

> to help teachers untangle the complex world of the arts and RE and choose for themselves the point at which they wish to begin their deployment of the arts, aware not only of the presuppositions, questions and potential dangers but also the many educational opportunities to be derived.

(Miller 2003: 211)

In practice, the borders between the arts, spirituality and religion are significantly blurred. Precisely because religious educators do not sufficiently disentangle the deeper layers of aetiology behind their approaches, we have instance of the following.

Thus, for Lat Blaylock, a leading UK religious educator, suggests that all artistic forms – literary, musical, visual – in whatever period, have similar aesthetic validity and spiritually egalitarian legitimacy. Blaylock (2012) even extends the remit of the arts to relatively underexplored areas; for example 'spiritual music', 'a source of spiritual life and an energising power in all human life', where from 'Bob Dylan to Beethoven, from Bob Marley to Buddhist chant, music expresses the spiritual'. A 'Spirited Arts' competition organized by the National Association of Religious Education illustrates where such thinking may lead. One competition winner was Eilish Marron's 'Walk in the Woods'; she comments:

> In the assessment we were asked to create a piece of artwork in response to the question where is God? 'I believe that God is where you want him to be. God is where you ask him to be and where you need him to be, you just need to ask him. I think that God is a part of everyone that believes in him. But I also think that he is in heaven to help the dead. So my art work shows that anyone can be your God.

(Marron 2012)

If religious education has lost its rootedness in the sacred or things set apart as holy, in terms of the presentation of religion, it is precisely the lack of a divide between the sacred and profane that enables all to become sacred; even the formerly profane does not simply encroach upon but becomes conceived itself as holy ground.

Summary

The arts are, then, no less neutral an epistemological ground *vis-à-vis* religion than are the sciences. In as fundamental ways, the arts have offered alternative grounds conceived not through critical philosophy but through new understandings of human being, an aesthetic of religious education. The arts cannot be separated from those epistemological shifts which shaped modernity. There are thus two sides to this Enlightenment. The one well-trodden is the path of rationalism, which emboldened the natural scientific method and enabled the shaping of new sciences. The other is that which reflected – once traditional, theological understandings of religion were discarded or adapted – the non-rational space that still remained as a source of meaning. This found expression in aesthetic theories which emerged as an integral part of Enlightenment.

It can therefore be tempting to see Romanticism and Enlightenment in oversimplified opposition (see Holmes 2009). Romanticism as a response to the reason of philosophers, scientists and technocrats and the industrial, disenchanted world it created. But Enlightenment philosophers also esteemed the sublime. Indeed, they enshrined it as that residual empty space which they left once they had de-sacralized everything else.

It is this *other* Enlightenment and the Romanticism in which such ideas found fuller and more direct expression that is the root of those emphases in religious education which stress creativity, self-expression and even see them in terms of 'spirituality'.

These ideals – art as expression of the human spirit and art democratized – would become the cornerstone of modern liberal societies its religious education. Art becomes an expression of freedom, as foundational as any other of the intellectual or political freedoms. From the Enlightenment onwards, such an aesthetic incorporates particular views of human history: the aesthetic is an expression of an unfolding history of being itself; the aesthetic which supports a particular political history of the people's freedom, art democratized. The aesthetic can also be an existential freedom in the light of the meaningless absurdity not only of history but existence.

9   The holy and the idea of the holy

Introduction

A separation of religious education from the religious life has entailed, necessitated, a series of alternate epistemological grounds. This has provided a critical distance between the holy and the idea of the holy. Enlightenment, as the chosen starting point for such developments, I have shown throughout, is neither a true beginning, most importantly because the Enlightenment had many immediate and ancient origins, nor (as I shall elaborate in this chapter) an adequate or sufficient end. The eighteenth century remains, however, a decisive historical marker from which contemporary, religious education has progressively formed epistemological frames of reference from the modernity out of which it emerged.

Thus, philosophical models see the object lesson of religious education to make thinkers and proto-philosophers; sociocultural models see the object lesson of religious education as creating ethnographic, cultural explorers; psychological models see the learner as a seeker after personal meaning and fulfilment, 'spiritual with religion'; phenomenological models see the object lesson of religious education as creating a detached observer of religion who is perpetually distanced from it; ever more prevalent political models, emphasizing the public face of religion, see teaching and learning in religious education as concerned with the creation of citizens and even activists; aesthetic models see a role for the arts in religious education, not simply the noting of art in religious contexts but also religious education classrooms as forums, through the expressive arts, for creativity as spirituality, the artist as spiritual seeker. These approaches to religion have been appropriated by religious education and become the epistemological filters through which religion is conceived and the subject justified.

Modern religious education can thus be defined as the search for epistemological grounds within intellectual traditions which rejected the holy, not only as a form of knowledge but as an orientation in life. The implications therefore far exceed disputes about forms of knowledge or legal–political contexts which constrain them. The grounds sought are also moral. From such grounds, it becomes necessary in educational terms to apply such understandings to lived experience, as a guide to life. An epistemological problem therefore becomes a moral, even existential one. An epistemological separation of the holy from the idea of the holy tends ultimately tends also towards separation of the learned from the holy life.

The holy life

Three principles guard the dividing line between the holy and the idea of the holy and prevent incursions from the one to the other. First, and above all, the principle of *rationality* (autonomy of reason, freedom of will and action, personal and political); second, the principle of *secularity* (a directness of purpose to worldly concern by removing the transcendent as a term accessible to reason); and, third, the principle of *temporality* (an understanding of *time* which, given the first two principles, focuses on the here and now). Where religion is retained within secular frameworks, if it is to be acceptable, it must be reset according to these 'enlightened' epistemological parameters. For Kant, it is religion 'within the bounds of reason', for psychologists mental health and wellbeing, in sociopolitical frameworks, society's wellbeing (again, Rousseau's 'civil religion', Kant's 'Kingdom of Heaven on Earth', Dewey's 'religion of humanity'), and so forth.

Ghiloni (2011) expresses favourably expresses for religious education, a this-worldly focus as a 'Coda', 'Our Garden is the World': 'Drawings of Dewey's ideal school reveal the heart of his educational philosophy. The school building was to be situated amid a network of other institutions and influences, including business, home, libraries, the university, gardens, parks, and the countryside.' For Ghiloni, 'Dewey's "one Earth" pedagogy provides an excellent image for interreligious education as an adventurous place of growth and exploration' (Ghiloni 2011: 491). Acknowledging that such images 'are not always promoted within solitary religious traditions', he unfavourably contrasts with the seventeenth century hymnist Isaac Watts (1674–1748). In particular Ghiloni cites Watts' depiction of the church:

> We are a garden walled around,
> Chosen and made peculiar ground;
> A little spot enclosed by grace,
> Out of the world's wide wilderness.

(Ghiloni 2011)

Not this for Dewey or for Ghiloni; for them, there are no sharply marked-off enclosures, no distinction between this world and any other, 'Our garden is the world' (Dewey 1988: 122–3; cited Ghiloni 2011: 491). 'Whereas,' comments Ghiloni, 'Dewey's school leads out into the garden and then out into the park and then out into the open countryside, Watts' church is a fortified patch, barricaded against the weeds of the world'. Ghiloni asks 'what would Dewey do?'. The response, speculates Ghiloni, would be 'a plethora of changes to the practice of religious education and theology'. Such adaptations include 'religious experience; the doctrine of creation; theological method; the relationship between doctrine and practice; and the doctrine of revelation' (Ghiloni 2011: 491; see also Ghiloni 2012).

Ghiloni's use of the garden imagery, and Dewey's, could not be more ironic, resonating with obvious parallels to another garden. Ghiloni's use of language, conscious or otherwise, continues to show the transference of theology into this educational vision, as in the *'grace'* of a Deweyan model, undefined by 'doctrinal subject matter'. Nothing better demonstrates the shift from a holy to secular ground.

Ghiloni's use of Isaac Watts provides a neat and unconfused metaphor for his thinking – he makes plain what he is saying. To separate the model from 'doctrinal subject matter', though, is curious. We might cite another of Isaac Watts' hymns, far more well known: 'When I Survey the Wondrous Cross'. The first verse opens:

When I survey the wondrous cross
On which the Prince of glory died,
My richest gain I count but loss,
And pour contempt on all my pride.

(Watts, published 1707)

Perhaps we might remove the doctrinal context from this verse? What of Dewey's garden, so lauded by Ghiloni? Isaac Watts had not only anticipated but also saw emerge such philosophy in his own time. Isaac Watts' hymn ends:

Were the whole realm of nature mine,
That were an offering far too small;
Love so amazing, so divine,
Demands my soul, my life, my all.

(Watts, published 1707)

I have suggested that modern, secular religious education, in mirroring modern, secular thought, attempts to maintain the separation of religious education from the religious life, to guard that epistemological border between the holy and the idea of the holy, constantly attempting to ensure that religious education remains critically distanced from the object of its study.

Here Habermas elaborates how epistemological – rational, secular, temporal – grounds become a teleological and thus an existential limit:

A devout person pursues her daily rounds by drawing on belief. Put differently, true belief is not only a doctrine, believed content, but also a source of energy that the person who has a faith taps performatively and thus nurtures his or her entire life. This totalizing trait of a mode of believing that infuses the very pores of daily life runs counter...to any flimsy switchover of religiously rooted political convictions onto a different cognitive basis.

(Habermas 2006: 8)

The secular can never fully appropriate the sacred. I have demonstrated the manner of such attempts across philosophy and theology, the natural sciences, the social and psychological sciences, phenomenology, in politics, and even in aesthetics. I have shown too how religious education in its modern forms has attempted to foreground the subject through various appropriations of these to provide new grounds for the subject once religious education is separated from the religious life.

Re-examination of religious lives, I suggest, reveals antinomies to those principles which mark such alternate grounds which frame such appropriations, outlined above as: rationality, temporality, secularity. The antinomies may be framed as: *faith* (that God alone is the ground, known but never fully knowable); the *eternal* (where God alone is ground, the temporal may manifest but is not the fulfilment of the holy); *sanctification* (where God alone grounds purpose, the world is an instrument not an end of the holy life). Modern religious education in its appropriations - from philosophy, the natural, social and psychological sciences, from phenomenology, from political interest, from aesthetic preoccupations – in maintaining critical distance rests its ground firmly to differing degrees on the rational, the temporal, the secular. As Ghiloni reminds us of Dewey, the Coda is that 'The World is Our Garden'. Religious education epistemologically foregrounds *such* critical distance as to foreclose such *lived* engagement.

To demonstrate this foreclosure, I draw examples from hagiography – from the Greek *hagios*, the sacred – of lives sanctified by an orientation to the holy. I present three consciously unsophisticated accounts: from the medieval (St Bernard of Clairvaux), the early modern (St Alphonsus Ligouri) and the modern (St Thérèse of Lisieux). Each life represents one aspect of the respective antinomies more acutely: faith and reason (St Bernard of Clairvaux), temporal and eternal (St Alphonsus Ligouri), secularity and sanctification (St Thérèse of Lisieux).

From the critical perspectives considered in previous chapters, these, it is important to note, might be considered wasted lives; their entire, existential orientation deluded and misguided. For all the influence they might exert on others, these deluded lives might be considered also to have been, in the broadest sense, politically harmful. As noted, Nietzsche reflects on his alter-ego meeting the saint praying in the forest, again, 'Could it be possible! This old saint in the forest hath not yet heard of it, that God is dead!' (Nietzsche 1974: 41).

Faith and reason: St Bernard of Clairvaux

St Bernard of Clairvaux (1090–1153), abbot, adviser to popes, counsellor of kings, was a reformer of medieval monasticism and founder of the Cistercian Order who had enormous impact on twelfth-century religious and political life (Birkedal 2012). But Bernard of Clairvaux, defender of the Crusades, scourge of heretics, was also a controversial figure in his time and still divides theological opinion. To modern liberal thinkers, Bernard represents the worst aspects of medieval ecclesiastic power upheld by obscurantist scholasticism, a dogged devotion to obedience; to the conservative-minded, Bernard is the upholder of orthodoxy through the affirmation of faith and revelation over reason. The most significant meeting which exemplifies disagreement over Bernard is in the latter's confrontation with Peter Abelard (1079–1142), arguably the leading exponent of the new learning, the first stirring of European Renaissance (Brower and Guilfoy 2004).

Bernard's confrontation with Peter Abelard can be read as a coda for the great divisions which would fragment medieval Christendom. Abelard's story can be read, too, as an account of intellectual repression against which Reformation and Enlightenment fought. Bernard was a defender of 'faith not as an opinion but as a certitude', Abelard the proponent of reason. Abelard, initially an orthodox scholastic philosopher and theologian, influenced considerably by St Anselm (1033–1109), even his opponents recognized his brilliance. A profoundly original thinker who often transgressed Catholic orthodoxy, Abelard began to see value in the transgression, modelling the individuality of a person's intellectual fathoming of faith in ways which would characterize figures like Huss and Wycliffe and later reformers in the Reformation proper. Abelard met controversy in 1121, when a synod condemned as heretical his work on the Trinity. Exiled from Paris, his secluded life was intermittently broken by invitations to lecture. By repute a gifted teacher, his lectures were events. In 1139, one of Bernard's fellow Cistercians, William of St Thierry, reopened the suspicions around Abelard's orthodoxy by denouncing him as an unreformed heretic. William of St Thierry's denunciation might have attracted little attention but for Abelard's history and for the fact that William of St Thierry made his declaration to the Holy See. Bernard, as the leading figure by then of the Cistercian Order, inevitably became involved. In private conversation, Abelard assured Bernard that he would retract his views. Ecclesiastical history seems to record that he retained them. At a synod of bishops convened at Sens in 1141, Abelard was formally denounced for heresy. Refusing to make a defence when accused by Bernard, Abelard appealed to the Pope. Innocent subsequently confirmed the denunciation of the bishops and of Bernard. Abelard died in 1142. To later Reformers, as to Enlightenment thinkers, Bernard's intractable attitude was symptomatic of all the medieval Church's authoritarianism freedom denying, repressive in matters of faith as much as intellect.

In Evans' (2000) terms, for all his involvement in theological and political dispute, Bernard was committed to 'a different sort of learning'; it was not for Bernard a matter of scholarly accomplishments by which progress in the religious life was to be measured, for: 'Both learned and unlearned may aspire to a properly Christian "love of God"' (Evans 2000: 49). Bernard would not have even described his discourses as theology, while his disputes with such as Abelard were a matter of settling a philosophical disputation of practical, pastoral concern. It was not a matter of winning an argument. Bernard considered Abelard's attempts to comprehend God by reason alone to be a mark of pride. It is plausible, therefore, to read in Bernard's defence of his own condemnation of Abelard emergent tensions which would unfold throughout the Renaissance and reach their height in the Reformation and their resolution in the Enlightenment. The meeting of Bernard and Abelard can be read not only as a watershed of medieval ecclesiastical dissent but also as a coda for its decline; not least because there were conflicts contemporaneous with the Bernard–Abelard conflict which had political as much as theological intent, even if, in the twelfth century, they had largely negligible effect. Thus, one of the most prominent disciples of Abelard, Arnold of Brescia, prompted direct rebellions against papal authority, which would resonate with later Reformation disputes. But Arnold of Brescia, in calling for a revolt of citizenry modelled on a polity of the ancient Roman republic, can also be read as a precursor to the revolutions of the eighteenth century as far back as the twelfth.

The emphasis on faith over reason then had practical political implications, too. Although the Enlightenment is read above all as a triumph of secular political power over ecclesiastical hegemony, in tensions between state and church, Augustine gives primacy to theological guidance over temporal governance simply because the former is enduring and the latter transient. The rule applies to ecclesiastical governance as much as the governance of states. In Bernard's time, that perspective still held. In *On Consideration*, written by way of pastoral advice to Pope Eugenius, he placed contemplation and self-examination above public even *ecclesiastical* duty. Bernard is, in this regard, an important figure in the history of scholasticism and the Renaissance. Scholasticism originally referred to a teacher associated with the system of schools created across the Holy Roman Empire by Charlemagne, overseen by Alcuin of York. The leading proponents would ensure the primacy of pastoral theology – that is, the saving of souls – above the merely speculative or rational. Leading 'schoolmen' who would have exerted influence on Bernard included John Scotus Erigena, 'the Irishman' (c.800–c.877); Berengarius of Tours (999–1088); Lanfranc (1005–1089), Roscelin, the reputed founder of Nominalism (condemned at the Council of Soissons, 1092); William of Champeaux (1070–1121); Abelard himself, who had been a student of Roscelin and William of Champeaux; and Anselm (1033–1109). As one of Bernard's translators, George Lewis, remarks, whatever one may think of scholasticism 'it would be doing great injustice to represent these figures as mere triflers, hair-splitters, verbal quibblers, syllogistic conjurers...Nor would it be right to represent them as in revolt against authority' for the 'revolt was not so much against authority, as against logic...He hated heresies as foes to practical life, as disturbers of the devotion of monasteries' (Bernard of Clairvaux 1908: 125).

'The utmost caution must be exercised,' writes Bernard, 'so as to avoid confusion, lest the uncertainties of opinion crystallize into articles of faith, or the foundation verities of faith become the questionable matter of opinion'. Reason, 'the poor, weak blade of our intellect', supports not opposes revelation, allowing in our present to view 'darkly as in a mirror, the only way for the present of seeing God at all'. In the eternal state,

> the veil shall have been utterly removed from the things of which we are now assured by faith...The Saints, therefore, comprehend. Do you ask how? If you are holy you have comprehended, and know; if you are not, be holy and you shall know by your own experience.
>
> (Bernard of Clairvaux 1908: 166–7)

On Consideration is a reminder to Eugenius that 'the things which are above you...do not call for action, but for contemplation. Bernard recognizes four kinds of contemplation. The first and highest is 'admiration of the Divine Majesty' when, if 'the heart be cleansed, free from vice, and relieved of the burden of its sins, it may hereby be easily raised to things above' and 'the admiring soul may sometimes also for brief intervals be even kept entranced with wonder and amazement' (Bernard of Clairvaux 1908: 171). The second 'must attend the first, for it beholds the judgements of God'. It 'may violently shock the beholder with the fearful vision' and thus put 'vice to flight'; in so doing, the level of contemplation is firmly based in virtue, it 'initiates in wisdom, preserves humility'. As with St Benedict's twelve steps of the ladder of humility – expressed in chapter 7 of *The Rule* of St Benedict – for Bernard, too, humility is the foundation of all virtues, as pride is the cardinal enemy of the religious life: 'If humility, forsooth, be insecure, the whole structure of the virtues is nothing but a ruin.' The third kind of contemplation is 'busy with, or rather leisurely surveys, past benefits', is manifest in gratitude of heart, is the character of one 'mindful of the love of the benefactor'. The fourth kind, 'forgetting the things that are behind, rests in the expectation of the promises alone; inasmuch as it is meditation on eternity, for the things promised are eternal, it fosters a spirit of long-suffering, and gives strength to perseverance' (Bernard of Clairvaux 1908: 167–9). Nothing places emphasis on faith over reason in more acute focus than this priority given to contemplation over action. Its primacy puts into sharp relief worldly concerns.

Eternal and temporal: St Alphonsus Ligouri

Christianity's denial of the world was amongst the most common of all ancient charges against it. In Roman times, the accusation that Christianity was harmful to the state was defended against even from the first century. In the eighteenth century, the charge was made by Gibbon that Christianity's other-worldliness was no less than cause of the collapse of Rome itself. Paine declared that the role of religion in governance was the most primitive – religion was politically regressive, restraining social progress. The contemporary charge made by Rousseau was that Christianity was antithetical to present-day society for these very other worldly concerns. Strictly speaking, therefore, what is often loosely referred to as political theology in early Christianity is rather the recognition of the limit of the political and the greater need for the theological. In Augustine's *City of God*, theology limits politics (Augustine 1998, 2001, 2003); in Schmitt's (2005) *Political Theology*, politics limits theology. Between these is the history of tension in Western civilization between the secular and the sacred. The goal of one is society; the goal of the other salvation. To achieve the former is to be a good citizen; to achieve the latter is to be a good citizen of heaven.

Alphonsus Ligouri (1696–1787) was canonized 1839 and, in 1871, he was declared a Doctor of the Church. 'Banquets, entertainments, theatres,' he declared, 'these are the pleasures of the world, but pleasures which are filled with the bitterness of gall and sharp thorns. Believe me who have experienced it, and now weep over it'. A successful Neapolitan lawyer from an early age (doctor of law at 16), his departure from the law and the courts occurred in 1723. A lawsuit between a Neapolitan nobleman and the Grand Duke of Tuscany had at stake half a million ducats. The young Alphonsus approached the case with his usual confidence. He sat with expectation of victory. He had never lost a case. Tradition does not relate which side he was representing but the opposing counsel declared: 'Your arguments are wasted breath. You have overlooked a document which destroys your whole case'. He is handed the document, reads it, reads it again, is dismayed, and then distraught, admitting defeat, declaring, 'You are right. I have been mistaken. This document gives you the case'. Ligouri is inconsolable. Details are incomplete but dramatic, the flight from secular professional entanglements indisputable. 'World,' he declares, 'I know you now. Courts, you shall never see me more'. For three days he fasted. In professional humiliation he saw revealed his pride. Praying to know what path his life should now take an answer came on 28 August 1723, when Ligouri was making in his customary act of charity a hospital for 'incurables'. In the hospital amongst the dying, Ligouri feels himself surrounded by light and he hears an interior voice commanding him: 'Leave the world and give thyself to Me'. Ligouri afterwards visits the Church of the Redemption of Captives, laying the sword he carried at the foot of the statue of Our Lady, making there and then a resolution to enter the religious life. Although he will later be the founder of the Redemptorists, in the first stages of his conversion of life, he offers himself to the novitiate of the Oratory, labouring for souls, as tradition tells us, among the poor and uneducated of Naples. He follows the priestly vocation for the next six decades, founds the Redemptorist Order and, over those six decades, authors many works of pastoral theology, his youthful conversion experience and worldly detachment their coda, and none more so than *Preparation for Death*.

Alphonsus Ligouri begins *Preparation for Death* with the visualization of the deceased. Description is vivid and deliberately disturbing, imagination as much as reason utilized to convince of the urgency of irrevocable choices made while living:

> Consider that as you have acted on the occasion of the death of friends and relatives, so others will act on the occasion of your death. The living take part in the scene. They occupy the possessions and offices of the deceased; but the dead are no longer remembered – their name is scarcely ever mentioned. In the beginning, their relatives are afflicted for a short time; but they will soon be consoled by the share of the property of the deceased which falls to them. Thus in a short time your death will be rather a source of joy; and in the very room in which you have breathed forth your soul . . . others will dance, and eat, and play, and laugh as before. And where will your soul then be?
>
> (Ligouri 1982: 4–5)

Such descriptions force readers' reflections to the temporal limit of their human condition, in which time is a gift, the use of which will have eternal consequences.

Ligouri's main themes are the finality that death brings to worldly existence, the shortness of life, the absolute certainty of death, the need to think continually of our last moment, the need for perpetual preparedness (chapters 2–5). In chapters 6 through to 9, he variously contrasts the state of being at death of the sinner, the indifferent, neglectful and worldly Christian, their regrets and inability to ability to correct their lives now their lives are over, with (in chapter 8) the just for whom death is a victory and an 'entrance to life' (in chapter 9). Chapters 10 through to 14 are Ligouri's practical and constant preparedness for death above all by a progressive detachment from an ephemeral world. Time is our currency. Our eternal destination depends on how we spend this currency. Salvation is not only 'our most important affair' but 'our only affair'. In the final chapters (13 and 14), he further impresses on the vanity of the world and on earthly life as a journey to eternity.

For Ligouri, this is the most urgent topic of pastoral theology, the only ultimate focus of pastoral theology. It differs from a detached scholastic reflection on the meaning of life or the possibility of life after death; still more does Ligouri differ from a philosophy of religion in which theories of life and death, the existence of the soul, the form of survival after death, are a matter of more urgency than argument.

Sanctification and secularity: St Thérèse of Lisieux

Marie-Francoise-Thérèse Martin, after her death known as Thérèse of Lisieux (1873–1897), were it not for her spiritual autobiography, *The Story of a Soul*, is likely to have been forgotten. She was born of a bourgeois family, in Alençon, France. Like Bernadette of Lourdes, her religious life blossomed where religion had been considered bigotry in, of all centuries, the nineteenth, in, of all countries, France, the heart of post-Enlightenment Europe.

As a child she describes how, 'During recreation I often gave myself up to serious thoughts, while from a distance I watched my companions at play'. Her other great pleasure was to 'search carefully for any poor little birds that had fallen dead under the big trees' and to bury them 'with great ceremony, all in the same cemetery, in a special grass plot'. 'Sometimes', she writes,

> I told stories to my companions, and often even the big girls came to listen; but soon our mistress, very rightly, brought my career as an orator to an end, saying she wanted us to exercise our bodies and not our brains.
>
> (Thérèse of Lisieux 1996: 81)

She talks of overcoming friendship offered and rejected; of one contemporary at school in particular she remarks: 'Nevertheless I still love my little school friend, and continue to pray for her, for God has given me a faithful heart, and when once I love, I love forever'. From these experiences she asks: 'How can a heart given up to human affections be closely united to God?'

> It seems to me that it is impossible. I have seen so many souls, allured by this false light, fly right into it like poor moths, and burn their wings, and then return, wounded, to Our Lord, the Divine fire which burns and does not consume. I know well Our Lord saw that I was too weak to be exposed to temptation, for, without doubt, had the deceitful light of created love dazzled my eyes, I should have been entirely consumed. Where strong souls find joy and practise detachment faithfully, I only found bitterness. No merit, then, is due to me for not having given up to these frail ties, since I was only preserved from them by the Mercy of God.
>
> (Thérèse of Lisieux 1996: 81)

She compares the work of God in her life to that of a 'very clever doctor' whose child had fallen. He attends the child with his surgeon's skills, heals the child. She imagines another scenario. The doctor, knowing that the child would stumble, removes the stone from the path, preventing the foreseen injury (Thérèse of Lisieux 1996: 83–4). 'God gave me the grace of knowing the world just enough to despise it and separate myself from it' (Thérèse of Lisieux 1996: 73).

She had often asked herself why God had preferences, 'why all souls did not receive an equal measure of grace'. 'I was filled with wonder,' she writes, 'when I saw extraordinary favours showered on great sinners like St Paul, St Augustine, St Mary Magdalen, and many others, whom He forced, so to speak, to receive His grace' (Thérèse of Lisieux 1996: 13–14).

At fifteen, wishing to enter the Carmelite convent in which two of her sisters were enclosed, Thérèse and her father make a pilgrimage to Rome to make direct petition to Pope Leo XIII, her request having been denied by her local bishop. The Pope advises she must defer to the local authorities. She writes of her tears and her insistence at this news given directly by Leo XIII and how she had literally to be carried away by the papal guards. Her experiences in Rome, where

> everything retains its stamp of antiquity. . . How shall I describe the feel-
> ings which thrilled me when I gazed on the Coliseum? At last I saw the
> arena where so many Martyrs had shed their blood for Christ. My first
> impulse was to kiss the ground sanctified by their glorious combats.
> (Thérèse of Lisieux 1996: 129–30)

But she encounters disappointment. The 'soil has been raised, and the real arena is now buried at the depth of about twenty-six feet', because of excavations the centre of which was 'nothing but a mass of rubbish' protected by seemingly insurmountable barriers to entry:

> But was it possible to be in Rome and not go down to the real Coliseum?
>   I uttered a cry of joy and called out to my sister: 'Come, follow me,
> we shall be able to get through'... As the warriors of old felt their
> courage grow in face of peril, so our joy increased in proportion to the
> fatigue and danger we had to face to attain the object of our desires.
> Celine, more foreseeing than I, had listened to the guide. She remem-
> bered that he had pointed out a particular stone marked with a cross, and
> had told us it was the place where the Martyrs had fought the good
> fight. She set to work to find it, and having done so we threw ourselves
> on our knees on this sacred ground.
> (Thérèse of Lisieux 1996: 130–1)

Yet she compares herself, although of little learning, to the cleverest of theologians, making the flowers of the field analogy for which she would be forever associated, understanding that God's 'love is revealed as perfectly in the most simple soul who resists His grace in nothing as in the most excellent soul'

... in fact since the nature of love is to humble oneself, if all souls resembled those of the Holy Doctors who illumined the Church with the clarity of their teachings, it seems God would not descend so low when coming to their heart. But he created the child who knows only how to make feeble cries heard ... It is to their hearts that God deigns to lower Himself. These are the wild flowers whose simplicity attracts him. When coming down in this way God manifests his infinite grandeur. Just as the sun shine simultaneously on the tall cedars and on each little flower as though it were alone on Earth, so Our Lord is occupied particularly with each soul as though there were no others like it.

(Thérèse of Lisieux 1996: 14)

Yet the 'little flower' of Lisieux would, in a short time after her death, be herself recognized as one of the Doctors of her Church.

She died of tuberculosis aged twenty-four. *Story of a Soul* was published posthumously, two years after her death. By 1907, Pope Pius X described Thérèse of Lisieux as 'the greatest saint of modern times'. On 19 October 1997, Thérèse was proclaimed a Doctor of the Church, in recognition of her theological influence, although she published nothing in her lifetime, an honour accorded to St Augustine of Hippo, St Bernard of Clairvaux, and her Carmelite predecessors, St Theresa of Avila and St John of the Cross. Thérèse, the youngest Doctor of the Church, 'leading a very simple and hidden life but who, after her death and the publication of her writings, became one of the best-known and best-loved saints' (John Paul II 1997).

The learned and the holy life

Enlightenment rationality was both epistemic and moral. Epistemically, it grounded knowledge based on reason – argument, logic, evidence – and reason elevated individual autonomy (moral and intellectual) as the freedom to choose, an idea as much as a life. Rational autonomy in religious education here consists in supposed radical epistemological openness. Yet, this freedom to choose is necessarily set by the frames of knowledge which define it. Their definitions of knowledge contain respective rational, secular, temporal ends for that knowledge. Opportunities abound for limitless comment on the holy as an object of study for sociological or psychological analysis or for political use or aesthetic fulfilment. Critical distance permits little recognition of the limits of learning in relation to the holy life.

The sense of the limitedness of learning in comparison to the holy life, personal sanctification and salvation above all other concerns, for teacher and student, permeates all pre-Enlightenment Christian history and is most abundantly evident in St Augustine of Hippo, a philosopher and theologian whose remarkable legacy is to have revered not only by Catholic and Protestant but also by secular philosophy (Stump and Kretzmann 2001).

St Augustine (354–430) is one of the towering figures of Western intellectual thought, whose influence on philosophy and theology extends far beyond his own Catholic Christian tradition (Pelikan *et al.* 2009). Augustine is most well known for an autobiographical work and biographies (Lancel 2002; O'Donnell 2006) chart a long life that, as we have noted, remains influential. The central event of his life as he narrates it is found in his *Confessions* (Augustine 1983). In this accessible work can be a found a synthesis of all Augustinian thought. Written around 395, in the years immediately following his conversion, *Confessions* provides rich incidental detail of life in North Africa in the time of late Roman Empire, written before the fall of Rome. The format of a self-narrated life story seems commonplace, yet *Confessions* was and remains a remarkable innovation in literary form. It was a Christian apologetic in an age of apologetics, expressed in personal terms, a story of a life addressed to the Creator of his life, a narrative addressed to God, the author addressing the Great Author.

The sense of a life as a calling to live according to will of God amidst conflicting calls from the world is evident in Augustine's schooling, university studies, love of philosophy and literary competition, an academic career. Augustine's conversion is progressive; he thinks he has decided one path and takes another. The great hindrance, Augustine realizes, is his intellectual superiority. In chapter VIII of Book VIII, Augustine speaks rhetorically to his friend Alypius: 'What is wrong with us? What is this you have heard? The unlearned rise and take heaven by storm, and we, with our learning, see where we wallow in flesh and blood' (Augustine 1983: 197).

At the core of *Confessions* is the dramatic moment of conversion in a garden in Milan. In anguish he laments there, 'How long, how long, tomorrow and tomorrow? Why not now?'. The moment of conversion arises from the chance reading of a text. He hears the voice of a child say 'Pick it up and read it, pick it up and read it'. He opens a copy of 'the apostle's book' (Paul's letter to the Romans) and opening a page at random reads, Romans 13: 13–14. The verses are an admonition against a life which condemns itself. 'I did not want to read on', he writes, 'there was no need. Instantly at the end of this sentence, as if a light of confidence had been poured into my heart, all the darkness of my doubt fled away'. Combining a deeply self-critical appraisal of a sinful life – a directionless hedonism, his academic and literary ambition – with theological reflection, his frank and explicit account of his many failings as a man would have been regarded by his ecclesiastical peers as potentially harmful not only to his own moral reputation but to that of the Church. Augustine's work provides a salutary synthesis not of theological abstraction but of deep conviction of the urgency of response to the saving grace of God. For Augustine, reason is a means of understanding faith – faith seeking understanding – and defending faith when faith is under attack from unbelieving reason. As such, he shaped not only the contours of medieval Catholic theology for the next thousand years but was beloved of all the Protestant Reformers, especially Martin Luther. However, *Confessions* is neither a work of formal theology nor less philosophy but a spiritual roadmap for lost souls.

Augustine's life after conversion was spent in monastic retreat but his intellectual brilliance was soon recognized and, although his pastoral skills were untested and his formal conversion to Christianity new, he was appointed bishop of Hippo, an episcopal seat from which, for the rest of his life, Augustine exerted immense theological, pastoral and political influence. It was as Bishop that he wrote *City of God*, his treatise on secular and ecclesiastical authority, notably determining the realms of the Earthly city and the city of God, a work which, as with all Augustine's theology, has salvation as the only true objective. Augustine's theology has at its core the notion that human destiny is not this world but the world to come. For Augustine, earthly purpose, and thus education's only purpose, was the city of God. False teaching was held to be an obstacle to the attainment of heaven. Augustine's most prominent counter-heretical studies are elaborations of the doctrine of how this salvation may be attained. Centrally Augustine's theological preoccupation was with the doctrine of grace, especially against Pelagius, who claimed personal moral effort, aided by asceticism, could achieve salvation, minimising the need for God's grace.

Importantly, however, Augustine legitimizes the use of classical, pagan learning if it is used in the service of salvific goals. In *On Christian Doctrine* (Augustine 1890, 2008), Augustine deals with the use of rhetoric or the means of effective communication in Christian teaching. Ends, not means, are important, 'a teacher should govern his words, not let the words govern him'. Yet, truth more than the manner of its expression is important,

> to teach what is right and to refute what is wrong' and 'in the performance of this task to conciliate the hostile, to rouse the careless, and to tell the ignorant both what is occurring at present and what is probable in the future.
>
> (Augustine 2008: 78)

His training in rhetoric is used to differentiate between types of learners. Once 'hearers are friendly, attentive, and ready to learn ... the remaining objects are to be carried out in whatever way the case requires'. Above all however the teacher should model in life the doctrine espoused, for 'whatever may be the majesty of the style, the life of the speaker will count for more in securing the hearer's compliance' (Augustine 1890). For Augustine, however, learning which does not serve salvific ends is worthless.

Throughout subsequent centuries, within the medieval Church, there existed strong traditions that emphasized holiness above all things and especially above learning. This counter-movement, not exactly anti-intellectual, was a contemplative counterpoint to the considerable and increasing emphasis placed on learning throughout the Renaissance, a tension that is evident already in the meeting of Abelard and Bernard. Thomas à Kempis is a prime example from that contemplative tradition which urges the importance of salvation over scholarship.

Thomas à Kempis was born in 1380 in Kempen near Dusseldorf. In his late teenage years, he travelled to Zwolle to the monastery at Mount St. Agnes. In 1406, he took his final profession or vows and was ordained priest in 1413. It is likely that the four short books that comprise *The Imitation of Christ* were written at this time. The earliest and anonymous date is 1418 and the first codex of the work dates from 1441. Although Thomas's authorship was subsequently contested, no contemporary scholar supports this. He died in 1471, aged 92. Destroyed in 1573, during the Reformation, today there is little archaeological trace of the original monastery where Thomas à Kempis spent 63 years of his long life. Of his many books Thomas à Kempis is remembered most for *The Imitation*. In a 1494 address to Peter Danhausser, publisher of a late fifteenth century edition of the *Imitation*, Prior Pirkhamer, commending the work of Thomas à Kempis, wrote, 'Nothing more holy, nothing more honourable, nothing more religious, nothing in fine more profitable for the Christian commonweal can you ever do than to make known these works of Thomas à Kempis' (Scully 1912).

The early pages of *The Imitation of Christ* warn of the limitations of scholarship as a means of attaining to sanctity. 'I would,' writes Thomas à Kempis, 'rather feel contrition than be able to define it'. And he warns his many readers across the centuries that knowledge of the religious life is separated by a chasm from those who have the knowledge but do not experience its truth: 'If you knew the whole Bible by heart, and all the teachings of the philosophers, how would this help you without the grace and love of God?' (Thomas à Kempis 1952: 27). Knowledge in itself is a natural good but what is knowledge without the means of using that knowledge for salvation: 'Everyone naturally desires knowledge, but of what use is knowledge itself without fear of God?' And he warns,

> Restrain an inordinate desire for knowledge, in which is found much anxiety and deception. The learned always wish to appear so, and desire recognition of their wisdom. But there are many matters, knowledge of which brings no advantage to the soul.
>
> (Thomas à Kempis 1952: 28–9)

And should the learned even within the religious life feel complacent, the warnings of the responsibility of using that knowledge as a means to sanctification are clear: 'The more complete and excellent your knowledge, the more severe will be God's judgement on you, unless your life be the more holy'. He thus advises avoidance of conceit and a constant guard against pride in knowledge. 'If you desire to learn anything to your advantage, then take delight in being unknown and unregarded' (Thomas à Kempis 1952: 29).

Conclusion

A now rarely referred to American President, Grover Cleveland (1837–1908), is probably best known by a (non-inclusive) aphorism: 'A man is known by the company he keeps'. Religious education, too, can be known from the company it keeps. Philosophers, scientists, sociologists, psychologists, phenomenologists, politicians, artists are among a diverse company. It is this company – adversaries and advocates of religion – whose frames of knowledge ground considerations of the holy; it is now something or rather an idea to be dissected, not a path to be lived.

Perhaps after all it is a matter of the company one keeps. If one had a choice of company, who would it be? We have seen that the choices made are as stark as that, in adversarial terms, with the unambiguous rejection of religious company. The choice is not always as stark but imagining it so can be an illuminating exercise. Let the seeming differences be considerable: the company of Kant or St Thérèse of Lisieux; Durkheim or St Bernard; Freud or St Augustine; Marx or à Kempis; Weber or St Alphonsus Ligouri. An epistemological problem soon becomes therefore a moral one; put simply, a matter of choice in how to lead one's life. The critical distance between the holy and the idea of the holy soon becomes a moral and existential distance from the holy life, between the learned and the holy life.

No modern philosopher expressed the frustration with academic philosophy more than Kierkegaard, who saw in the cold rationalism of Enlightenment a dissociation of philosophy from lived experience. Its loss of urgency about fundamental questions of existence had made philosophical doubt a commonplace assumption. He makes this plain in the opening of *Fear and Trembling*, remarking of the crowd now following 'the significant march of modern philosophy':

> This preliminary movement they have therefore all of them made, and presumably with such ease that they do not find it necessary to let drop a word about the how; for not even he who anxiously and with deep concern sought a little enlightenment was able to find any such thing, any guiding sign, any little dietetic prescription, as to how one was to comport oneself in supporting this prodigious task. 'But Descartes did it.' Descartes, a venerable, humble and honest thinker, whose writings surely no one can read without the deepest emotion, did what he said and said what he did. Alas, alack, that is a great rarity in our times! Descartes, as he repeatedly affirmed, did not doubt in matters of faith.
>
> (Kierkegaard, 1941: 1, also 2013)

For Kierkegaard, existential questions acquire not speculative importance but *urgency*.

In the lives of those who live out such faith, it is apparent that some of the greatest of saints are unlearned, less socially adept, far from academically brilliant and yet (in their traditions) they outshine in sanctity the nobly born and privileged or learned. Adversaries and advocates alike might suggest that sanctity thus pursued is a mark of social or psychological or intellectual deficiencies; that to laud the unlearned is obscurantist. Yet critical distance does or can mark a separation of the holy from the holy life and formal learning, gift though it may be, is not in the holy life seen as the highest of gifts. I take one further life of a man, according to his own testimony born of humble circumstances, of limited education, a man who spent some proportion of this life in a prison and who exerted as much influence as those more educated of his age – Locke, Newton, Milton – one John Bunyan.

John Bunyan (1628–1688) was born in Elstow, near Bedford, England. In his autobiographical *Grace Abounding*, he opens his life with an account of his 'descent', which was 'of a low and inconsiderable generation', his 'father's house being of that rank that is meanest, and most despised of all the families in the land . . . Wherefore, I have not here, as others, to boast of noble blood, or of any high-born state'. He writes:

> But yet, notwithstanding the meanness and inconsiderableness of my parents, it pleased God to put it into their hearts, to put me to school, to learn both to read and write; the which I also attained, according to the rate of other poor men's children: though, to my shame, I confess, I did soon lose that I had learned, even almost utterly, and that long before the Lord did work His gracious work of conversion upon my soul.
>
> (Bunyan 2002: para. 2)

John Bunyan's unhappy, even tormented childhood, he describes in a few vivid paragraphs, when he was

> greatly afflicted and troubled with the thoughts of the fearful torments of hell-fire; still fearing, that it would be my lot to be found at last among those devils and hellish fiends, who are there bound down with the chains and bonds of darkness, unto the judgment of the great day.
>
> (Bunyan 2002: para. 6)

> These things, I say, when I was but a child, but nine or ten years old, did so distress my soul, that then in the midst of my many sports and childish vanities, amidst my vain companions, I was often much cast down.
>
> (Bunyan 2002: para. 7)

At sixteen, he worked in his father's indeterminate trade, a 'mechanic', the year his mother and sister died and his father remarried.

With home life so altered, Bunyan joined the Puritan army, which was disbanded in 1646. His youth, which overlaps with his military experience, he describes with the same self-reproach as Augustine: 'I was the very ringleader of all the youth that kept me company, in all manner of vice and ungodliness' (Bunyan 2002: para. 8). The army disbanded, Bunyan returned to Elstow and married, a time which in *Grace Abounding* he describes as a period of great spiritual turmoil, where yet

> *...the scriptures could not agree in the salvation of my soul...*And now remained only the hinder part of the tempest, for the thunder was gone beyond me, only some drops did still remain, that now and then would fall upon me; but because my former frights and anguish were very sore and deep, therefore it oft befall me still, as it befalleth those that have been scared with fire.
>
> (Bunyan 2002: para. 227, emphasis in original)

His conversion, like Augustine's, is sudden, marked and unexpected, when 'one day, as I was passing in the field, and that too with some dashes on my conscience, fearing lest yet all was not right, suddenly this sentence fell upon my soul, *Thy righteousness is in heaven*'. Accompanied by heavenly visions, seen with 'the eyes of my soul', Bunyan's initial joy turns fretful when he cannot find the passage to authenticate his vision. He discovers a close proximity in 1 Corinthians 1: 30, and 'by this word I saw the other sentence true'.

Following from his conversion experience in 1653, he joined St. John's Church in Bedford, attracted by the pastor John Gifford's oratory and prayerfulness. Becoming deacon after two years, Bunyan's own oratory and personal devotion were recognized by others as a call to preach. A call to preach was not a licence. He was challenged but, it seems, uncharged in 1658. His reputation as a preacher spread, in part from a controversy with the Quakers, whose faith in their own inner light tended to lessen a reliance on scripture which, for Bunyan, was anathema. With the Restoration of Charles I to the throne, revived pressures for conformity to the established Anglican Church drew Bunyan to the attention of magistrates, aware that he preached without licence. In his own account of his arrest and indictment (in a supplement to *Grace Abounding*), he reports of his examination before Justice Keelin, Justice Chester, Justice Blundale, Justice Beecher, and Justice Snagg, that he was

> That John Bunyan, of the town of Bedford, labourer, being a person of such and such conditions, he hath (since such a time) devilishly and perniciously abstained from coming to church to hear Divine service, and is a common upholder of several unlawful meetings... to the great disturbance and distraction of the good subjects of this kingdom, contrary to the laws of our sovereign lord the King, etc.
>
> (Bunyan 2002: 95)

Bunyan, found guilty, spent the next twelve years in Bedford jail. During this time, he wrote *Grace Abounding*, publishing the first edition in 1666.

Released in 1672, and at liberty for the three subsequent years, he was rearrested on similar charges in the autumn of 1675 and spent that winter and the spring of 1676 again in Bedford jail. Beyond *Grace Abounding*, the classic account of these events remains John Brown's (1830–1922) *John Bunyan: His Life, Times and Work* (Brown 1902) Imprisonment seems to have been favourable to Bunyan's literary productiveness. In the latter period of incarceration, he wrote *Pilgrim's Progress* (1678, 'the second part', 1784).

The narrator opens with a description of his wandering 'through the wilderness of this world' and finding 'a den', a place of seclusion, he dreams the tale of the pilgrim:

> I dreamed, and behold, I saw a man clothed with rags, standing in a certain place, with his face from his own house, a book in his hand, and a great burden upon his back. I looked and saw him open the book, and read therein; and as he read, he wept and trembled; and not being able longer to contain, he brake out with a lamentable cry, saying, 'What shall I do?'.
>
> (Bunyan 2008: 11–12)

The man become utterly distracted and preoccupied with his plight, walking like his narrator, 'solitarily in the fields, sometimes reading, and sometimes praying. Bunyan continues:

> Now I saw, upon a time, when he was walking in the fields, that he was (as he was wont) reading in his book, and greatly distressed in his mind; and as he read, he burst out, as he had done before, crying, 'What shall I do to be saved?'
>
> (Bunyan 2008: 11–12)

Seeking an answer to that question becomes the eponymous pilgrim's motivation for leaving home and family, symbols of worldly attachment, to seek salvation.

Meeting Evangelist, the latter asks his business: 'Sir, I perceive, by the book in my hand, that I am condemned to die, and after that to come to judgment; and I find that I am not willing to do the first, nor able to do the second'. Evangelist asks why he might be unwilling to die 'since this life is attended with so many evils'? Pilgrim fears the burden on his back will sink him lower than the grave, and 'the thoughts of these things make me cry'. Evangelist asks: 'If this be thy condition, why standest thou still?' He does not know where to go. Evangelist 'gave him a parchment roll, and there was written within, "Fly from the wrath to come"' (Bunyan 2008: 13–14).

It is with this prompt that Christian makes his pilgrim flight from the world. He is mocked by many and some take the trouble to dissuade him, to persuade him back. He, however, has seen that the city where he lived is 'the city of Destruction'. The pilgrim tries to persuade them to join him. One of his interlocutors, Obstinate, unimpressed, replies:

'What . . . and leave our friends and our comforts behind us!'

Yes, said Christian, (for that was his name) because that all which you forsake is not worthy to be compared with a little of that I am seeking to enjoy; and if you will go along with me, and hold it, you shall fare as I myself; for there, where I go, is enough and to spare. Come away, and prove my words.

(Bunyan 2008: 14–15)

Obstinate asks, 'What are the things you seek, since you leave all the world to find them?' Christian replies, 'I seek an inheritance incorruptible, undefiled, and that fadeth not away; and it is laid up in heaven, and safe there, to be bestowed, at the time appointed, on them that diligently seek it' (Bunyan 2008: 15).

John Bunyan died in London on 31 August 1688. Literary renown he took seemingly as lightly as imprisonment and persecution, as trifles in a mere pilgrimage through this world. For, like Augustine and Thomas à Kempis, the attitude of Bunyan to those great literary talents he had was to regard them *as gifts*. Prior to the fame which was to come with *Pilgrim's Progress*, in *Grace Abounding* he states:

Thus therefore I came to perceive that, though gifts in themselves were good, to the thing for which they are designed, to wit, the edification of others; yet empty, and without power to save the soul of him that hath them, if they be *alone*.

(Bunyan 2002: para. 301)

Gifts 'alone, were dangerous, not in themselves, but because of those evils that attend them that have them, to wit, pride, desire of vain glory, self-conceit, etc.' (Bunyan 2002: para. 301). The world as earthly pilgrimage was not simply a literary device; through it, Bunyan preserved pertinacity with a seeming lightness of heart, in rejection as in acclaim.

I suggested from the outset that Enlightenment was as much an attitude as an epistemology. From the century *before* Enlightenment, John Bunyan's confessions – *Grace Abounding* – and his allegorical *Pilgrim's Progress*, in their humility and simple piety, already anticipated in rejoinder the philosophical brilliance of Kant and those who followed after. In that century *after* Kant, Kierkegaard warned that the real philosophical questions are not merely speculative but pressingly existential. Freedom has its responsibilities and brings its choices. It may be a question of intellectual taste and preference or a matter of graver urgency.

References

Abdillah, M. (2013) 'Religious Education in Indonesia', in D. H. Davis and E. Miroshnikova (eds), *The Routledge International Handbook of Religious Education*, London: Routledge, 150–5.

Ackroyd, P. (2008) *Newton*, London: Doubleday.

Addams, J. (1911) 'The Social Situation: Religious Education and Contemporary Social Conditions' *Religious Education*, 6 (2): 145–52.

Alam, M., Shaifullah Mehedi, A. T. M. and Malmud, N. (2013) 'Religious Education in Bangladesh' in D. H. Davis and E. Miroshnikova (eds), *The Routledge International Handbook of Religious Education*, London: Routledge, 46–53.

Alberts, W. (2010) 'The Academic Study of Religions and Integrative Religious Education in Europe', *British Journal of Religious Education*, 32 (3): 275–90.

Alexander, D. L. (ed.) (1988) *Christian Spirituality: Five Views of Sanctification*, Downers Grove, IL: ivpress.

Alexander, H. A. (2003) 'Moral Education and Liberal Democracy: Spirituality, Community, and Character in an Open Society', *Educational Theory*, 53 (4): 367–87.

Alexander, H. A. (ed.) (2004) *Spirituality and Ethics: Philosophical, Theological and Radical Perspectives*, Brighton: Sussex Academic Press.

Alexander, H. A. and Agbaria, A. K. (eds) (2012) *Commitment, Character, and Citizenship: Religious Education in Liberal Democracy*, London: Routledge.

Alisauskiene, M. (2013) 'Religious Education in Lithuania' in D. H. Davis and E. Miroshnikova (eds), *The Routledge International Handbook of Religious Education*, London: Routledge, 212–16.

Almond, P. C. (1984) *Rudolf Otto: An Introduction to His Philosophical Theology*. Chapel Hill, NC: University of North Carolina Press.

Altemeyer, B. (1981) *Right-Wing Authoritarianism*, Winnipeg: University of Manitoba Press.

Altemeyer, B. (1988) *Enemies of Freedom: Understanding Right-Wing Authoritarianism*, San Francisco, CA: Jossey-Bass.

Altemeyer, B. (1996) *The Authoritarian Specter*, Cambridge, MA: Harvard University Press. Altemeyer, B. and Hunsberger, B. (1992) 'Authoritarianism, Religious Fundamentalism, Quest, and Prejudice', *International Journal for the Psychology of Religion*, 2 (2): 113–33.

Altemeyer, B. and Hunsberger, B. (2004) 'A Revised Religious Fundamentalism Scale: The Short and Sweet of It', *International Journal for the Psychology of Religion*, 14 (1): 47–54.

Alves, C. (1966a) 'Recent Experiments in Religious Education – 1', *Learning for Living* 6 (1): 6–9.

Alves, C. (1966b) 'Recent Experiments in Religious Education – 2', *Learning for Living*, 6 (2): 21–4.

Ameriks, K. (ed.) (2000) *The Cambridge Companion to German Idealism*, Cambridge: Cambridge University Press.

Ames, E. S. (1931) 'Our Machine Age', *Religious Education*, 26 (8): 600–6.

Amor, A. (2001) 'The Role of Religious Education in the Pursuit of Tolerance and Non-Discrimination', UN: International Consultative Conference on School Education in Relation with Freedom of Religion and Belief, Tolerance and Non-Discrimination.

Anandarajah, G. and Hight, E. (2001) Spirituality and Medical Practice: using the HOPE questions as a practical tool for spiritual assessment. *American Family Physician*, 63, 81–92.

AoC (2013) United Nations Alliance of Civilizations. Available online at www.unaoc.org/

Apostolos-Cappadona, D. (2006) 'Introduction to the New Edition', in G. Van Der Leeuw, *Sacred and Profane Beauty: The Holy in Art*, trans. by D. E. Green, Oxford: Oxford University Press, xxi–xxv.

Aquinas, T. (2002) *Aquinas: Political Writings*, trans. R. W. Dyson, Cambridge: Cambridge University Press.

Arendt, H. (2004) *The Origins of Totalitarianism*, New York: Schocken Books.

Argyle, M. (1958) *Religious Behaviour*, London: Routledge and Kegan Paul.

Argyle, M. (1987) *The Psychology of Happiness*, London: Methuen.

Argyle, M. (2000) *Psychology and Religion: An Introduction*. London: Routledge.

Argyle, M. (2002) 'State of the Art: Religion', *The Psychologist*, 15 (1): 22–6.

Argyle, M. and Beit-Hallahmi, B. (1997) *The Psychology of Religious Behaviour, Belief and Experience*, London: Routledge.

Arnett Dixon, D. (1978) 'Spirituality, World Religions and Education', *Religious Education*, 73 (3): 345–50.

Arnold, M. (1993) *Arnold: 'Culture and Anarchy' and Other Writings*, ed. S. Collini, Cambridge: Cambridge University Press.

Aron, R. (1957) *The Opium of the Intellectuals*, trans. T. Kilmartin. New York: Doubleday.

Arthur, C. J. (1985) 'Religion, 'Identity and Maturity: Some Remarks on Erikson's 'Eight Ages of Man' and Religious Education', *British Journal of Religious Education*, 7 (2): 48–75.

Arthur, J. and Holdsworth, M. (2012) 'The European Court of Human Rights, Secular Education and Public Schooling', *British Journal of Educational Studies*, 60 (2): 129–49.

Arthur, J., Gearon, L. and Sears, A. (2010) *Education, Politics, Religion*, London: Routledge.

Arweck, E. and Nesbitt, E. (2010a) 'Plurality at Close Quarters: Mixed-Faith Families in the UK', *Journal of Religion in Europe* 3 (1), 155–82.

Arweck, E. and Nesbitt, E. (2010b) 'Close Encounters? The Intersection of Faith and Ethnicity in Mixed-Faith Families', *Journal of Beliefs and Values*, 31 (1), 39–52.

Arweck, E. and Nesbitt, E. (2010c) 'Young People's Identity Formation in Mixed-Faith Families: Continuity or Discontinuity of Religious Traditions?', *Journal of Contemporary Religion*, 25 (1), 67–87.

Astley, J. (2012) 'A Theological Reflection on the Nature of Religious Truth', in Astley, J., Francis, L. J., Robbins, M. and Selcuk, M. (eds) (2012) *Teaching Religion, Teaching Truth*, Bern: Peter Lang, 241–62.

Astley, J. and Francis, L. J. (2010) 'Promoting Positive Attitudes Towards Science and Religion Among Sixth-Form Pupils: Dealing with Scientism and Creationism', *British Journal of Religious Education* 32 (3): 189–200.

Astley, J., Francis, L. J., Robbins, M. and Selcuk, M. (eds) (2012) *Teaching Religion, Teaching Truth: Theoretical and Empirical Perspectives*, Bern: Peter Lang.

Atkinson, H. A. (1927) 'The Relation of State Schools to Religion in France, Germany, England and Canada', *Religious Education*, 22 (3): 241–7.

Aubrey, E. E. (1928) 'Teaching the Bible in an Age of Science', *Religious Education* 23 (2): 149–53.

Audi, R. (2005) 'Moral Foundations of Liberal Democracy, Secular Reasons, and Liberal Neutrality Toward the Good', *Notre Dame Journal of Law, Ethics, & Public Policy*, 19 (3): 197–218.

Audi, R. and Wolterstorff, N. (1997) *Religion in the Public Sphere*, New York: Rowman and Littlefield.

Augustine, St (1890) *On Christian Doctrine*, trans. J.F. Shaw, A Select Library of the Nicene and Post-Nicene Fathers of the Christian Church, New York: The Christian Literature Co. Available online at www9.georgetown.edu/faculty/jod/augustine/ddc.html

Augustine, St (1983) *Confessions*, trans. E. M. Blaiklock, London: Hodder and Stoughton.

Augustine, St (1998) *Augustine: The City of God against the Pagans*, trans. R. W. Dyson, Cambridge: Cambridge University Press.

Augustine, St (2001) *Augustine: Political Writings*, eds E. M. Atkins and R. J. Dodaro, Cambridge: Cambridge University Press.

Augustine, St (2003) *City of God*, rev. edn., trans. H. Bettenson, London: Penguin.

Augustine, St (2008) *On Christian Teaching*, trans. R. P. H. Green, Oxford: Oxford University Press.

Babie, P. and Mylius, B. (2013) 'Religious Education in Australia', in D. H. Davis and E. Miroshnikova (eds), *The Routledge International Handbook of Religious Education*. London: Routledge, 23–31.

Bailey, A. E. (1871) *The Use of Art in Religious Education*, Princeton: Princeton Theological Seminary. Available online at http://archive.org/details/useofartinreligi00bail

Bakunin, M. (1991) *Bakunin: Statism and Anarchy*, ed. M. Shatz. Cambridge: Cambridge University Press.

Ball, T. and Bellamy, P. (eds) (2003) *The Cambridge History of Twentieth-Century Political Thought*, Cambridge: Cambridge University Press.

Balodis, R. (2013) 'Religious Education in Latvia' in D. H. Davis and E. Miroshnikova (eds), *The Routledge International Handbook of Religious Education*, London: Routledge, 202–11.

Barendt, E. (2011) 'Teaching Evolution, Creationism and Intelligent Design in US Schools (With Some European Comparisons)' in M. Hunter-Henin (eds) *Law, Religious Freedoms and Education in Europe*, Farnham: Ashgate, 267–82.

Barnes, L. P. (2000) 'Ninian Smart and the Phenomenological Approach to Religious Education', *Religion*, 30 (4): 315–32.

Barnes, L. P. (2001a) 'The Contribution of Professor Ninian Smart to Religious Education', *Religion*, 31 (4): 317–19.

Barnes, L. P. (2001b) 'What is Wrong with the Phenomenological Approach to Religious Education?' *Religious Education*, 96 (4): 445–61.

Barnes, L. P. (2006) 'The Misrepresentation of Religion in Modern British (Religious) Education' *British Journal of Educational Studies*, 54 (4): 395–411.

Barnes, L. P. (2007a) 'The Disputed Legacy of Ninian Smart and Phenomenological Religious Education: A Critical Response to Kevin O'Grady', *British Journal of Religious Education*, 29 (2): 157–68.

Barnes, L. P. (2007b) 'Michael Hand, Is Religious Education Possible? *Studies in Philosophy and Education*, 27 (1): 63–70.

Barnes, L. P. and Wright, A. (2006) 'Romanticism, Representations of Religion and Critical Religious Education', *British Journal of Religious Education*, 28 (1): 65–77.

Barrett, B. B. (2012) *What Is Psychoanalysis? 100 Years after Freud's 'Secret Committee'*. London: Routledge.

Barrett, J. L. (2011) *Cognitive Science, Religion, and Theology: From Human Minds to Divine Minds*, West Conshohocken, PA: Templeton Press.

Barrett, J. L. (2012) *Born Believers: The Science of Children's Religious Belief.* Free Press.

Barth, K. (1934) 'No! Answer to Emil Brunner,' in E. Brunner and K. Barth, *Natural Theology*, trans. P. Fraenkel. London: Centenary Press, 65–128.

Barth, K. (2012) *Karl Barth's Church Dogmatics: An Introduction and Reader* ed. R. M. Allen. New York: T. and T. Clark.

Bartholomew, C. G. (1998) 'Babel and Derrida: Postmodernism, Language and Biblical Interpretation', *Tyndale Bulletin*, 49 (2): 305–28.

Bastow, D. (1976) 'Otto and Numinous Experience', *Religious Studies*, 12 (2): 159–76.

Bates, D. (1996) 'Christianity, Culture and Other Religions (Part 2): F. H. Hilliard, Ninian Smart and the 1988 Education Reform Act', *British Journal of Religious Education*, 18 (2): 85–102.

Bates, D., Durka, G. and Schweitzer, F. (eds) (2005) *Education, Religion and Society*, London: Routledge.

Batteux, C. (1746) *Les Beaux Arts Reduits à un Même Principe*, Paris: Chez Durand.

Batteux, C. (1747) *Cours de Belles-Lettres, ou, Principes de la Littérature*, Paris: Desaint.

Bauman, Z. (1989) *Modernity and the Holocaust*, Cambridge: Polity.

Baumfield, V. and Cush, D. (2012) 'A Gift from the Child: Curriculum Development in Religious Education'. *British Journal of Religious Education*, 34 (3): 227–30.

Baumfield, V. M., Conroy, J. C., Davis, R. A. and Lundie, D. C. (2012) 'The Delphi Method: Gathering Expert Opinion in Religious Education', *British Journal of Religious Education*, 34 (1): 5–19.

Bausor, J. and Poole, M. (2002) 'Science-and-Religion in the Agreed Syllabuses – An Investigation and Some Suggestions', *British Journal of Religious Education*, 25 (1): 18–32.

Beard, C. (1932) *A Charter for the Social Sciences in Schools. Part 1 of a Report of the Commission on the Social Studies of the American Historical Association*, New York: Charles Scribner's Sons.

Beattie, T. (2007) *The New Atheists: The Twilight of Reason and the War on Religion*, London: Darton, Longman and Todd.

Beilin, H. (1992) 'Piaget's Enduring Contribution to Developmental Psychology', *Developmental Psychology*, 28, 191–204.

Beiser, F. C. (ed.) (1993) *The Cambridge Companion to Hegel*, Cambridge: Cambridge University Press.

Beiser, F. C. (2000) 'The Enlightenment and Idealism', *The Cambridge Companion to German Idealism*, Cambridge: Cambridge University Press.

Beiser, F. C. (ed.) (2008) *Cambridge Companion to Hegel and Nineteenth-Century Philosophy*. Cambridge: Cambridge University Press.

Beit-Hallahmi, B. (2012) 'Studying Atheism and the Psychology of Religiosity', *Religion, Brain and Behavior*, 2 (1): 25–7.

Bellah, R. (1967) 'Civil Religion in America', *Daedalus* 96 (1): 1–21.

Bellah, R. (1968) *Beyond Belief*, Berkeley: University of California Press, 163–90.

Bellah, R. N. (2011) *Religion in Human Evolution: From the Paleolithic to the Axial Age*. Boston: Belknap Press of Harvard University Press.

Bellah, R. N. (2012) 'Religion in Human Evolution Revisited: Response to Commentators' *Religion, Brain and Behavior*, 2 (3): 260–70.

Berger. P. (ed.) (1999) *The Desecularization of the World*, Washington, DC: Ethics and Public Policy Center.

Berger, P. L. (1967) *The Sacred Canopy* (New York: Doubleday).

Berger, P. L. (1970) *A Rumor of Angels: Modern Society and the Rediscovery of the Supernatural*, Garden City, NY: Doubleday.

Berger, P. L. and Luckmann, T. (1966) *The Social Construction of Reality: A Treatise in the Sociology of Knowledge*, New York: Doubleday.Berger, P., Davie, G. and Fokas, E. (2008) *Religious America, Secular Europe?* Aldershot: Ashgate.

Bernard of Clairvaux, St (1908) *On Consideration*, trans. G. Lewis, Oxford: Clarendon Press.

Bernstein, P. S., Chave, E. J. and Macelwane, F. J. (1940) 'The Inter-Relationship of Religion and Democracy', *Religious Education*, 35 (3): 141–51.

Berry, D. L. (1983) 'A Strategy for Considering Truth Claims in Teaching Religion', *Religious Education*, 78 (2): 218–31.

Bertram-Troost, G. D. (2011) 'Mitigating the Impact of Religious Diversity in Schools for Secondary Education: A Challenging but Necessary Exercise', *British Journal of Religious Education*, 33 (2): 271–83.

Bielefeldt, H. (2012) 'Freedom of Religion or Belief – A Human Right Under Pressure', *Oxford Journal of Law*, 1 (1): 15–35.

Biesta, G. (2010) 'This is My Truth, Tell Me Yours'. Deconstructive Pragmatism as a Philosophy for Education' *Educational Philosophy and Theory*, 42 (7): 710–27.

Biesta, G. (2011) 'Philosophy, Exposure, and Children: How to Resist the Instrumentalisation of Philosophy in Education', *Journal of Philosophy of Education*, 45 (2): 305–19.

Binns, C. A. P. (1982) 'Soviet Secular Ritual: Atheist Propaganda or Spiritual Consumerism?' *Religion in Communist Lands*, 10 (3): 298–309.

Bion, W. R. (1955) 'Language and the Schizophrenic', in M. Klein, P. Heimann and R. E. Money-Kyrle (eds) *New Directions in Psycho-analysis*, London: Tavistock, 220–39.

Bion, W. R. (1962) 'A Theory of Thinking', *International Journal of Psycho-Analysis*, 43, 306–10.

Bion, W. R. (1992) *Cogitations*, London: Karnac Books.

174   *References*

Birkedal, M. (2012) *The Cambridge Companion to the Cistercian Order*. Cambridge: Cambridge University Press.

Black, D. M. (eds) (2006) *Psychoanalysis and Religion in the 21st Century: Competitors or Collaborators?* London: Routledge.

Blaylock, L. (2012) 'Teaching Religion and Science: Effective Pedagogy and Practical Approaches for RE Teachers', *British Journal of Religious Education*, 34 (2): 224–6.

Bleazby, J. B. (2012) 'Dewey's Notion of Imagination in Philosophy for Children', *Education and Culture*, 28 (2): 95–111.

Blevins, D. G. (2011) 'Brain Matters: A Journey with Neuroscience and Religious Education', *Religious Education*, 106 (3): 246–51.

Boas, F. (1911) *The Mind of Primitive Man: A Course of Lectures Delivered Before the Lowell Institute, Boston, Mass., and the National University of Mexico, 1910–1911*, San Diego: Ulan Press.

Boethius, A. (2012) *The Consolation of Philosophy*, trans. S. Goins and B. H. Wyman, San Francisco: Ignatius Press.

Boisen, A. T. (1928) 'The Psychiatric Approach to the Study of Religion', *Religious Education*, 23 (3): 201–7.

Bonhoeffer, D. (2001) *The Cost of Discipleship*, London: SCM.

Bowie, B., Peterson, A. and Lynn Revell, L. (2012) 'Post-Secular Trends: Issues in Education and Faith', *Journal of Beliefs and Values*, 33 (2): 139–41.

Boyer, P. (2001) *Religion Explained*, New York: Basic Books.

Brelsford, T. (2005) 'Lessons for Religious Education from Cognitive Science of Religion', *Religious Education*, 100 (2): 174–91.

Brickner, B. R. (1938) 'What Liberty Does Religion Require?', *Religious Education*, 33 (4): 212–17.

Bringuier, J. C. (1980) *Conversations with Jean Piaget*, Chicago, IL: University of Chicago Press.

Broadie, A. (ed.) (2003) *The Cambridge Companion to the Scottish Enlightenment*, Cambridge: Cambridge University Press.

Brooke, J. H. (1991) *Science and Religion: Some Historical Perspectives*, Cambridge: Cambridge University Press.

Brower, J. E. and Guilfoy, K. (eds) (2004) *The Cambridge Companion to Abelard*, Cambridge: Cambridge University Press.

Brown, C. G. (2006) *Religion and Society in Twentieth-Century Britain*, London: Pearson.

Brown, C. G. (2009) *The Death of Christian Britain*, London: Routledge.

Brown, J. (1902) *John Bunyan: His Life, Times and Work*. London: Isbister. Available online at http://archive.org/stream/johnbunyanhislif01browuoft#page/n9/mode/2up

Bruce, S. (2002) *God is Dead: Secularization in the West*, Oxford: Blackwell.

Bruce, S. (2003) *Politics and Religion*, Cambridge: Polity.

Buchanan, M. T. (2005) 'Pedagogical Drift: The Evolution of New Approaches and Paradigms in Religious Education', *Religious Education*, 100 (1): 20–37.

Bullivant, S. (2008) 'Research Note: Sociology and the Study of Atheism', *Journal of Contemporary Religion*, 23 (3): 363–8.

Bullivant, S. and Ruse, M. (eds) (2013) *The Oxford Handbook of Atheism*, Oxford: Oxford University Press.

Bultmann R. (1953) *Kerygma and Myth*, London: SPCK.

Bunyan, J. (2002) *Grace Abounding to the Chief of Sinners*, transcribed from the 1905 Religious Tract Society edition by D. Price. Project Gutenberg eBook available online at www.gutenberg.org/files/654/654-h/654-h.htm

Bunyan, J. (2006) *Grace Abounding to the Chief of Sinners*, London: Penguin.

Bunyan, J. (2008) *Pilgrim's Progress*, London: Penguin.

Burke, E. (2009) *Reflections on the Revolution in France*, ed. L. G. Mitchell, Oxford: Oxford University Press.

Burleigh, M. (2006) *Earthly Powers: Religion and Politics in Europe from the Enlightenment to the Great War*, London: Harper Perennial.

Burleigh, M. (2007) *Sacred Causes: The Clash of Religion and Politics from the Great War to the War on Terror*, London: HarperCollins.

Burnham, D. (2000) *An Introduction to Kant's Critique of Judgment*, Edinburgh: Edinburgh University Press.

Burnham, J. C. (ed.) (2012) *After Freud Left: A Century of Psychoanalysis in America*, Chicago, IL: Chicago University Press.

Bushman, B. J., Ridge, R. D., Das, E., Key, C. W. and Busath, G. L. (2007) 'When God Sanctions Killing: Effect of Scriptural Violence on Aggression', *Psychological Science*, 18 (3): 204–7.

Calhoun, C., Mendieta, E. and van Antwerpen, J. (2013) *Habermas and Religion*, Cambridge: Polity.

Calvin, J. and Luther, M. (1991) *Luther and Calvin on Secular Authority*, ed. and trans. by Harro Höpfl, Cambridge: Cambridge University Press.

Camara, F. K. and Seck, A. (2013) 'Religious Education in Senegal', in D. H. Davis and E. Miroshnikova (eds), *The Routledge International Handbook of Religious Education*. London: Routledge, 300–9.

Camus, A. (2000a) *The Rebel*, London: Penguin.

Camus, A. (2000b) *The Outsider*, London: Penguin.

Camus, A. (2005) *The Myth of Sisyphus*, London: Penguin.

Canetti-Nisim, D. (2004) 'The Effect of Religiosity on Endorsement of Democratic Values: The Mediating Influence of Authoritarianism.' *Political Behavior*, 26 (4): 377–98.

Caputo, J. D. (2002) *Philosophy and Theology*, Nashville: Abingdon Press.

Caputo, J. D. and Vatimmo, G. (2009) *After the Death of God*, New York: Columbia University Press.

Carr, D. (1994) Knowledge and Truth in Religious Education. *Journal of Philosophy of Education*, 28 (2): 221–38.

Carr, D. (1996) 'Rival Conceptions of Spiritual Education', *Journal of Philosophy of Education*, 30 (2): 159–78.

Carr, D. (2007) 'Religious Education, Religious Literacy and Common Schooling: A Philosophy and History of Skewed Reflection', *Journal of Philosophy of Education*, 41 (4): 659–73.

Carr, D. (2012) 'Post-Secularism, Religious Knowledge and Religious Education', *Journal of Beliefs and Values*, 33 (2): 157–68.

Carr, D. and Alexander, H. A. (2005) 'Philosophical Issues in Spiritual Education and Development', in E. C. Roehlkepartain, P. E. King, L. Wagener and P. L. Benson (eds) *The Handbook of Spiritual Development in Childhood and Adolescence*, Thousand Oaks, CA: Sage, 73–91.

Carr, D. and Haldane, J. (eds) (2003) *Philosophy, Spirituality and Education*, London: RoutledgeFalmer.

Casanova, J. (1994) *Public Religions in the Modern World*, Chicago, IL: Chicago University Press.

Cassidy, D. (1992) *Uncertainty: The Life and Science of Werner Heisenberg*, New York: W.H. Freeman.

Cavan, J. D. and Cavan, R. S. (1928) 'Educational Sociology – A New Foundation Science', *Religious Education*, 23 (5): 482–90.

Cavan, J. D. and Cavan, R. S. (1930) 'The Adolescent in American Psychology and Sociology', *Religious Education*, 25 (2): 154–65.

Cavan, R. S. (1932) 'Methods of Studying Personality', *Religious Education*, 27 (1): 50–5.

Cepar, D. (2013) 'Religious Education in the Republic of Slovenia', in D. H. Davis and E. Miroshnikova (eds), *The Routledge International Handbook of Religious Education*, London: Routledge, 318–24.

Chambers, R. (1993) *Vestiges of the Natural History of Creation and Other Evolutionary Writings*, ed. J. A. Secord. Chicago, IL: University of Chicago Press.

Chater, M. and Erricker, C. (2012) *Does Religious Education Have a Future?* Oxford: Routledge.

Cimino, R. and Smith, C. (2011) 'The New Atheism and the Formation of the Imagined Secularist Community', *Journal of Media and Religion*, 10 (1): 24–38.

Clark, E. A. (2013) 'Religious Education in the United States of America', in D. H. Davis and E. Miroshnikova (eds), *The Routledge International Handbook of Religious Education*, London: Routledge, 375–82.

Clayton, J. (2001) 'Chairman Ninian', *Religion*, 31 (4): 321–2.

CoE (2008a) *Recommendation CM/Rec(2008)12 of the Committee of Ministers to Member States on the Dimension of Religions and Non-religious Convictions Within Intercultural Education*, Strasbourg: Council of Europe. Available online at https://wcd.coe.int/ViewDoc.jsp?id=1386911&Site=CM

CoE (2008b) *White Paper on Intercultural Dialogue CM(2008)30 'Living Together as Equals'*, Strasbourg: Council of Europe. Available online at www.coe.int/t/dg4/intercultural/whitepaper_interculturaldialogue_2_EN.asp

Coe, G. A. (1917) 'Religious Education and General Education', *Religious Education*, 12 (2): 123–8.

Coe, G. A. (1922) 'Religious Education and Political Conscience', *Religious Education*, 17 (6): 430–5.

Coe, G. A. (1932) 'A Charter for the Social Sciences in the Schools', *Religious Education*, 27 (7): 641–2.

Coe, G. A. (1940) 'Religion, Education, Democracy', *Religious Education*, 35 (3): 131–7.

Coles, R. (1986) *The Moral Life of Children*, New York: Atlantic Monthly Press.

Coles, R. (1992) *The Spiritual Life of Children*, New York: T. and T. Clark.

Collicutt, J. (2011) 'Psychology, Spirituality, Religion', *The Psychologist* 24 (4): 250–1.

Comte, A. (1998a) *Comte: Early Political Writings*, ed. H. S. Jones, Cambridge: Cambridge University Press.

Comte, A. (1998b) *Auguste Comte and Positivism: The Essential Writings*, ed. G. Lenzer, New York: Transaction.

Commonwealth (2007) *Civil Paths to Peace: Report of the Commonwealth Commission on Respect and Understanding*, Commonwealth Commission on Respect and Understanding, London: Commonwealth Secretariat.

Condorcet, Marquis de (2012) *Condorcet: Political Writings*, trans. S. Lukes and N. Urbinati. Cambridge: Cambridge University Press.

Conroy, J. C., Lundie, D. and Baumfield, V. (2012) 'Failures of meaning in religious education', *Journal of Beliefs and Values*, 33 (3): 309–23.

Cook, C., Powell, A. and Sims, A. (eds) (2009) *Spirituality and Psychiatry*, London: RCPsych Publications.

Cooling, T. (1990) 'Science and Religious Education – Conflict or Co-operation?' *British Journal of Religious Education*, 13 (1): 35–42.

Cooling, T. (2005) 'The Search for Truth: Postmodernism and Religious Education', *Journal of Beliefs and Values*, 26 (1): 87–93.

Cooling, T. (2009) *Doing God in Education*, London: THEOS.

Copley, T. (1996) 'A Tribute to John Hull: A Review of Editorials in *Learning for Living* and the *British Journal of Religious Education*, 1971–1996' *British Journal of Religious Education*, 19 (1): 5–12.

Copley, T. (2000) *Spiritual Development in the State School*. Exeter: University of Exeter Press.

Copley, T. (2004) *Teaching Religion*. Exeter: Exeter University Press.

Copley, T. (2005) *Indoctrination, Education and God*, London, S.P.C.K.

Corless, R. (2001) 'A Smart Teacher: A Reminiscence of Ninian Smart' *Religion* 31 (4): 323–4.

Council of Europe (2011) Parliamentary Assembly, Committee on Culture, Science and Education, *The Dangers of Creationism in Education*, Doc. 11375, 17 September. Strasbourg: Council of Europe. Available online at http://assembly.coe.int/ASP/Doc/XrefViewHTML.asp?FileId=11751&Language=EN

Cox. E. (1967) *Sixth Form Religion*, London: SCM.

Cox, E. (1971) 'Changes in Attitudes Towards Religious Education and the Bible Among Sixth Form Boys and Girls', *British Journal of Educational Psychology*, 41 (3): 328–41.

Cox, E. (1983) 'Understanding Religion and Religious Understanding', *British Journal of Religious Education*, 6 (1): 3–13.

Cox, H. (1965) *The Secular City*, New York: Macmillan.

Cox, J. L. (2006) *A Guide to the Phenomenology of Religion: Key Figures, Formative Influences and Subsequent Debates*, London: Continuum.

Coyle, A (2011) 'Critical Responses to Faith Development Theory: A Useful Agenda for Change?', *Archive for the Psychology of Religion*, 33 (3): 281–98.

Crain, W. C. (1985) *Theories of Development*, New York: Prentice-Hall.

Crawford, M. and Rossiter, G. (1996) 'The Secular Spirituality of Youth: Implications for Religious Education' *British Journal of Religious Education*, 18 (3): 133–43.

Crump Miller, R. (1991) 'The Educational Philosophy of William James', *Religious Education*, 86 (4): 619–34.

Csikszentmihalyi, M. and Csikszentmihalyi, I. S. (2006) *A Life Worth Living: Contributions to Positive Psychology*, New York: Oxford University Press.

Csinos, D. M. (2009) 'Nurturing Children's' Spirituality: Christian Perspectives and Best Practices', *Religious Education*, 104 (2), 217–20.

Culliford, L. (2002) 'Spirituality and Clinical Care', *British Medical Journal*, 325 (7378) 1434–5.

Culliford, L. (2007) 'Taking a Spiritual History', *Advances in Psychiatric Treatment*, 13, 212–19.

Cunningham, A. (2001) 'Obituary for Ninian Smart', *Religion*, 31 (4): 325–6.

Cupitt, D. (2003) *The Sea of Faith*, 3rd edn., London: SCM.

Dacey, A. (2012) *The Future of Blasphemy: Speaking of the Sacred in an Age of Human Rights*. London: Continuum.

D'Angelo, G. (2013) 'Religious Education in Sudan', in D. H. Davis and E. Miroshnikova (eds), *The Routledge International Handbook of Religious Education*, London: Routledge, 336–42.

Darwin, C. (2008) 'Autobiography' [1876] in *Evolutionary Writings: Including the Autobiographies*, ed. J. A. Secord, Oxford: Oxford University Press.

Darwin, C. (2011) *On the Origin of Species: The Illustrated Edition*, ed. David Quammen. Sterling Signature.

Davidson, R. F. (1947) *Rudolf Otto's Interpretation of Religion*, Princeton: Princeton University Press.

Davie, G. (2001) *Global Civil Religion: A European Perspective Sociology of Religion*, 62 (4), 455–73.

Davies, B. and Leftow, B. (eds) (2004) *The Cambridge Companion to Anselm*, Cambridge: Cambridge University Press.

Davis, A. (2010) 'Defending Religious Pluralism for Religious Education', *Ethics and Education*, 5 (3): 189–202.

Davis, C., Milbank, J. and Zizek, S. (eds) (2005) *Theology and the Political: The New Debate*, Durham, NC: Duke University Press.

Davis, D. H. and Miroshnikova, E. (2013) *The Routledge International Handbook of Religious Education*. London: Routledge.

Dawkins, R. (2007) *The God Delusion*, London: Transworld Paperbacks.

Dawkins, R. (2010) *The Greatest Show on Earth*, London: Black Swan.

Dawson, G. E. (1909) 'The Biological Sciences and Religious Education', *Religious Education*, 4 (5): 437–41.

Dawson, G. E. (1906) 'The Child's Self-expression and Religious Education', *Religious Education*, 1 (3): 83–7.

Day, D. (1985) 'Religious Education Forty Years On: A Permanent Identity Crisis', *British Journal of Religious Education*, 7 (2): 55–63.

Day, V. (2008) *The Irrational Atheist: Dissecting the Unholy Trinity of Dawkins, Harris, and Hitchens*. Dallas, TX: Benbella Books.

de Berg, K. (2011) 'Joseph Priestley Across Theology, Education, and Chemistry: An Interdisciplinary Case Study in Epistemology with a Focus on the Science Education Context', *Science and Education*, 20 (7/8): 805–30.

de Berg, K. (2012) 'The Enlightenment and Joseph Priestley's Disenchantment with Science and Religion', *Christian Perspectives on Science and Technology*, 8: 1–13.

de Montesquieu, C. (1989) *Montesquieu: The Spirit of the Laws*, ed. A. M. Cohler, B. C. Miller and H. S. Stone, Cambridge: Cambridge University Press.

de Montesquieu, C. (1999) *Considerations on the Causes of the Greatness of the Romans and Their Decline*, trans. D. Lowenthal, New York: Hackett.

de Souza, M., Durka, G., Engebretson, K. and Jackson, R. (eds) (2007) *International Handbook of the Religious, Moral and Spiritual Dimensions in Education*, Amsterdam: Springer.

de Souza, M., Francis, L. J., O'Higgins-Norman, J. and Scott, D. G. (eds) (2009) *International Handbook of Education for Spirituality, Care and Wellbeing*, Amsterdam: Springer.

de Vries, H. and Sullivan, L. E. (eds) (2006) *Political Theologies: Public Religions in a Post-Secular World*, London: Continuum.

Deems, M. M. (1949) 'Making Our Religion Contemporary', *Religious Education*, 44 (4): 204–10.

Degler, C. N. (1989) *Culture versus Biology in the Thought of Franz Boas and Alfred L. Kroeber, German Historical Institute Washington DC Annual Lecture Series No. 2*, New York: Berg. Available online at www.ghi-dc.org/publications/ghipubs/annual/al02.pdf

Degler, C. N. (1992) *In Search of Human Nature: The Decline and Revival of Darwinism in American Social Thought*, Oxford: Oxford University Press.

Degler, C. N., Hyatt, M. and Duden, B. (1989) *Culture Versus Biology In the Thought of Franz Boaz and Alfred L. Kroeber*, New York: Berg, 1989.

Dennett, D. (2007) *Breaking the Spell: Religion as a Natural Phenomenon*, London: Penguin.

Dericquebourg, R. (2013) 'Religious Education in France', in D. H. Davis and E. Miroshnikova (eds), *The Routledge International Handbook of Religious Education*, London: Routledge, 113–21.

Derrida, J. (1984) *Margins of Philosophy*, Chicago, IL: University of Chicago Press.

Derrida, J. (2001) *Writing and Difference*, London: Routledge.

Derrida, J. (2002) *Acts of Religion*, London: Routledge.

Desmond, A. J. (1995) *Huxley: The Devil's Disciple*, London: Michael Joseph.

Deutsch, E. (2001) 'A Tribute to Ninian Smart', *Religion*, 31 (4): 327.

Dewey, J. (1916) *Democracy and Education: An Introduction to the Philosophy of Education*, New York: Macmillan.

Dewey, J. (1991) *A Common Faith*, New Haven: Yale University Press.

Dewey, J. (1980) *Art as Experience*, New York: Perigree.

Dewey, J. (1988) *Individualism, Old and New. The Later Works of John Dewey, in J. A. Boydston (ed.)*, Carbondale and Edwardsville: Southern Illinois University Press.

Dewey, J. (1997) *Experience and Education*, New York: Free Press.

Dewey, J. (2008a) *The Collected Works of John Dewey, 1882–1953*, 3rd edn., ed. J. Boydston. Carbondale and Edwardsville: Southern Illinois University Press.

Dewey, J. (2008b) *The Collected Works of John Dewey, 1882–1953*, electronic version. Available online at www.nlx.com/collections/133/

Diderot, D. (1992) *Diderot: Political Writings*, ed. J. Hope Mason and R. Wokler, Cambridge: Cambridge University Press.

Diderot, D. and d'Alembert, J. (1976) *Rameau's Nephew/D'Alembert's Dream*, trans. L. Tancock, London: Penguin.

Dilthey, W. (2010) *Wilhelm Dilthey: Selected Works, Volume III: The Formation of the Historical World in the Human Sciences*, Princeton: Princeton University Press.

Donnelly, J. (2002) *Universal Human Rights in Theory and Practice*, Ithaca, NY: Cornell University Press.

Dowling, E. M. and Scarlett, W. G. (eds) (2005) *Encyclopedia of Spiritual and Religious Development in Childhood and Adolescence*, Thousand Oaks: Sage.

Dreyfus, H. L. and Wrathall, M. A. (eds) (2009) *A Companion to Phenomenology and Existentialism*, Oxford: Blackwell.

Drumheller, S. J. (1968) 'A Jung Oriented Rationale for a Program for Moral Education', *Religious Education*, 63 (2): 131–5.

du Plessis, L. M. (2013) 'Religious Education in South Africa', in D. H. Davis and

E. Miroshnikova (eds), *The Routledge International Handbook of Religious Education*, London: Routledge, 325–8.

Durka, G. and Smith, J. (1979) *Aesthetic Dimensions in Religious Education*, New York: Paulist Press.

Durkheim, E. (2001) *The Elementary Forms of the Religious Life*, Oxford: Oxford University Press.

Durkheim, E. (2006) *On Suicide*, trans. R. Buss, London: Penguin.

Durkheim, E. (2009) *The Evolution of Educational Thought: Lectures on the Formation and Development of Secondary Education in France* (Selected Writings on Education). London: Routledge.

Durham, W. C. (2013) 'Introduction', in D. H. Davis and E. Miroshnikova (eds), *The Routledge International Handbook of Religious Education*, London: Routledge.

Ecklund, E. H. and Scheitle, C. P. (2007) 'Religion Among Academic Scientists: Distinctions, Disciplines, and Demographics', *Social Problems*, 54 (4): 289–307.

Ecklund, E. H., Park, J. Z. and Sorrell, K. L. (2011) 'Scientists Negotiate Boundaries Between Religion and Science', *Journal for the Scientific Study of Religion*, 50: 552–69.

Eisenstadt, S. N. (2000) 'Multiple Modernities', *Daedalus* 129 (Winter) 1–30.

Eisenstadt, S. N. (2002) *Multiple Modernities*, New York: Transaction Publishers.

el-Hakim, J. (2013) 'Religious Education in Syria', in D. H. Davis and E. Miroshnikova (eds), *The Routledge International Handbook of Religious Education*, London: Routledge, 357–60.

Eliade, M. (1957) *The Sacred and the Profane: The Nature of Religion*, Orlando, FL: Harcourt.

Elliott, H. S. (1941) 'Religion in the Educational Experience of Children and Youth', *Religious Education*, 36 (4): 195–211.

Emerson, R. (2003) 'The Contexts of the Scottish Enlightenment', in A. Broadie (ed.), *The Cambridge Companion to the Scottish Enlightenment*, Cambridge: Cambridge University Press, 9–30.

Enger, T. (1992) 'Religious Education Between Psychology and Theology', *Religious Education*, 87 (3): 435–45.

Engebretson, K., de Souza, M., Durka, G. and Gearon, L. (eds) (2010) *International Handbook of Inter-religious Education*, Amsterdam: Springer.

English, L. M., D'Souza, M. O. and Chartrand, L. (2003) 'A 10-year Retrospective of the *British Journal of Religious Education: An Analysis of Contents and Contributors*', *British Journal of Religious Education*, 25 (4): 308–19.

English, L. M., D'Souza, M. O. and Chartrand, L. (2005) 'Analysis of Contents, Contributors, and Research Directions: Mapping Publication Routes in the Journal', *Religious Education*, 100 (1): 6–19.

Erricker, C. (2001) 'Professor Ninian Smart', *International Journal of Children's Spirituality*, 6 (1): 129–30.

Erricker, C. (2001) 'Shall We Dance? Authority, Representation, and Voice: The Place of Spirituality in Religious Education', *Religious Education*, 96 (1): 20–35.

Erricker, J., Clive Erricker, C. and Ota, C. (eds) (2001) *Spiritual Education: Cultural, Religious and Social Differences*, Sussex: Sussex Academic Press.

Evans, D. E. (1944) 'Religious Education and Some of its Critics', *Religion in Education*, 11 (2): 33–8.

Evans, G. R. (2000) *Bernard of Clairvaux*, Oxford: Oxford University Press.

Evans, R. (1973) *Jean Piaget, the Man and His Ideas*, New York: Dutton.

Evans-Pritchard, E. E. (1937) *Witchcraft, Oracles and Magic Among the Azande*, Oxford: Oxford University Press.

Evans-Pritchard, E. E. (1940) *The Nuer: A Description of the Modes of Livelihood and Political Institutions of a Nilotic People*, Oxford: Oxford University Press.

Evans-Pritchard, E. E. (1969) *Theories of Primitive Religion*, Oxford: Oxford University Press.

Evans-Pritchard, E. E. (1956) *Nuer Religion*, Oxford: Oxford University Press.

Everington, J., ter Avest, I., Bakker, C. and van der Want, A. (2011) 'European Religious Education Teachers' Perceptions of and Responses to Classroom Diversity and their Relationship to Personal and Professional Biographies', *British Journal Of Religious Education*, 33 (2), 241 – 256.

EWTN (2013) The Syllabus. Pope Pius IX. Available online at www.ewtn.com/library/papaldoc/p9syll.htm

Falconer, R. A. (1913) 'Science and Religion as Factors in Progress', *Religious Education*, 8 (3): 340–4.

Falconer, R. A. (1928) 'Difficulties for Religion in an Age of Science', *Religious Education*, 23 (4): 278–88.

Farias, V., Margolis, J. and Rockmore, T. (eds) (1991) *Heidegger and Nazism*, Philadelphia, PA: Temple University Press.

Fenn, R. (1977) 'The Relevance of Bellah's "Civil Religion" Thesis to a Theory of Secularization', *Social Science History*, 1(4), 502–11.

Fenn, R. (1978) *Towards a Theory of Secularization*, Storrs, CT: Society for Scientific Study of Religion.

Ferrari, S. (2013a) 'Religious Education in the European Union', in D. H. Davis and E. Miroshnikova (eds), *The Routledge International Handbook of Religious Education*, London: Routledge, 100–3.

Ferrari, A. (2013b) 'Religious Education in Italy', in D. H. Davis and E. Miroshnikova (eds), *The Routledge International Handbook of Religious Education*, London: Routledge, 175–80.

Feuerbach, L. (1854) *The Essence of Christianity*, trans. G. Eliot, London: John Chapman. Available online at www.marxists.org/reference/archive/feuerbach/works/essence/index.htm

Fisher, C. M. (1936) 'The Place of Religious Education in the Social Revolution – and the Nazis', *Religious Education*, 31 (1): 46–52.

Fitzpatrick, S. (2002) *The Commissariat of Enlightenment: Soviet Organization of Education and the Arts under Lunacharsky, October 1917–1921*, Cambridge: Cambridge University Press.

Flanagan, K. and Jupp, P. C. (eds) (2009) *A Sociology of Spirituality*, Farnham: Ashgate.

Fletcher, J. (1997) *Situation Ethics: The New Morality*, New York: John Knox Press.

Foucault, M. (1994) *The Order of Things: An Archaeology of the Human Sciences*, London: Vintage.

Fowler, J. W. (1981) *Stages of Faith: The Psychology of Human Development and the Quest for Meaning*, San Francisco: Harper and Row.

Fowler, J. W. (2001) 'Faith Development Theory and the Postmodern Challenges', *International Journal for the Psychology of Religion*, 11 (3): 159–72.

Francis, L. J. (2005), *Faith and Psychology: Personality, Religion and the Individual*, London: Darton, Longman and Todd.

Francis, L. J., Gibson, H. M. and Fulljames, P. (1990) 'Attitudes towards Christianity, Creationism, Scientism and Interest in Science Among 11–15 Year Olds', *British Journal of Religious Education*, 13 (1): 4–17.

Francis, L. J., Robbins, M. and Astley, J. (eds) (2005) *Religion, Education and Adolescence: International Empirical Perspectives*, Cardiff: University of Wales Press.

Francis, L. J., Robbins, M., and Astley, J. (eds) (2009) *Empirical Theology in Texts and Table: Qualitative, Quantitative and Comparative Perspectives*, Leiden: Brill.

Frayn, M. (1998) *Copenhagen*, London: Methuen.

Frazer, J. G. (1993) *The Golden Bough: A Study in Magic and Religion*, Ware, Herts: Wordsworth.

Freathy, R. and Parker, S. (2010) 'The Necessity of Historical Inquiry in Educational Research: The Case of Religious Education', *British Journal of Religious Education*, 32 (3): 229–43.

Freathy, R. J. K. (2008) 'Three Perspectives on Religious Education and Education for Citizenship in English Schools, 1934–1944: Cyril Norwood, Ernest Simon and William Temple', *British Journal of Religious Education*, 30 (2): 103–12.

Freehof, S. B. , Hough, L. H., Luccock, H. E., Mather, K. F. and Rugh, C. E. (1932) 'Sin and Salvation in an Age of Science and Machinery', *Religious Education*, 27 (5): 392–407.

Freud, S. (1985) *Civilization, Society and Religions: Group Psychology and the Analysis of the Ego, Future of an Illusion and Civilization and Its Discontents*, London: Penguin.

Freud, S. (1990) *Origins of Religion: Totem and Taboo and Moses and Monotheism*, London: Penguin.

Freud, S. (1991) *The Interpretation of Dreams*, A. Richards (ed.), London: Penguin.

Freud, S. (2001) *Complete Psychological Works Of Sigmund Freud, Vol. 13: Totem and Taboo and Other Works*, London: Vintage.

Friedner, L. (2013) 'Religious Education in Sweden', in D. H. Davis and E. Miroshnikova (eds), *The Routledge International Handbook of Religious Education*, London: Routledge, 343–8.

Friedrich, C. J. and Brzezinski, Z. (1967) *Totalitarian Dictatorship and Autocracy*, New York: Praeger.

Fromm, E. (1957) *Man for Himself: An Inquiry Into the Psychology of Ethics*, New York: Holt.

Fromm, E. (1959) *Psychoanalysis and Religion*, The Terry Lectures Series, New Haven: Yale University Press.

Fromm, E. (1994) *Escape from Freedom*, New York: Holt.

Fromm. E. (2001) *The Fear of Freedom*, London: Routledge.

Furlong, J. and Lawn, M. (eds) (2010) *Disciplines of Education*, London: Routledge.

Fukuyama, F. (2006) *The End of History and the Last Man*, New York: Free Press.

Fylypovych, L. and Gavrilova, N. (2013) 'Religious Education in Ukraine', in D. H. Davis and E. Miroshnikova (eds), *The Routledge International Handbook of Religious Education*, London: Routledge, 361–6.

Gadamer, H.-G. (2004) *Truth and Method,* new edn., London: Continuum.

Garcimartin Montero, C. (2013) 'Religious Education in Spain', in D. H. Davis and E. Miroshnikova (eds), *The Routledge International Handbook of Religious Education*. London: Routledge, 329–35.

Gardner, P. (1993) 'Should We Teach Children to be Open-Minded? Or, is the Pope

Open-Minded about the Existence of God?', *Journal of Philosophy of Education*, 27: 39–43.

Gates, B. (2011) 'Religious Education as Encounter. A Tribute to John M Hull', *British Journal of Religious Education*, 33 (3): 355–7.

Gay, P. (1989) *A Godless Jew: Freud, Atheism, and the Making of Psychoanalysis*, New Haven: Yale University Press.

Gearon, L. (2001) 'A Spirituality of Dissent: Religion, Culture and Post-Colonial Criticism', *International Journal of Children's Spirituality*, 6 (3): 289–98.

Gearon, L. (2002) 'Human Rights and Religious Education: Some Postcolonial Perspectives', *British Journal of Religious Education*, 24 (2): 140–51.

Gearon, L. (2006) *Freedom of Expression and Human Rights: Historical, Literary and Political Contexts*, Brighton: Sussex Academic Press.

Gearon, L. (2008) 'Religion, Politics and Pedagogy: Historical Contexts', *British Journal of Religious Education*, 30 (2): 93–102.

Gearon, L. (2012) 'European Religious Education and European Civil Religion', *British Journal of Religious Education*, 60 (2): 151–69.

Gearon, L. (2013a) *MasterClass in Religious Education*, London and New York: Bloomsbury.

Gearon, L. (2013b) The King James Bible and the Politics of Religious Education: Secular State and Sacred Scripture', *Religious Education*, 108 (1): 9–27.

Gearon, L. (2013c) 'The Counter Terrorist Classroom: Religion, Education, Security', *Religious Education*, 108 (2).

Geertz, C. (1973) *The Interpretation of Cultures*, New York: Basic Books.

Geertz, C. (1999) '*A Life of Learning*', The 1999 Charles Homer Haskins Lecture, American Council of Learned Societies Occasional Paper No. 45, New York: ACLS. Available online at www.acls.org/Publications/OP/Haskins/1999_CliffordGeertz.pdf

Gennadievna Romanova, E. (2013) 'Religious Education in Modern Russia' in D. H. Davis and E. Miroshnikova (eds), *The Routledge International Handbook of Religious Education*. London: Routledge, 287–94.

Ghiloni, A. J. (2011) 'Interreligious Education: What Would Dewey Do?', *Religious Education*, 106 (5): 476–93.

Ghiloni, A. J. (2012) *John Dewey Among the Theologians*, New York: Peter Lang.

Gibbon, E. (2000) *The History of the Decline and Fall of the Roman Empire*, London: Penguin.

Gifford, A. (1885) 'Lord Adam Gifford's Will', *Gifford Lectures*. Available online at www.giffordlectures.org/will.asp

Gifford, A. (2013) 'The Biography of Adam Lord Gifford', *Gifford Lectures*. Available online at www.giffordlectures.org/biography.asp

Gilson, E. (1990) *The Spirit of Mediaeval Philosophy*, Notre Dame, IN: University of Notre Dame Press.

Gilson, E. (1994) *The Christian Philosophy of St. Thomas Aquinas*, Notre Dame, IN: University of Notre Dame Press.

Ginges, J., Hansen, I. G. and Norenzayan, A. (2009) 'Religion and Support for Suicide Attacks.' *Psychological Science*, 20, 224–30.

Gleason, A. (1997) *Totalitarianism: The Inner History of the Cold War*, New York: Oxford University Press.

Gold, D. (2003) *Aesthetics and Analysis in Writing on Religions: Modern Fascinations*, Berkeley: University of California Press.

Gold, D. (2004) 'On the Aesthetics of Interpreting Religious Life', *Revista de Estudos da Religião*, 4, 1–6.

Golding, C. (2011) 'Educating Philosophically: The Educational Theory of Philosophy for Children', *Educational Philosophy and Theory*, 43 (5): 413–14.

Goldman, R. J. (1964) *Religious Thinking From Childhood to Adolescence*, London: Routledge and Kegan Paul.

Goldman, R. J. (1969) *Readiness for Religion*, London: Routledge.

Goldstein, W. S. (1999) 'Patterns of Secularization and Religious Rationalization in Emile Durkheim and Max Weber', *Implicit Religion*, 12 (2): 229–47.

Goldstein, W. S. (2009) 'Secularization Patterns in the Old Paradigm', *Sociology of Religion*, 70 (2): 157–78.

Gonzalez, M. C. (2013) 'Religious Education in Mexico', in D. H. Davis and E. Miroshnikova (eds), *The Routledge International Handbook of Religious Education*, London: Routledge, 227–35.

Gouveia, J. B. (2013) 'Religious Education in Portugal', in D. H. Davis and E. Miroshnikova (eds), *The Routledge International Handbook of Religious Education*, London: Routledge, 272–9.

Grace, G. (2004) 'Making Connections for Future Directions: Taking Religion Seriously in the Sociology of Education', *International Studies in Sociology of Education*, 14 (1): 47–56.

Gray, J. (2008) *Black Mass: Apocalyptic Religion and the Death of Utopia*. London: Penguin.

Gray, R. (2011) *After the Fall: American Literature Since 9/11*, Oxford: Wiley-Blackwell.

Greenwood Peabody, F. (1909) 'The Social Conscience and the Religious Life', *Religious Education*, 4 (1): 1–6.

Greer, J. E. (1984a) 'Fifty Years of the Psychology of Religion in Religious Education (Part One)', *British Journal of Religious Education*, 6 (2): 93–8.

Greer, J. E. (1984b) 'Fifty Years of the Psychology of Religion in Religious Education (Part Two)', *British Journal of Religious Education*, 7 (1): 23–8.

Gregory, M. (2011) 'Philosophy for Children and Its Critics', *Journal of Philosophy of Education*, 45 (2): 199–219.

Gregory, M and Granger, D. (2012) 'John Dewey on Philosophy and Childhood', *Education and Culture*, 28 (2): 1–25.

Goldburg, P. (2004) 'Towards a Creative Arts Approach to the Teaching of Religious Education with Special Reference to the Use of Film', *British Journal of Religious Education*, 26 (2): 175–84.

Gottlieb, E. (2006) 'Development of Religious Thinking', *Religious Education*, 101 (2): 242–60.

Grimmitt, M. (ed.) (2000) *Pedagogies of Religious Education*, Great Wakering, Essex: McCrimmon Publishing.

Grimmitt, M. (ed.) (2010) *Religious Education and Social and Community Cohesion*, Great Wakering, Essex: McCrimmon Publishing.

Guyer, P. (ed.) (1992) *Cambridge Companion to Kant*, Cambridge: Cambridge University Press.

Guyer, P. (ed.) (2003) *Kant's Critique of the Power of Judgment: Critical Essays*, Lanham: Rowman and Littlefield.

Guyer, P. (2005) *Values of Beauty: Historical Essays in Aesthetics*. Cambridge: Cambridge University Press.

Guyer, P. and Wood, A. W. (1998) 'Introduction to *The Critique of Pure Reason*,' in Kant, I. *Critique of Pure Reason*, trans. and ed. P. Guyer and A. W. Wood, Cambridge: Cambridge University Press, 2.

Guyette, F. W. (2009) 'Human Rights Education and Religious Education: From Mutual Suspicion to Elective Affinity', *British Journal of Religious Education*, 31 (2): 129–39.

Haag, A. (1912). Syllabus. In the Catholic Encyclopedia. New York: Robert Appleton Company. Available online at www.newadvent.org/cathen/14368b.htm

Habermas, J. (2006) 'Religion in the Public Square', *European Journal of Philosophy*, 14 (1): 1–25.

Habermas, J. (2008) Between Naturalism and Religion: Philosophical Essays, Cambridge: Polity.

Hackett, R. J. J. (2001) 'Ninian Smart: On Buttonholes and Missing Dimensions', *Religion*, 31 (4): 329–30.

Hall, E. (1987) 'Fantasy in Religious Education: A Psychological Perspective', *British Journal of Religious Education*, 10 (1): 41–8.

Hall, J., Francis, L. and Callaghan, B. (2011) 'Faith and Psychology in Historical Dialogue', *The Psychologist*, 24 (4): 260–2.

Hammond, J. and Hay, D. (1992) '"When You Pray" Go To Your Private Room: A Reply to Adrian Thatcher', *British Journal of Religious Education*, 14 (3): 145–50.

Hammond, J. Hay, D. Moxon, J., Netto, B., Robson, K. and Straughier G (1990) *New Methods in Religious Education Teaching: An Experiential Approach*, London: Oliver and Boyd.

Hampson, N. (1990) *The Enlightenment*, London: Penguin.

Hammond, N. (2003) 'Pascal's *Pensées* and the Art of Persuasion', in N. Hammond (ed.) *Cambridge Companion to Pascal*, Cambridge: Cambridge University Press, 235–52.

Hancock, P. L. and Skinner, B. J. (eds) (2000) *The Oxford Companion to the Earth*, Oxford: Oxford University Press.

Hand, M. (2006) *Is Religious Education Possible? A Philosophical Investigation*, London: Continuum.

Hand, M. (2007) 'A Response to Philip Barnes', *Studies in Philosophy and Education*, 27 (1): 71–5.

Hannam, J. (2010) *God's Philosophers: How the Medieval World Laid the Foundations of Modern Science*, London: Icon Books.

Hargrove, B. (1978) 'Dilemmas of the New Spirituality', *Religious Education*, 73 (3): 259–65.

Harner, N. C. (1932) 'Is Religious Education to Become a Science?' *Religious Education*, 27 (3): 202–8.

Harner, N. C. (1950) 'Crucial Challenges to Present Day Religious Education', *Religious Education*, 45 (3): 159–64.

Harris, M. (1978) 'A Model for Aesthetic Education', *New Catholic World*, 221 170–4.

Harris, M. (1987a) 'Fantasy: Entrance Into Inwardness', *British Journal of Religious Education*, 10 (1): 72–8.

Harris, M. (1987b) *Teaching and Religious Imagination*, New York: Harper Collins.

Harris, S. (2006) *The End of Faith: Religion, Terror, and the Future of Reason*, New York: Free Press.

Harris, S. (2007) *Letter to a Christian Nation*, New York: Bantam.

Harris, S (2011) *The Moral Landscape: How Science Can Determine Human Values*, New York: Random House.

Harrison, P. (ed.) (2010) *The Cambridge Companion to Science and Religion*, Cambridge: Cambridge University Press.

Hart, K. (2000) *The Trespass of the Sign: Deconstruction, Theology and Philosophy*, 2nd edn., New York: Fordham.

Hartshorne, H. (1922) 'Can Growth in Religion Be Measured?', *Religious Education*, 17 (3): 224–9.

Harvey, J. W. (1950) 'Translator's Preface to the Second Edition', Otto, R. (1917) *The Idea of the Holy*, Oxford: Oxford University Press, ix–xix.

Hashim, R. (2013) 'Religious Education in Malaysia' in D. H. Davis and E. Miroshnikova (eds), *The Routledge International Handbook of Religious Education*, London: Routledge, 217–26.

Haussmann, W. (1993) '"Walking in Other People's Moccasins?" Openness to Other Religions in Confessional Religious Education: Possibilities and Limits', *British Journal of Religious Education*, 15 (2): 12–22.

Hawking, S. (1998) *A Brief History of Time: From Big Bang To Black Holes*, New York: Bantam.

Hawking, S. and Mlodinow, L. (2011) *The Grand Design*, London: Transworld.

Hay, D. (1987) *Exploring Inner Space: Scientists and Religious Experience*, London: Continuum.

Hay, D. and Nye, R. (2006) *The Spirit of the Child*, London: Jessica Kingsley.

Haynes, J. (ed.) (2008) *The Handbook of Religion and Politics*, London, Routledge.

Haynes, J. (ed.) (2009) *Religion and Politics*, London, Routledge.

Hayward, M. (2012) 'The Use of Italian Renaissance Art in Victorian Religious Education', *British Journal of Religious Education*, 34 (3): 360–3.

Heater, D. (2004) *Citizenship: the Civic Ideal in World History, Politics and Education*. Manchester: Manchester University Press.

Heelas, P., Woodhead, L. Seel, B. Szerszynski, B. and Tusting, K. (2004) *The Spiritual Revolution: Why Religion is Giving Way to Spirituality*, Oxford: Wiley-Blackwell.

Hegel, G. W. F. (1910) *Phenomenology of Mind*, trans. J. B. Baillie, London: Macmillan.

Hegel, G. W. F. (1981) *Lectures on the Philosophy of World History*, trans. and ed. H. Barr Nisbet and D. Forbes, Cambridge: Cambridge University Press.

Hegel, G. W. F. (1991) *Elements of the Philosophy of Right*, trans. and ed. A. W. Wood and H. B. Nisbet, Cambridge: Cambridge University Press.

Hegel, G. W. F. (1999) *Hegel: Political Writings*, trans. and ed. Lawrence Dickey and H. B. Nisbet, Cambridge: Cambridge University Press.

Heidegger, M. (1978) *Being and Time* (new ed.), Oxford: Wiley-Blackwell.

Heilbron, J. L. (2003) *The Oxford Companion to the History of Modern Science*, Oxford: Oxford University Press.

Heisenberg, W. (2000) *Physics and Philosophy: The Revolution in Modern Science*, London: Penguin.

Heywood, D. (2008) 'Faith Development Theory: A Case for Paradigm Change', *Journal of Beliefs and Values*, 29, 263–72.

Hick, J. (2004) *An Interpretation of Religion: Human Responses to the Transcendent* (2nd ed.), London: Palgrave Macmillan.

Hiltner, S. (1943) 'Clinical Education in Religion and Mental Hygiene', *Religious Education*, 38 (3): 152–9.

Hiltner, S. (1956) 'Counseling Viewed as Part of the Educational Process', *Religious Education*, 51 (6): 414–15.

Hiltner, S. and Rogers, W. R (1962) 'Research on Religion and Personality Dynamics', *Religious Education*, 57 (4): 128–40.

Himmelfarb, G. (2008) *The Roads to Modernity: The British, French and American Enlightenments*, London: Vintage.

Hinnells, J. R. (2001) 'Ninian Smart: Some Personal Memories', *Religion* 31 (4): 333–5.

Hitchens, C. (2007) *The Portable Atheist: Essential Readings for the Non-Believer*, Da Capo Press.

Hitchens, C. (2009) *God Is Not Great: How Religion Poisons Everything*, New York: Twelve.

Hobbes, T. (1996) *Leviathan*, Oxford: Oxford University Press.

Hobbes, T. (1998) *Hobbes: On the Citizen*, ed. R. Tuck and M. Silverthorne, Cambridge: Cambridge University Press.

Hobsbawm, E. (1988) *The Age Of Capital: 1848–1875*, London: Abacus.

Hobsbawm, E. (1994) *The Age Of Revolution: 1789–1848*, London: Abacus.

Hobsbawm, E. (1995) *Age of Extremes: The Short Twentieth Century 1914–1991*, London: Abacus.

Hobson, P. R. (1999) *Religious Education in a Pluralist Society: The Key Philosophical Issues*, The Woburn Education Series, London: RoutledgeFalmer.

Hodgson, P. C. (2012) *Shapes of Freedom: Hegel's Philosophy of World History in Theological Perspective*, Oxford: Oxford University Press.

Holley, R. (1978) *Religious Education and Religious Understanding: An Introduction to the Philosophy of Religious Education*, London: Routledge and Kegan Paul.

Holmes, R. (2009) *The Age of Wonder: How the Romantic Generation Discovered the Beauty and Terror of Science*, London: Harper.

Hood, R. W. (ed.) (1995) *Handbook of Religious Experience*, Birmingham, AL: Religious Education Press.

Hood, R. W., Spilka, B., Hunsberger, B. and Gorsuch, R. (1996) *The Psychology of Religion: An Empirical Approach*, New York: Guilford Press.

Hood, R. W., Hill, P. C. and Spilka, B. (2009) *The Psychology of Religion: An Empirical Approach*, 2nd edn. New York: Guilford Press.

Houston Clark, W. (1959) 'The Psychology of Religion and the Understanding of Man in Religious Education', *Religious Education* 54 (1): 18–23.

Hoy, D. C. (2009) *The Time of Our Lives: A Critical History of Temporality*, Cambridge, MA: MIT Press.

Hubben, W. (1937) 'The Totalitarian Mind', *Religious Education*, 32 (3): 172–4.

Huber, M. A. (1988) 'Learning through Fantasy Games', *British Journal of Religious Education*, 10 (2): 72–8.

Hughes-Warrington, M. (2007) *Fifty Key Thinkers on History*, 2nd edn., London: Routledge.

Hull, J. M. (1978) 'From Christian Nurture to Religious Education', *Religious Education*, 73: 124–43.

Hull, J. M. (1997) 'Theological Conversation with Young Children'. *British Journal of Religious Education*, 20 (1): 7–13.

Hull, J. M. (2003) 'The Blessings of Secularity: Religious Education in England and Wales', *Journal of Religious Education*, 51 (3): 51–8.

Hume, D. (1757) *Four Dissertations. I. The Natural History of Religion. II. Of the*

Passions. III. Of Tragedy. IV Of the Standard of Taste, London: Millar. Available online at www.davidhume.org/texts/fd.html

Hume, D. (2009) *Dialogues Concerning Natural Religion Dialogues and Natural History of Religion*, ed. J. C. A. Gaskin, New York: Oxford University Press.

Hunsberger, B. E. and Altemeyer, B. (2003) *Atheists: A Groundbreaking Study of America's Nonbelievers*, New York: Prometheus.

Hunter-Henin, M. (2011) *Law, Religious Freedoms and Education in Europe*, Farnham: Ashgate.

Husserl, E. (1927) 'Phenomenology', Edmund Husserl's article for the Encyclopaedia Britannica trans. R. E. Palmer, *Journal of the British Society for Phenomenology*, 2 (2): 77–90.

Husserl, E. (1970) *The Crisis of European Sciences and Transcendental Phenomenology: An Introduction to Phenomenological Philosophy*, Evanston, IL: Northwestern University Press.

Hyde, B. (2008a) *Children and Spirituality: Searching for Meaning and Connectedness*, London and Philadelphia: Jessica Kingsley.

Hyde, B. (2008b) 'I Wonder What You Think Really, Really Matters? Spiritual Questing and Religious Education', *Religious Education*, 103 (1): 32–47.

Hyde, K. (1984) 'Twenty Years after Goldman's Research', *British Journal of Religious Education*, 7 (1): 5–7.

Hyde, K. E. (1990) *Religion in Childhood and Adolescence: A Comprehensive Review of the Research*, Birmingham: AL, Religious Education Press.

Hyslop-Margison, E. J. and Peterson, P. (2012) 'Epistemic Epistemic Evaluation of Religious Claims in Public Schools: A Response to Suzanne Rosenblith', *Religion and Education*, 39 (1): 3–12.

Ibadov, R. (2013) 'Religious Education in Azerbaijan' in D. H. Davis and E. Miroshnikova (eds), *The Routledge International Handbook of Religious Education*, London: Routledge, 39–45.

Independent (2010) 'Martin Rees: "We Shouldn't Attach any Weight to what Hawking says about God" As Martin Rees steps down as head of the Royal Society, he tells Steve Connor why he would like to see "Peaceful Coexistence" between Science and Religion' [Profile], *The Independent*, 27 September. Available online at www.independent.co.uk/news/people/profiles/martin-rees-we-shouldnt-attach-any-weight-to-what-hawking-says-about-god-2090421.html

Inzlicht, M., Tullett, A. M. and Good, M. (2011) 'The Need to Believe: A Neuroscience Account of Religion as a Motivated Process', *Religion, Brain and Behavior*, 1 (3): 192–212.

Isaac, J. C. (2003) 'Critics of Totalitarianism', in T. Ball and P. Bellamy (eds) *The Cambridge History of Twentieth Century Thought*, Cambridge: Cambridge University Press, 181–201.

Jackson, R. (1997) *Religious Education: An Interpretive Approach*, London: Hodder Murray.

Jackson, R. (2004) *Rethinking Religious Education and Plurality*, London: Routledge.

Jackson, R. (2008) 'The Evolution of the British Journal of Religious Education: 30th and 74th birthdays', *British Journal of Religious Education*, 31 (3): 183–6.

Jackson, R. (2009) 'The Council of Europe and Education about Religious Diversity', *British Journal of Religious Education*, 31 (2): 85–90.

Jackson, R. (2011a) 'Religion, Education, Dialogue and Conflict', *British Journal of Religious Education*, 33 (2), 105–10.

Jackson, R. (2011b) 'The Interpretive Approach as a Research Tool: Inside the REDCo Project', *British Journal of Religious Education*, 33 (2): 189–208.

Jackson, R. (2012) Religious Education and Social and Community Cohesion: An Exploration of Challenges and Opportunities', *British Journal of Religious Education*, 34 (1): 101–4.

Jackson, R. and Fujiwara, S. (2007) 'Towards Religious Education for Peace', *British Journal of Religious Education*, 29 (1): 1–14.

Jackson, R. and O'Grady, K. (2007) 'Religious Education in England: Social Plurality, Civil Religion and Religious Education Pedagogy', in R. Jackson, S. Miedema, W. Weisse and J.-P. Willaime (eds), *Religion and Education in Europe*, Münster: Waxmann, 181–202.

Jackson, R., Miedema, S., Weisse, W. and Willaime, J.-P. (eds) (2007) *Religion and Education in Europe: Developments, Contexts and Debates*. Münster: Waxmann.

James, W. (1985) *The Varieties of Religious Experience: A Study in Human Nature*, London: Penguin.

Jawoniyi, O. (2012) 'Children's Rights and Religious Education in State-Funded Schools: An International Human Rights Perspective', *International Journal of Human Rights*, 16 (2): 337–57.

John Paul II (1997) *Divina Amoris Scienita: Saint Thérèse of the Child Jesus and The Holy Face is Proclaimed a Doctor of the Universal Church*, Apostolic Letter of His Holiness Pope John Paul II, 19 October. Rome: Libreria Editrice Vaticana. Available online at www.vatican.va/holy_father/john_paul_ii/apost_letters/documents/hf_jp-ii_apl_19101997_divini-amoris_en.html

John Paul II (1998) *Fides et Ratio: Encyclical Letter of the Supreme Pontiff John Paul II to the Bishops of the Catholic Church on the Relationship Between Faith and Reason*, Rome: Libreria Editracie Vaticana. Available at www.vatican.va/holy_father/john_paul_ii/encyclicals/documents/hf_jp-ii_enc_15101998_fides-et-ratio_en.html

Jones, J. W. (2012) *Blood That Cries Out From the Earth: The Psychology of Religious Terrorism*, New York: Oxford University Press.

Joshi, S. T. (2011) *The Unbelievers: The Evolution of Modern Atheism*, Prometheus Books.

Jung, C. G. (1968) *Man and His Symbols*, New York: Random House.

Jung, C. G. (1981) *The Archetypes and the Collective Unconscious*. Collected Works of C. G. Jung, Vol. 9 Part 1, trans. R. F. C. Hull, Princeton, NJ: Princeton University Press.

Jung, C. G. (1989) *Memories, Dreams, Reflections* ed. A. Jaffe, trans. C. Winston and R. Winston, London: Vintage.

Jung, C. G. (2010) *The Undiscovered Self: With Symbols and the Interpretation of Dreams*, trans. R. F. C. Hull and S. Shamdasani, Princeton, NJ: Princeton University Press.

Kandinsky, W. (1911) *Concerning the Spiritual in Art*, trans. M. T. H. Sadler, Toronto: Dover Publications.

Kant, I. (1784) *An Answer to the Question: 'What is Enlightenment?'*. Available online at www.columbia.edu/acis/ets/CCREAD/etscc/kant.html

Kant, I. (1788) *Critique of Practical Reason*, trans. T. Kingsmill Abbott, London: Longmans, Green and Company. Available online at www2.hn.psu.edu/faculty/jmanis/kant/critique-practical-reason.pdf

Kant, I. (1909) *Critique of Practical Reason*, trans. T. Kingsmill Abbott, London: Longmans, Green and Company.

Kant, I. (1981) *Observations on the Feeling of the Beautiful and the Sublime*, Berkeley: California University Press.

Kant, I. (1991) *Kant: Political Writings*, trans. H. S. Reiss and H. B. Nisbet, Cambridge: Cambridge University Press.

Kant, I. (1996a) *Religion and Rational Theology*, trans. and ed. A. W. Wood and G. di Giovanni, The Cambridge Edition of the Works of Immanuel Kant, Cambridge: Cambridge University Press.

Kant, I. (1996b) 'Religion within the Boundaries of Mere Reason' in *Religion and Rational Theology*, trans. A. W. Wood and G. di Giovanni, Cambridge: Cambridge University Press, 39–216.

Kant, I. (1996c) 'The End of All Things' in *Religion and Rational Theology* ed. and trans. A. W. Wood and G. di Giovanni, Cambridge: Cambridge University Press, 217–32.

Kant, I. (1996d) *The Conflict of the Faculties* in *Religion and Rational Theology*, trans. A. W. Wood and G. di Giovanni, Cambridge: Cambridge University Press, 233–328.

Kant, I. (1997) *Lectures on Metaphysics*, trans. P. Guyer and E. Matthews, Cambridge: Cambridge University Press.

Kant, I. (1999a) *Critique of Pure Reason*, trans. P. Guyer and A. W. Wood, Cambridge: Cambridge University Press.

Kant, I. (1999b) *Practical Philosophy*, trans. M. J. Gregor, A. W. Wood, Cambridge: Cambridge University Press.

Kant, I. (2002) *Theoretical Philosophy after 1781*, ed. P. Guyer and A. W. Wood, trans. G. Hatfield, M. Friedman, H. Allison and P. Heath, Cambridge: Cambridge University Press.

Kant, I. (2003) *Theoretical Philosophy, 1755–1770, trans. D. Walford and R. Meerbote.* Cambridge: Cambridge University Press.

Kant, I. (2004) *Prolegomena to Any Future Metaphysics: That Will Be Able to Come Forward as Science: With Selections from the Critique of Pure Reason*, rev. edn., trans. G. Hatfield, Cambridge: Cambridge University Press.

Kant, I. (2007a) *Critique of Judgment*, trans. J. C. Meredith, Oxford: Oxford University Press.

Kant, I. (2007b) 'Lectures on Pedagogy' (1803) in Kant, ed. I. G. Zöller and R. B. Louden, trans. R. B. Louden, *Anthropology, History, and Education*, Cambridge: Cambridge University Press, 337–485.

Kant, I. (2011) *Anthropology, History, and Education*, trans. R. B. Louden and G. Zöller, Cambridge: Cambridge University Press.

Kaplan, G. and Parsons, W. (eds) (2010) *Disciplining Freud on Religion: Perspectives from the Humanities and Social Sciences*, Lanham: Lexington.

Kelsey, M. T. (1970) 'God, Education and the Unconscious', *Religious Education*, 65 (3): 227–34.

Kennedy, D. (2012) 'Lipman, Dewey and the Community of Philosophical Inquiry', *Education and Culture*, 28 (2): 36–53.

Keysar, A. (2012) 'Atheism and Secularity', *Journal of Contemporary Religion*, 27 (1): 141–4.

Khan, K.-ur-R. and Javed Mian, Q. (2013) 'Religious Education in Pakistan' in D. H. Davis and E. Miroshnikova (eds), *The Routledge International Handbook of Religious Education*, London: Routledge, 251–5.

Kierkegaard, S. (1941) *Fear and Trembling*, trans. W. Lowrie, Princeton, NJ:

Princeton University Press. Available online at www.religion-online.org/showbook.asp?title=2068

Kierkegaard, S. (2008) *The Sickness Unto Death*, London: Penguin.

Kierkegaard, S. (2013) *Fear and Trembling*, trans. W. Lowrie, Princeton, NJ: Princeton University Press.

King, U. (2007) 'Religious Education and Peace: An Overview and Response', *British Journal of Religious Education*, 29, (1): 115–24.

Kiviorg, M. (2013) 'Religious Education in Estonia' in D. H. Davis and E. Miroshnikova (eds), *The Routledge International Handbook of Religious Education*, London: Routledge, 90–9.

Kohlberg, L. (1981) *The Philosophy of Moral Development: Moral Stages and the Idea of Justice*, New York: Harper and Row.

Koenig, H., McCullough, M. and Larson, D. (eds) (2001) *Handbook of Religion and Health*, New York: Oxford University Press.

Kotiranta, M. (2013) 'Religious Education in Finland' in D. H. Davis and E. Miroshnikova (eds), *The Routledge International Handbook of Religious Education*, London: Routledge, 104–12.

Konigsberger, G. and Kubarth, L. (2013) 'Religious Education in Austria', in D. H. Davis and E. Miroshnikova (eds), *The Routledge International Handbook of Religious Education*, London: Routledge, 32–8.

Kretzmann, N. and Stump, E. (eds) (1993) *The Cambridge Companion to Aquinas*, Cambridge: Cambridge University Press.

Kristensen, W. B. (1960) *The Meaning of Religion: Lectures in the Phenomenology of Religion*, Dordrecht: M. Nijhoff.

Kruglanski, A. W., Crenshaw, M., Post, J. M. and Victoroff, J. (2008) 'What Should This Fight Be Called? Metaphors of Counterterrorism and Their Implications', *Psychological Science in the Public Interest*, 8 (3): 97–133.

Kukla, R. (ed.) (2011) *Aesthetics and Cognition in Kant's Critical Philosophy*, Cambridge: Cambridge University Press.Lamb, R. (2001) 'Always Teaching, Always Gracious: Reflections on Ninian Smart', *Religion*, 31 (4): 341–2.

Lacan, J. (2007) *Écrits: The First Complete Edition in English*, trans. B. Fink, New York: W. W. Norton and Company.

Lancel, S. (2002) *St. Augustine*, London: SCM.

Larson, G. J. (2001) 'Ninian Smart', *Religion*, 31 (4): 343.

Lealman, B. (1982a) 'The Ignorant Eye: Perception and Religious Education', *British Journal of Religious Education*, 4 (2): 59–63.

Lealman, B. (1982b) 'Blue Wind and Broken Image' 'Drum, Whalebone and Dominant X' 'model for creativity' in D. H. Webster and M. F. and Tickner (eds) *Religious Education and the Imagination*, Aspects of Education, 28, Hull: University of Hull Institute of Education.

Lealman, B. (1993) 'Drum, Whalebone and Dominant X: A Model for Creativity' in D. Starkings (ed.) *Religion and the Arts in Education: Dimensions of Spirituality*, London: Hodder and Stoughton, 55–66.

Lederman, L. (1993) *The God Particle: If the Universe Is the Answer, What Is the Question?* New York: Dell.

Lee, J. M. (1973) *The Flow of Religious Instruction: A Social Science Approach*, Birmingham: Religious Education Press.

Leech, A. J. (1989) 'Another Look at Phenomenology and Religious Education', *British Journal of Religious Education*, 11 (1): 70–5.

LeFebvre, P. (1959) 'Religion and the Teaching of the Social Sciences', *Religious Education*, 54 (1): 49–53.

Leirvik, O. (2008) 'Religion in School, Interreligious Relations and Citizenship: The Case of Pakistan', *British Journal of Religious Education*, 30 (2): 143–54.

Lerner, N. (2002) *Religion, Beliefs and International Human Rights*, New York: Orbis.

Levine, J. (1991) 'Giambattista Vico and the Quarrel between the Ancients and the Moderns', *Journal of the History of Ideas*, 52 (1): 55–79.

Lévi-Strauss, C. (1974) *Structural Anthropology*, New York: Basic Books.

Lévi-Strauss, C. (1994) *The Savage Mind*, London: Weidenfeld and Nicolson.

Lévi-Strauss, C. (2011) *Tristes Tropiques*, London: Penguin.

Lewis, L. and Chandley, N. (eds) (2012) *Philosophy for Children through the Secondary Curriculum*, London: Continuum International Publishing.

Lied, S. (2009a) '"It's Good to Talk": Dialogue and the Development of Mutual Understanding', *British Journal of Religious Education*, 31 (3): 183–5.

Lied, S. (2009b) 'The Norwegian Christianity, Religion and Philosophy subject KRL in Strasbourg', *British Journal of Religious Education*, 31 (3): 263–75.

Ligouri, St Alphonsus (1982) *Preparation for Death: Considerations on the Eternal Truths*, Charlotte, North Carolina: Tan.

Lindberg, D. C. (2008) *The Beginnings of Western Science: The European Scientific Tradition in Philosophical, Religious, and Institutional Context, Prehistory to A.D. 1450*, Chicago, IL: University of Chicago Press.

Lipman, M. and Sharp, A. M. (1978) 'Some Educational Presuppositions of Philosophy for Children', *Oxford Review of Education*, 4 (1): 85–90.

Lipman, M., Sharp, A. M. and Oscanyan, F. S. (1980) *Philosophy in the Classroom* (2nd ed.), Philadelphia, PA: Temple University Press.

Locke, J. (1988) *Locke: Two Treatises of Government*, ed. P. Laslett, Cambridge: Cambridge University Press.

Loobuyck, P. and Franken, L. (2011) 'Towards Integrative Religious Education in Belgium and Flanders: Challenges and Opportunities', *British Journal of Religious Education*, 33 (1): 17–30.

Loukes, H. (1961) *Teenage Religion*, London: SCM.

Loukes, H. (1963) *Readiness for Religion*, Wallingford, PA: Pendle Hill.

Lovat, T. J. (2001) 'In Defence of Phenomenology', *Religious Education*, 96 (2): 462–9.

Luckmann, T. (1966) *The Invisible Religion*, New York, Macmillan.

Lundie, D. (2010) '"Does RE Work?" An Analysis of the Aims, Practices and Models of Effectiveness of Religious Education in the UK', *British Journal of Religious Education*, 32 (2): 163–70.

Lyall, F. (2013) 'Religious Education in Scotland', in D. H. Davis and E. Miroshnikova (eds), *The Routledge International Handbook of Religious Education*, London: Routledge, 295–9.

Lyell, G. (1990) *Principles of Geology*, vol. 1, Chicago, IL: University of Chicago Press.

Lyell, G. (1991a) *Principles of Geology*, vol. 2, Chicago, IL: University of Chicago Press.

Lyell, G. (1991b) *Principles of Geology*, vol. 3, Chicago, IL: University of Chicago Press.

Lynch, G. (2007) *New Spirituality: An Introduction to Belief Beyond Religion*, London: I. B. Tauris.

MacCulloch, D. (2009) *Christianity: The First Three Thousand Years*, London: Penguin.

McGrath, A. (2007) *The Dawkins Delusion? Atheist Fundamentalism and the Denial of the Divine*, London: SPCK.

McGrath, A. (2010) *Science and Religion: A New Introduction*, Oxford: Wiley-Blackwell.

McGrath, A. (2011a) *Why God Won't Go Away: Engaging the New Atheism*, London: SPCK.

McGrath, A. (2011b) *Darwinism and the Divine: Evolutionary Thought and Natural Theology*, Oxford: Wiley-Blackwell.

McGuire, W. (ed.) (1974) *The Freud/Jung Letters: The Correspondence between Sigmund Freud and C. G. Jung*, Princeton, NJ: Princeton University Press.

MacIntyre, A. (2011) *God, Philosophy, Universities*, New York: Rowman and Littlefield.

McKenna, A. (2003) 'The Reception of Pascal's *Pensées* in the Seventeenth and Eighteenth Centuries', in N. Hammond (ed.), *Cambridge Companion to Pascal*, Cambridge: Cambridge University Press, 253–63.

McKinney, S. J. (2011) 'Is Religious Education Possible? By Michael Hand', *Journal of Philosophy of Education*, 45 (1): 163–5.

MacLean, H. A. (1928) 'Religious Curricula and Science', *Religious Education*, 23 (2): 141–8.

Magaldi-Dopman, D., Park-Taylor, J. and Ponterotto, J. G. (2011) 'Psychotherapists' Spiritual, Religious, Atheist or Agnostic Identity and their Practice of Psychotherapy: A Grounded Theory Study', *Psychotherapy Research*, 21 (3): 286–303.

Maghioros, N. (2013) 'Religious Education in Greece', in D. H. Davis and E. Miroshnikova (eds), *The Routledge International Handbook of Religious Education*, London: Routledge, 130–8.

Mahmood, T. (2013a) 'Religious Education in Asia', in D. H. Davis and E. Miroshnikova (eds), *The Routledge International Handbook of Religious Education*, London: Routledge, 19–22.

Mahmood, T. (2013b) 'Religious Education in India', in D. H. Davis and E. Miroshnikova (eds), *The Routledge International Handbook of Religious Education*, London: Routledge, 144–9.

Maier, H. (ed.) (2004) *Totalitarianism and Political Religions*, vol. I, trans. J. Bruhn, London: Routledge.

Maier, H. (ed.) (2007) *Totalitarianism and Political Religions*, vol. III, trans. J. Bruhn, London: Routledge.

Maier, H. and Schafer, M. (eds) (2007) *Totalitarianism and Political Religions*, vol. II, trans. J. Bruhn, London: Routledge.

Maoz, A. (2013) 'Religious Education in Israel', in D. H. Davis and E. Miroshnikova (eds), *The Routledge International Handbook of Religious Education*, London: Routledge, 166–74.

Marron, E. (2012) 'God: Who? Where? How? If? Walk in the Woods, Eilish Marron, Aged 14', *Spirited Arts*. Available online at www.natre.org.uk/spiritedarts/art11/god_who_where_how_if/gww11.php

Martin, D. (1978) *A General Theory of Secularization*, Oxford: Blackwell.

Martin, D. (2005) *On Secularization: Towards a Revised General Theory*, Aldershot: Ashgate.

Martin, F. and Fautre, W. (2013) 'Religious Education in Belgium', in D. H. Davis and E. Miroshnikova (eds), *The Routledge International Handbook of Religious Education*, London: Routledge, 54–61.

Martin, M. (ed.) (2007) *The Cambridge Companion to Atheism*, Cambridge: Cambridge University Press.

Martin, M. K. and de Pisón, M. (2006) 'From Knowledge to Wisdom: A New Challenge to the Educational Milieu with Implications for Religious Education', *Religious Education*, 100 (2): 157–73.

Marvell, J. (1976) 'Phenomenology and the Future of Religious Education', *Learning for Living*, 16 (1): 4–8.

Marx, K. (1994) *Marx: Early Political Writings*, trans. by R. A. Davis, Cambridge: Cambridge University Press.

Marx, K. (1996) *Marx: Later Political Writings*, ed. T. Carver, Cambridge: Cambridge University Press.

Marx, K. (1977) *Critique of Hegel's 'Philosophy Of Right'*, trans. J. O'Malley and A. Jolin, Cambridge: Cambridge University Press.

Marx, K. (2000) *Karl Marx: Selected Writings*, ed. D McLellan, Oxford: Oxford University Press.

Marx, K. and Engels, F. (1975–2005) *Marx/Engels Collected Works*, 50 vols., compiled and printed by Progress Publishers of the Soviet Union in collaboration with, London: Lawrence and Wishart and New York: International Publishers. Available online at the Marx/Engels Internet Archive www.marxists.org/archive/marx/works/cw/index.htm

Marx, K. and Engels, F. (2002) *The Communist Manifesto*, trans. S. Moore, London: Penguin.

Mason, M. (2003) 'Religion and Schools: A Human Rights-based Approach', *British Journal of Religious Education*, 25 (2): 117–28.

Mathews, S. (1937) 'What Liberty Does Religion Require?', *Religious Education*, 32 (3): 183–5.

Mavor, K. I., Boala, M. J. and Louis, W. R. (2009) 'Right-wing Authoritarianism, Fundamentalism and Prejudice Revisited: Removing Suppression and Statistical Artefact', *Personality and Individual Differences*, 46 (5–6) 592–7.

Mavor, K. I., Louis, W. and Laythe, B. (2011) 'Religion, Prejudice, and Authoritarianism: Is RWA a Boon or Bane to the Psychology of Religion?', *Journal for the Scientific Study of Religion*, 50 (1): 22–43.

Midgley, M. (2007) 'Intelligent Design Theory and Other Ideological Problems', *Journal of the Philosophy of Education Society of Great Britain*, (15) 1–48.

Miedema, S. and Bertram-Troost, G. (2008) 'Democratic Citizenship and Religious Education: Challenges and Perspectives for Schools in the Netherlands', *British Journal of Religious Education*, 30 (2): 123–32.

Mill, J. S. (1989) *J. S. Mill: 'On Liberty' and Other Writings*. Cambridge: Cambridge University Press.

Miller, J. (2003) 'Using the Visual Arts in Religious Education: An Analysis and Critical Evaluation', *British Journal of Religious Education*, 25 (3): 200–13.

Miller, J. (2013) 'REsilience, Violent Extremism and Religious Education'. *British Journal of Religious Education*, 188–200.

Miller, L. J. (ed.) (2012) *The Oxford Handbook of Psychology and Spirituality*, New York: Oxford University Press.

Milo L. and Whittaker, M. L. (1932) 'Adolescent Religion in Relation to Mental Hygiene', *Religious Education*, 27 (9): 811–17.

Moore, A. J. (1987) 'A Social Theory of Religious Education', *Religious Education*, 82 (3): 415–25.

Moore, M. E. and Wright, A. M. (eds) (2008) *Children, Youth, and Spirituality in a Troubling World*, St. Louis: Chalice.

Moracikova, M. (2013) 'Religious Education in the Slovak Republic', in D. H. Davis and E. Miroshnikova (eds), *The Routledge International Handbook of Religious Education*, London: Routledge, 310–17.

Moriarty, M. (2003) 'Grace and Religious Belief in Pascal', in N. Hammond (ed.), *Cambridge Companion to Pascal*, Cambridge: Cambridge University Press, 144–61.

Morizot, J. (2011) '18th Century French Aesthetics', *The Stanford Encyclopedia of Philosophy*, Winter 2011 edn., ed. E. N. Zalta. Available online at http://plato.stanford.edu/archives/win2011/entries/aesthetics-18th-french/

Morris, P. (2001) 'Ninian Smart: Comparative Theologian, Poet, Philosopher, and Global Citizen' *Religion*, 31 (4): 353–4.

Moulin, D. (2012) 'Religious Education in England After 9/11', *Religious Education*, 107 (2): 158–73.

Mountford, B. (2011) *Christian Atheist: Belonging without Believing*, London: O Books.

Moyar, D. and Quante, M. (2011) *Hegel's Phenomenology of Spirit: A Critical Guide*, Cambridge: Cambridge University Press.

Müller, F. M. (1889–1893) *Gifford Lectures* (Collected Works, vols. 1–4): *Natural Religion* (1889), *Physical Religion* (1891), *Anthropological Religion* (1892), *Theosophy, or Psychological Religion* (1893). Available online at www.giffordlectures.org/Author.asp?AuthorID=127

Munsey, B. (1980) *Moral Development, Moral Education and Kohlberg*, Birmingham, AL: Religious Education Press.

Mussen, P. (ed.) *Handbook of Child Psychology*, London: John Wiley and Sons.

Nash, D. (2010) *Blasphemy in the Christian World: A History*, New York: Oxford University Press.

Navarro Floria, J. G. (2013) 'Religious Education in Latin American Countries', in D. H. Davis and E. Miroshnikova (eds), *The Routledge International Handbook of Religious Education*. London: Routledge, 197–201.

Neiman, A. V. (1999) 'Religious Belief and Education for Spirituality after the Enlightenment', *Religious Education*, 94 (4): 428–41.

Nelson, J. (2010) 'The Evolving Place of Research on Religion in the American Educational Research Association', *Religion and Education*, 37 (1): 60–86.

Nesbitt, E. (2009) 'The Teacher of Religion as Ethnographer', in P. B. Clarke (ed.), *The Oxford Handbook of the Sociology of Religion*, Oxford and New York: Oxford University Press, 965–85.

Netto, B (1989) 'On Removing Theology from Religious Education', *British Journal of Religious Education*, 11 (3): 163–8.

Neusner, J. (2001) 'Remembering Ninian Smart', *Religion*, 31 (4): 355–6.

Newcombe, S. (2013) 'Religious Education in the United Kingdom', in D. H. Davis and E. Miroshnikova (eds), *The Routledge International Handbook of Religious Education*, London: Routledge, 367–74.

Niebuhr, H. R. (1960) *Radical Monotheism and Western Culture*, New York: Harper and Row.

Nietzsche, F. (1974) *Thus Spoke Zarathustra*, trans. R. J. Hollingdale, London: Penguin.

Nietzsche, F. (2006) *Nietzsche: 'On the Genealogy of Morality' and Other Writings*, ed. K. Ansell-Pearson, trans. C. Diethe, Cambridge: Cambridge University Press.

Nietzsche, F. (2008) *Beyond Good and Evil: Prelude to a Philosophy of the Future*, ed. M. Faber and R. C. Holub, Oxford: Oxford University Press.

Norton, D. F. and Taylor, J. (eds) (2008) *The Cambridge Companion to Hume*, 2nd edn., Cambridge: Cambridge University Press.

Nye, R. (2009) *Children's Spirituality*, London: Church House.

O'Donnell, J. J. (2006) *Augustine: A New Biography*, London: Harper.

O'Grady, K. (2005) 'Professor Ninian Smart, Phenomenology and Religious Education', *British Journal of Religious Education*, 27 (3): 227–37.

Oliverio, S. (2012) 'Accomplishing Modernity: Dewey's Inquiry, Childhood and Philosophy', *Education and Culture*, 28 (2): 54–69.

O'Mahony, C. (2013) 'Religious Education in Ireland', in D. H. Davis and E. Miroshnikova (eds), *The Routledge International Handbook of Religious Education*, London: Routledge, 156–65.

Oppenheim, W. (1990) *Europe and the Enlightened Despots*, London: Hodder Arnold.

Osbeck, C. (2012) 'More Purpose than Meaning in RE: A Response to James Conroy, David Lundie, and Vivienne Baumfield', *Journal of Beliefs and Values*, 33 (3): 325–8.

OSCE (2007) Office for Democratic Institutions and Human Rights, *Toledo Guiding Principles on Teaching about Religions and Beliefs in Public Schools Prepared by the ODIHR Advisory Council of Experts on Freedom of Religion or Belief*, Warsaw: OSCE/ODIHR. Available online at www.osce.org/odihr/29154

Oser, F., and Gmünder, P. (1991) *Religious Judgement: A Developmental Approach*, Birmingham, AL: Religious Education Press.

Oser, F. K. (1994) 'The Development of Religious Judgment' in B. Puka (ed.), *Fundamental Research in Moral Development*, New York: Garland, 375–96.

Otto, R. (1917) *Das Heilige – Über das Irrationale in der Idee des Göttlichen und sein Verhältnis zum Rationalen* [The Holy: On the Irrational in the Idea of the Divine and Its Relation to the Rational], 2nd edn., 2004. Munich: C. H. Beck.

Otto, R. (1950) *The Idea of the Holy: An Inquiry into the Non-rational Factor in the Idea of the Divine and Its Relation to the Rational*, 2nd edn., trans. John W. Harvey, London/Oxford/New York: Oxford University Press, 1950.

Otto, R. (1962) *Mysticism East and West: A Comparative Analysis of the Nature of Mysticism*, New York: Macmillan.

Padilla, N. (2013) 'Religious Education in Argentina', in D. H. Davis and E. Miroshnikova (eds), *The Routledge International Handbook of Religious Education*, London: Routledge, 13–18.

Pahud de Martanges, R. and Suess, R. (2013) 'Religious Education in Switzerland', in D. H. Davis and E. Miroshnikova (eds), *The Routledge International Handbook of Religious Education*, London: Routledge, 359–66.

Paine, T. (1984) *Rights of Man*, Penguin Classics, London: Penguin.

Paine, T. (1995) *Thomas Paine: Collected Writings: Common Sense/The Crisis/Rights of Man/The Age of Reason/Pamphlets, Articles, and Letters*, New York: Library of America.

Paley, W. (2008) *Natural Theology*, eds M. D. Eddy and D. Knight, Oxford: Oxford University Press.

Palmer, M. (1997) *Freud and Jung on Religion*, London: Routledge.

Palmer, M. (2010) *The Atheist's Creed*, Cambridge: Lutterworth Press.

Pals, D. L. (2006) *Eight Theories of Religion*, 2nd edn., Oxford: Oxford University Press.

Pargament, K. (1999) 'The Psychology of Religion and Spirituality? Yes and No', *International Journal for the Psychology of Religion*, 9 (1): 3–16.

Parker, S., Freathy, R. and Francis, L. J. (eds) (2012) *Religious Education and Freedom of Religion and Belief*, Oxford: Peter Lang.

Parsons, T. (1967) *Sociological Theory and Modern Society*, New York: Free Press.

Pascal, B. (1660) *Pensées*, trans. W.F. Trotter. Grand Rapids, MI: Christian Classics Ethereal Library. Available online at www.ccel.org/p/pascal/pensees/

Pavel Tavala, E. (2013) 'Religious Education in Romania', in D. H. Davis and E. Miroshnikova (eds), *The Routledge International Handbook of Religious Education*. London: Routledge, 280–6.

Pearson, B. A. (2001) 'A Personal Tribute to Ninian Smart', *Religion*, 31 (4): 357–8.

Pelikan, J. Fitzgerald, A. D., Cavadini, J. C. and Djuth, M. (eds) (2009) *Augustine Through the Ages: An Encyclopedia*, New York: William B Eerdmans.

Pereira, A. (2013) 'Religious Education in Uruguay' in D. H. Davis and E. Miroshnikova (eds), *The Routledge International Handbook of Religious Education*. London: Routledge, 383–90.

Petersen, J. (2004) 'The History of the Concept of Totalitarianism in Italy' in Maier, H. (ed.) *Totalitarianism and Political Religions*, vol. I, trans. J. Bruhn, London: Routledge, 3–21.

Phillips, D. C. (2008) 'John Dewey', *Stanford Encyclopedia of Philosophy*, Spring 2009 edn. Available online at http://plato.stanford.edu/entries/education-philosophy/

Piaget, J. (1928) *Judgment and Reasoning in the Child*, London: Routledge and Kegan Paul.

Piaget, J. (1952) 'Autobiography' in E. G. Boring, H. S. Langfeld, H. Werner, and R. M. Yerks (eds), *A History of Psychology in Autobiography*, Worchester, MA: Clark University Press, 237–56.

Piaget, J. (1953) *Origins of Intelligence in the Child*, London: Routledge and Kegan Paul.

Piaget, J. (1957) *Construction of Reality in the Child*, London: Routledge and Kegan Paul.

Pickering, M. (1993) *Auguste Comte: Volume 1: An Intellectual Biography*, Cambridge: Cambridge University Press.

Pickering, M. (2009a) *Auguste Comte: Volume 2: An Intellectual Biography*, Cambridge: Cambridge University Press.

Pickering, M. (2009b) *Auguste Comte: Volume 3: An Intellectual Biography*, Cambridge: Cambridge University Press.

Pickering, W. S. F. and Walford, G. (eds) (2000) *Durkheim's Suicide: A Century of Research and Debate*, London: Routledge.

Pike, M. A. (2008) 'Faith in citizenship? On teaching children to believe in liberal democracy', *British Journal of Religious Education*, 30 (2): 113–22.

Pinkard, T. P. (1996) *Hegel's Phenomenology: The Sociality of Reason*, Cambridge: Cambridge University Press.

Pippin, R. (2008) 'The Absence of Aesthetics in Hegel's Aesthetics', in F. C. Beiser (ed.), *Cambridge Companion to Hegel and Nineteenth-Century Philosophy*, Cambridge: Cambridge University Press.

Podoprigora, R. (2013) 'Religious Education in Kazakhstan', in D. H. Davis and E.

Miroshnikova (eds), *The Routledge International Handbook of Religious Education*, London: Routledge, 191–6.

Polkinghorne, J. C. (2003) *Belief in God in an Age of Science*, New Haven, CT: Yale University Press.

Polkinghorne, J. C. (2007) *Science and Providence: God's Interaction with the World*, West Conshohocken, PA: Templeton Press.

Polkinghorne, J. C. (2012) *Science and Religion in Quest of Truth*, New Haven, CT: Yale University Press.

Poole, M. (1990) 'Science and Religion: A Challenge for Secondary Education', *British Journal of Religious Education*, 13 (1): 18–27.

Pope, H. (1910) 'Holiness', in *The Catholic Encyclopedia*, New York: Robert Appleton Company. Available online at www.newadvent.org/cathen/07386a.htm

Popper, K. (2011) *The Open Society and Its Enemies*, London: Routledge.

Power, W.L. (1973) 'Interpreting Man's Religion in Academe', *Religious Education*, 68 (6): 659–72.

Power, S. (2007) *A Problem from Hell: America and the Age of Genocide*, New York: Harper.

Priestley, J. G. (1981) Religious Story and the Literary Imagination', *British Journal of Religious Education*, 4 (1): 17–24.

Priestley, J. G. (1982) 'Teaching Transcendence', in Webster and Tickner (eds) *Religious Education and the Imagination, Aspects of Education*, Aspects of Education, 28, Hull: University of Hull Institute of Education.

Priestley, J. G. (1985) 'Towards Finding the Hidden Curriculum: A Consideration of the Spiritual Dimension of Experience in Curriculum Planning', *British Journal of Religious Education*, 7 (3): 112–19.

Priestley, J. G. (1996) *'Spirituality in the Curriculum', Hockerill Lecture*, Essex: Hockerill Educational Foundation.

Prieto, V. (2013) 'Religious Education in Colombia', in D. H. Davis and E. Miroshnikova (eds), *The Routledge International Handbook of Religious Education*, London: Routledge, 84–9.

Puolimatka, T. and Tirri, L. (2000) 'Religious Education in Finland: Promoting Intelligent Belief?' British Journal of Religious Education 23 (1): 38–44.

Radford, M. (2012) 'Faith and Reason in a Post Secular Age', *Journal of Beliefs and Values*, 33 (2): 229–40.

Ratliff, T. L. (2010) 'Educating for a "Spirituality of Dialogue": Theological Foundations, Hermeneutical Invitations, and Pedagogical Directions', *Religious Education*, 105 (4): 430–43.

Ratzinger, J. and Habermas, J. (2007) *The Dialectics of Secularization*, San Francisco: Ignatius.

Rawls, J. (1999) *The Law of Peoples*, Cambridge, MA: Harvard University Press.

Rawls, J. (2005) *Political Liberalism*, New York: Columbia University Press.

RCPSYCH (2013) 'Spirituality and Mental Health', Royal College of Psychiatrists, Available online at www.rcpsych.ac.uk/expertadvice/treatments/spirituality.aspx/

Reich, H. (1989) 'Between Religion and Science: Complementarity in the Religious Thinking of Young People', *British Journal of Religious Education*, 11 (2): 62–9.

Reich, H. (1990) 'Beliefs of German and Swiss Children and Young People about Science and Religion', *British Journal of Religious Education*, 13 (1): 65–73.

Reich, K. H. (2005) 'Stage-Structural Approach to Religious Development', in E. M.

Dowling and W. G. Scarlett (eds), *Encyclopedia of Spiritual and Religious Development in Childhood and Adolescence*, Thousand Oaks, CA: Sage, 431–7.

Reid Martin, A. (1943) 'Recent Trends on Psychiatry of Particular Significance for Religion', *Religious Education*, 38 (3): 131–42.

Reno, S. J. (1979) 'Distance in the Study of Religion', *British Journal of Religious Education*, 1 (3): 108–10.

Revell, L. (2008) 'Spiritual Development in Public and Religious Schools: A Case Study', *Religious Education*, 103 (1): 102–18.

Reynolds, T. E. (2002) 'Religion Within the Limits of History: Schleiermacher and Religion – A Reappraisal', *Religion*, 32 (1): 51–70.

Ricoeur, P. (1970) *Freud and Philosophy: An Essay on Interpretation*, trans. D. Savage, New Haven: Yale University Press.

Ricoeur, P. (1974) *The Conflict of Interpretations: Essays in Hermeneutics*, ed. D. Ihde, Evanston: Northwestern University Press.

Ricoeur, P. (1976) *Interpretation Theory: Discourse and the Surplus of Meaning*, Fort Worth: Texas Christian University Press.

Ricoeur, P. (1978) *The Rule of Metaphor: Multi-Disciplinary Studies in the Creation of Meaning in Language*, trans. R. Czerny, K. McLaughlin and J. Costello, Toronto: University of Toronto Press.

Ricoeur, P. (1980) *Essays on Biblical Interpretation*, ed. L. S. Mudge, Philadelphia: Fortress Press.

Rieff, P. (1979) *Freud: The Mind of the Moralist*, Chicago, IL: Chicago University Press.

Rieff, P. (2006) *Triumph of the Therapeutic: Uses of Faith After Freud*, Wilmington, Delaware: ISI Books.

Riggs, A. (1990) 'Biotechnology and Religious Education', *British Journal of Religious Education*, 13 (1): 56–64.

Riis, O. and Woodhead, L. (2012) *A Sociology of Religious Emotion*, New York: Oxford University Press.

Rist, J. (2001) 'Faith and Reason', in E. Stump, E. and N. Kretzmann (eds), *The Cambridge Companion to Augustine*, Cambridge: Cambridge University Press, 26–39.

Roberts, D. D. (2006) *The Totalitarian Experiment in Twentieth Century Europe: Understanding the Poverty of Great Politics,* London: Routledge.

Roberts, R. (2001) 'Ninian Smart and the First Years of Religious Studies at Lancaster University (1967–70)' *Religion* 31 (4): 361–2.

Robinson, J. A. T. (2001) *Honest to God*, London: SCM.

Roehlkepartain, E. C., King, P. E., Wagener, L. and Benson, P. L. (eds) (2005) *The Handbook of Spiritual Development in Childhood and Adolescence*, Thousand Oaks, CA: Sage.

Rogers, B. (2003) 'Pascal's Life and Times', in N. Hammond (ed.) *Cambridge Companion to Pascal*. Cambridge: Cambridge University Press, 4–19.

Rohlf, M. (2010) 'Immanuel Kant', *Stanford Encyclopedia of Philosophy*, Fall 2010 edn. Available online at http://plato.stanford.edu/entries/kant/#KanProThePurRea

Rohrwasser, M. (2004) 'Religious and Ecclesiastical Structures in Communism and National Socialism, and the Role of the Writer', in H. Maier (ed.), *Totalitarianism and Political Religions,* volume I, trans. J. Bruhn, London: Routledge, 335–50.

Rolfe, M. A. (1924) 'Teaching God to Students of Science', *Religious Education*, 19 (4): 246–51.

Rolfe, M. A. (1926) 'Teaching the Bible with the Purpose of Clearing the Students' Mind for an Understanding of the Religion of the Scientist', *Religious Education*, 21 (4): 371–7.

Rosenblith, S. (2012) 'Beyond Belief: Epistemic Evaluation of Religious Experiences', *Religion and Education*, 39 (1): 13–23.

Ross, J. E. (1932) 'Sin and Salvation in an Age of Science', *Religious Education*, 27 (10): 934–5.

Rousseau, J. J. (1914) *Profession of Faith of Savoyard Vicar* from C. W. Eliot (ed.) The Harvard Classics. Available online at www.bartleby.com/34/4/5.html/

Rousseau, J. J. (1997a) *Rousseau: 'The Social Contract' and Other Later Political Writings*, ed. V. Gourevitch, Cambridge: Cambridge University Press.

Rousseau, J. J. (1997b) *Rousseau: 'The Discourses' and Other Early Political Writings*, ed. V. Gourevitch, Cambridge: Cambridge University Press.

Roy, O. (2010) *Holy Ignorance: When Religion and Culture Part Ways*, New York: Columbia University Press.

Rushdie, S. (1990) *Is Nothing Sacred? Rushdie's Herbert Read Memorial Lecture, delivered February 6, 1990*, Cambridge: Granta. Available online at www.beartronics.com/rushdie.html

Saint-Simon, C.-H. (1976) 'Letters from an Inhabitant of Geneva to His Contemporaries' (1803), in *The Political Thought of Saint-Simon*, Oxford: Oxford University Press.

Saltzman, J. D. (2001) 'Tribute to Ninian Smart', *Religion*, 31 (4): 363.

Santana, G. F. (2013) 'Religious Education in Peru', in D. H. Davis and E. Miroshnikova (eds), *The Routledge International Handbook of Religious Education*, London: Routledge, 256–63.

Sartre, J.-P. (1970) *Nausea*, London: Penguin.

Sartre, J.-P. (2003) *Being and Nothingness: An Essay on Phenomenological Ontology*, London: Routledge.

Savage, S. and Boyd-Macmillan, E. (2008) *Transforming Conflict: Conflict Transformation Amongst Senior Church Leaders with Different Theological Stances*, Cambridge: Foundation for Church Leadership.

Sawicki, M. (1987) 'Historical Methods and Religious Education', *Religious Education*, 82 (3): 375–89.

Sawicki, M. (2011) 'Edmund Husserl', *Internet Encyclopedia of Philosophy*, University Park, PA: Pennsylvania State University. Available online at www.iep.utm.edu/husserl/

Sayers (2003a) 'Divine Therapy', *The Psychologist*, 16 (9): 466–7.

Sayers, J. (2003b) *Divine Therapy: Love, Mysticism and Psychoanalysis*, Oxford: Oxford University Press.

Schanda, B. (2013) 'Religious Education in Hungary', in D. H. Davis and E. Miroshnikova (eds), *The Routledge International Handbook of Religious Education*, London: Routledge, 139–43.

Schleiermacher, F. (1893) *On Religion: Speeches to its Cultured Despisers*, trans. J. Oman. London: K. Paul, Trench, Truber and Co./Grand Rapids, MI: Christian Classics Ethereal Library. Available online at www.ccel.org/ccel/schleiermach/religion.html/

Schmalzle, U. F. (2013) 'Religious Education in Germany', in D. H. Davis and E. Miroshnikova (eds), *The Routledge International Handbook of Religious Education*, London: Routledge, 122–9.

Schmid, A. P. (ed.) (2011) *The Routledge Handbook of Terrorism Research*. London and New York: Routledge.

Schmitt, C. (2005) *Political Theology: Four Chapters on the Concept of Sovereignty*, trans. G. Schwab, Chicago, IL: Chicago University Press.

Schreiner, P. (2008) 'Religious Education from a European Perspective', in P. Kieran and A. Hession (eds), *Exploring Religious Education*, Dublin: Veritas, 109–23.

Schroeder, G. L. (2009) *The Science of God*, New York: Free Press.

Schroeder, G. L. (2010) *God According to God*, New York: Free Press.

Schweitzer, F. (2005) 'Children's Right to Religion and Spirituality: Legal, Educational and Practical Perspectives', *British Journal of Religious Education*, 27 (2): 103–13.

Schweitzer, F. and Boschki, R. (2004) 'What Children Need: Cooperative Religious Education in German Schools – Results from an Empirical Study', *British Journal of Religious Education*, 26 (1): 33–44.

Schweitzer, F., Simojoki, H., Moschner, S. and Müller, M. (2012) 'Researching Religious Education Journals: Methodology and Selected Results from a German Study', *Journal of Beliefs and Values*, 33 (1): 83–93.

Scott, P. and W. T. Cavanaugh (eds) (2003) *The Blackwell Companion of Political Theology*, Oxford, Wiley-Blackwell.

Scully, V. (1912) 'Thomas à Kempis' in *The Catholic Encyclopedia*, New York: Robert Appleton Company. Available online at www.newadvent.org/cathen/14661a.htm

Sealey, J. (1982) 'Another Look at Smart's Six Dimensional Account of Religion', *British Journal of Religious Education*, 5 (1): 15–19.

Secord, J. A. (2003) *Victorian Sensation: The Extraordinary Publication, Reception, and Secret Authorship of Vestiges of the Natural History of Creation*, Chicago, IL: University of Chicago Press.

Seiple, C., Hooper, D. and Otis, P. (eds) (2011) *Routledge Handbook of Religion and Security: Theory and Practice*, London and New York, Routledge.

Seymour, J. L. (1995) 'Philosophy and Religious Education', *Religious Education*, 90 (3–4), 318–21.

Seymour, J. L. (2011a) 'The Canon of Religious Education', *Religious Education*, 106, (2): 119–20.

Seymour, J. L. (2011b) 'Brain Matters: Neuroscience, Creativity, and Diversity', *Religious Education*, 106 (3): 243–4.

Seymour, J. L. (2012) 'Theology, Education, and Social Science', *Religious Education*, 107 (4): 321–2.

Shabani, O. M. (2011) 'The Role of Religion in Democratic Politics: Tolerance and the Boundary of Public Reason', *Religious Education*, 106 (3): 332–46.

Sharma, A. (2001) 'Encountering Ninian Smart', *Religion*, 31 (4): 365–6.

Sharpe, E. F. (1975) 'The Phenomenology of Religion', *Learning for Living*, 15 (1): 4–9.

Sharpe, E. F. (2009) *Comparative Religion: A History*, Bristol Classical Press.

Sheldrake, P. (1996) *Spirituality and History: Questions of Interpretation and Method*, London: SPCK.

Shepherd, J. J. (2005) 'The Ninian Smart Archive and Bibliography', *Religion*, 35 (3): 167–97.

Shermer, M. (2011) *In Darwin's Shadow: The Life and Science of Alfred Russel Wallace: A Biographical Study on the Psychology of History*, Oxford: Oxford University Press.

Siegler, E. (2001) 'Ninian Smart, Teacher', *Religion*, 31 (4): 367–8.

Silcox, C. E. (1937) 'The Significance of Religious Freedom in the Modern World', *Religious Education*, 32 (3): 174–9.

Slee, N. (1992) '"Heaven in Ordinarie"' in B. Watson (ed.) *Priorities in Religious Education*, London: Falmer, 38–57.

Smart, N. (1962) 'The Christian and Other Religions', *Learning for Living*, 1 (3): 20–1.

Smart, N. (1967) 'A New Look at Religious Studies: The Lancaster Idea', *Learning for Living*, 7 (1): 27–9.

Smart, N. (1969) *The Religious Experience of Mankind*. London: Macmillan.

Smart, N. (1970) 'What is Truth in RE?', *Learning for Living*, 10 (1): 13–15.

Smart, N. (1972) 'Guest Editorial', *Learning for Living*, 11 (3): 5.

Smart, N. (1973) *The Science of Religion and the Sociology of Knowledge: Some Methodological Questions*, Princeton, NJ: Princeton University Press.

Smart, N. (1974) 'The Uniqueness of Christianity', *Learning for Living*, 13 (4): 136–8.

Smart, N. (1996) *Dimensions of the Sacred: An Anatomy of the World's Beliefs*, Berkeley and Los Angeles, CA: University of California Press.

Smart, N. (1998) *The World's Religions*, Cambridge: Cambridge University Press.

Smart, N. (1999) *Dimensions of the Sacred: An Anatomy of the World's Beliefs*, Berkeley: California University Press.

Smidt Hanson, B. (1983) 'Phenomenology of Religion: A Bridge Between the Scholarly Study of Religion and Religious Education', *British Journal of Religious Education*, 6 (1): 14–19.

Smith, A. (2008) *The Wealth of Nations, A Selected Edition*, ed. K. Sutherland, Oxford: Oxford University Press.

Smith, A. D. (2009) 'Otto's Criticisms of Schleiermacher', *Religious Studies*, 45 (2): 187–204.

Smith, B. and Woodruff Smith, D. (eds) (1995) *The Cambridge Companion to Husserl*, Cambridge: Cambridge University Press.

Smith, G. B. (1928) 'Nature of Science and of Religion and their Interrelation', *Religious Education*, 23 (4): 304–14.

Smith, L. (1993) *Necessary Knowledge: Piagetian Perspectives on Constructivism*, Hove, East Sussex: Lawrence Erlbaum.

Smith, L. (1997) 'Jean Piaget', in N. Sheehy, A. Chapman and W. Conroy (eds), *Biographical Dictionary of Psychology*, London: Routledge.

Smith, W. C. (1991) *The Meaning and End of Religion*, Minneapolis, MN: Augsburg.

Smith Leiper, H. (1938) 'What Liberty Does Religion Require?', *Religious Education*, 32 (3): 186–92.

Snelling, C. H. (1989) 'The Proper Study and the Chief End: The Relation of Religious Education and the Social Sciences', *Religious Education*, 84 (3): 428–53.

Socker, B. (2006) *Routledge Philosophy Guidebook to Derrida on Deconstruction*, London: Routledge.

Staebuck, E. D. (1929) 'Religious Psychology and Research Methods', *Religious Education*, 24 (9): 874–6.

Stannard, R. (1990) 'Science and Religion: How to Start an Argument', *British Journal of Religious Education*, 13 (1): 28–34.

Starbuck, E. (1911) *The Psychology of Religion*, 3rd edn., New York: Charles Scribner's Sons.

Stark, R. (1999a) 'Atheism, Faith, and the Social Scientific Study of Religion', *Journal of Contemporary Religion*, 14 (1): 41–62.

Stark, R. (1999b) 'Secularization, RIP', *Sociology of Religion*, 60 (3): 249–73.

Starkings, D. (ed.) (1993) *Religion and the Arts in Education: Dimensions of Spirituality*, London: Hodder and Stoughton.

Stedman Jones, G. (2002) 'The Reception of the Manifesto', in K. Marx, and F. Engels, *The Communist Manifesto*, London: Penguin, 14–26.

Stein, M. (1998) *Jung's Map of the Soul*, Chicago, IL: Open Court.

Stepan, A. C. (2000) 'Religion, Democracy, and the "Twin Tolerations"', *Journal of Democracy*, 11 (4): 37–57.

Strassner, M. (2011) *Religion, Education and the State: An Unprincipled Doctrine in Search of Meanings*, Farnham: Ashgate.

Streetman. R. F. (1980) 'Some Later Thoughts of Otto on the Holy', *Journal of the American Academy of Religion*, 48 (3): 365–84.

Streib, H. (2001a) 'Faith Development Theory Revisited: The Religious Styles Perspective', *International Journal for the Psychology of Religion*, 11 (3): 143–58.

Streib, H. (2001b) 'Fundamentalism as a Challenge for Religious Education', *Religious Education*, 96 (2): 227–44.

Streib, H. (2005) 'Theory: "Faith Development Research Revisited: Accounting for Diversity in Structure, Content, and Narrativity of Faith"', *International Journal for the Psychology of Religion*, 15 (2): 99–121.

Streib, H., Hood, R. W., Keller, B., Csof, R.-M. and Silver, C. F. (2009) *Deconversion*, Goettingen: Vandenhoech and Ruprecht.

Strenski, I. (2001) Ninian Smart and the Overcoming of Philosophy', *Religion*, 31 (4): 369–71.

Strhan, A. (2010) 'A Religious Education Otherwise? An Examination and Proposed Interruption of Current British Practice', *Journal of Philosophy of Education*, 44 (1): 23–44.

Stump, E. and Kretzmann, N. (eds) (2001) *The Cambridge Companion to Augustine*, Cambridge: Cambridge University Press.

Swann, M. (1985) *Education for All: Report of the Committee of Enquiry into the Education of Children From Ethnic Minority Groups*, Michael Swann, Chairman, London: HMSO. Available online at www.educationengland.org.uk/documents/swann

Sztokman, E. A. (2008) 'War, Terror, Girls and God', *British Journal of Religious Education*, 30 (2): 155–64.

Takahata, E. (2013) 'Religious Education in Japan', in D. H. Davis and E. Miroshnikova (eds), *The Routledge International Handbook of Religious Education*, London: Routledge, 181–91.

Talmon, J. L. (1961) *History of Totalitarian Democracy*, [1952], Mercury Books.

Tan, C. (2008) 'Creating 'Good Citizens' and Maintaining Religious Harmony in Singapore', *British Journal of Religious Education*, 30 (2): 133–42.

Tate, A. and Bradley, A. (2010) *The New Atheist Novel*, London: Continuum.

Taylor, C. (2007) *A Secular Age*, Cambridge MA: Harvard University Press.

Taylor, C. (2010) 'The Meaning of Secularism', *The Hedgehog Review*, 12 (3), 1.

Taylor, M. C. (1987) *A Erring: Post-modern A/theology*, Chicago, IL: University of Chicago Press.

Teece, G. (2010) 'Is it Learning About and from Religions, Religion or Religious

Education? And is it any Wonder Some Teachers Don't Get it?', *British Journal of Religious Education*, 32 (2): 93–103.

Teece, G. (2011) 'Too many Competing Imperatives? Does RE need to Rediscover its Identity?' *Journal of Beliefs and Values*, 32 (2): 161–72.

ter Avest, I., Jozsa, D-P., Knauth, T. Rosón, J and Skeie, G. (eds) (2008) *Dialogue and Conflict on Religion. Studies of Classroom Interaction in European Countries*, Münster: Waxmann.

Thapa, K. B. and Mukhia, B. B. (2013) 'Religious Education in Nepal', in D. H. Davis and E. Miroshnikova (eds), *The Routledge International Handbook of Religious Education*, London: Routledge, 236–42.

Thatcher, A. (1991) 'A Critique of Inwardness in Religious Education', *British Journal of Religious Education*, 14 (1): 22–7.

Thérèse of Lisieux, St. (1996) *The Story of a Soul: The Autobiography of Saint Thérèse of Lisieux*, trans. O. C. D. John Clarke, Washington: ICS Publications.

Thi Minh Ngoc, N. (2013) 'Religious Education in Vietnam' in D. H. Davis and E. Miroshnikova (eds), *The Routledge International Handbook of Religious Education*, London: Routledge, 391–5.

Thomas à Kempis (1952) *The Imitation of Christ*, trans. L. Sherley-Price, London: Penguin.

Thorson Plesner, I. (2013) 'Religious Education in Norway', in D. H. Davis and E. Miroshnikova (eds), *The Routledge International Handbook of Religious Education*, London: Routledge, 243–50.

Thouless, R. (1971) *An Introduction to the Psychology of Religion*, Cambridge: Cambridge University Press.

Tillich, P. (1973) *Systematic Theology: Reason and Revelation*, Chicago, IL: Chicago University Press.

Tillich, P. (1975) *Systematic Theology: Existence and the Christ*, Chicago, IL: Chicago University Press.

Tillich, P. (1976) *Systematic Theology: Life and the Spirit; History and the Kingdom of God*, Chicago, IL: Chicago University Press.

Torrey, R. A. (ed.) (1917) *The Fundamentals: A Testimony to the Truth*, Chicago, IL: Testimony Publishing Co. Available online at http://archive.org/stream/fundamentalstest17chic/fundamentalstest17chic_djvu.txt

Tracy, F., Greenwood Peabody, F. J. Davies, W. F. Churchill, W. F., King, H., Wright Gates, H., Butterfield, K. L. Hartshorne, H., Winchester, B. S., Lawrance, W. I., Porter St John, E. and Cope, H. F. (1917) 'Ideals and Methods of Religious Education for the Coming World Order', *Religious Education*, 12 (3): 181.

Trigg, R. (2007) *Religion in Public Life: Must Faith be Privatized?* Oxford: Oxford University Press.

Tschannen, O. (1991) 'The Secularization Paradigm', *Journal for the Scientific Study of Religion*, 30 (4): 395–415.

Tylor, E. B. (1871) *Primitive Culture: Researches into the Development of Mythology, Philosophy, Religion, Art and Custom*, London: John Murray.

UN (1948) *Universal Declaration of Human Rights*, New York: UN. Available online at www.un.org/en/documents/udhr/index.shtml

UN (1966) *International Covenant on Civil and Political Rights*, New York: UN. Available online at http://treaties.un.org/pages/ViewDetails.aspx?src=TREATY&mtdsg_no=IV-4&chapter=4&lang=en

UN (1981) *Declaration Against Declaration on the Elimination of All Forms of Intolerance and of Discrimination Based on Religion or Belief*, A/RES/36/55, New York: UN. Available online at www.un.org/documents/ga/res/36/a36r055.htm

UN (2010) *General Assembly Human Rights Council, Sixteenth Session, Agenda Item 3, Report of the Special Rapporteur on Freedom of Religion or Belief, Heiner Bielefeldt*, United Nations General Assembly Document A/HRC/16/53. New York: United Nations. Available online at www2.ohchr.org/english/bodies/hrcouncil/docs/16session/A-HRC-16-53.pdf.

UN (2012) *General Assembly Human Rights Council, Nineteenth Session, Agenda Item 3, Promotion and Protection of all Human Rights, Civil, Political, Economic, Social and Cultural Rights, Including the Right to Development*. United Nations General Assembly Document A/HRC/19/L.23. New York: United Nations. Available online at http://daccess-dds-ny.un.org/doc/RESOLUTION/LTD/G12/121/43/PDF/G1212143.pdf?OpenElement

UNESCO (2006) *Guidelines on Intercultural Education*, Geneva: UNESCO.

UNESCO (2011) *Contemporary Issues in Human Rights Education*, Geneva: UNESCO. Available online at www.theewc.org/uploads/content/UNESCO%20report.pdf/

USCIRF (1998) International Religious Freedom Act of 1998, Public Law 105-292, Washington DC: United States Commission on International Religious Freedom. Available online at www.uscirf.gov/about-uscirf/authorizing-legislation.html

Vaihinger, H. (1935) *The Philosophy of 'As If'*, trans. C. K. Ogden, London: Kegan Paul.

Van Buren, P. M. (1963) *The Secular Meaning of the Gospel*, New York: Macmillan.

van der Leeuw, G. (1933) *Phänomenologie der Religion* [*Phenomenology of Religion*]. Mohr: Tübingen.

van der Leeuw, G. (1963) *Religion in Essence and Manifestation: A Study in Phenomenology*, Oxford: Oxford University Press.

van der Leeuw, G. (2006) *Sacred and Profane Beauty: The Holy in Art*, trans. D.E. Green, Oxford: Oxford University Press.

Vansieleghem, N. and Kennedy, D. (2011) 'What is Philosophy for Children, What is Philosophy with Children – After Matthew Lipman?' *Journal of Philosophy of Education*, 45 (2):171–82.

Vansieleghem, N. and Kennedy, D. (eds) (2011a) *Philosophy for Children in Transition: Problems and Prospects*. Oxford: John Wiley and Sons.

Vatican (1864a) Pius IX *Quanta Cura (Condemning Current Errors)*, Available online at www.ewtn.com/library/encyc/p9quanta.htm/

Vatican (1864b) Pius IX 'A Syllabus Containing the most Important Errors of our time, which have been Condemned by our Holy Father Pius IX in Allocutions, at Consistories, in Encyclicals, and other Apostolic Letters [Syllabus of Errors]. Available online at www.papalencyclicals.net/Pius09/p9syll.htm

Vatican (1878) Leo XIII *Inscrutabili Dei Consilio*. Available online at www.vatican.va/holy_father/leo_xiii/encyclicals/documents/hf_l-xiii_enc_21041878_inscrutabili-dei-consilio_en.html/

Vatican (1907) *Pascendi Dominici Gregis*, Encyclical of Pope Pius X on the Doctrines of the modernists, Rome, 8 September. Available online at www.vatican.va/holy_father/pius_x/encyclicals/documents/hf_p-x_enc_19070908_pascendi-dominici-gregis_en.html/

Veitch, J. (2001) 'Creating a Legend: Recollections of an Up and Coming Ninian Smart, 1967–69', *Religion*, 31 (4): 373–7.

Vermeer, P. (2012) 'Meta-Concepts, Thinking Skills and Religious Education', *British Journal of Religious Education*, 34 (3): 333–47.

Versluys, K. (2009) *Out of the Blue: September 11 and the Novel*, New York: Columbia.

Veverka, F. B. (1987) 'Learning from History', *Religious Education*, 82 (3): 341–7.

Vico, G. B. (2002) *The First New Science*, trans. L. Pompa, Cambridge: Cambridge University Press.

Vidal, F. (1994) *Piaget before Piaget*, Cambridge: Harvard University Press.

Voegelin. E. (1999) *Modernity Without Restraint: The Political Religions*, Collected Works of Eric Voegelin, Vol. 5, ed. M. Henningsen. Columbia, MO: University of Missouri.

Voltaire (1994) *Voltaire: Political Writings*, D. Williams (ed.), Cambridge: Cambridge University Press.

von Harnack, A. (2009) *What is Christianity?* Minneapolis, MN: Fortress.

Wach, J. (1951) 'Rudolf Otto and the Idea of the Holy,' in J. Wach (ed.) *Types of Religious Experience: Christian and Non-Christian*, Chicago, IL: Chicago University Press, 209–27.

Ware, O. (2007) Rudolph [sic] 'Otto's Idea of the Holy: A Reappraisal', *The Heythrop Journal*, 48 (1): 48–60.

Warner, R. S. (1993) 'Work in Progress Toward a New Paradigm for the Sociological Study of Religion in the United States', *American Journal of Sociology*, 98 (5): 1044–93.

Warnock, M. (1990) 'Imagination – Aesthetic and Religious', *Theology*, LXXXIII (696) 403–9.

Watson, B. (ed.) (1990) *Priorities in Religious Education*, London: Falmer, 38–57.

Watson, B. (1993) 'The Arts as a Dimension of Religion' in D. Starkings (ed.), *Religion and the Arts in Education: Dimensions of Spirituality*, Sevenoaks: Hodder and Stoughton, 95–105.

Watson, J. (2004) 'Educating for Citizenship – the Emerging Relationship Between Religious Education and Citizenship Education', *British Journal of Religious Education*, 26 (3): 259–71.

Watson, J. (2008a) 'Can Children and Young People Learn from Atheism for Spiritual Development? A Response to the National Framework for Religious Education'. *British Journal of Religious Education*, 30 (1): 49–58.

Watson, J. (2008b) 'Spirituality in and Beyond Education, and the Start of a New Chapter of the Story', *International Journal of Children's Spirituality*, 13 (4): 305–7.

Watson, J. (2010) 'Including Secular Philosophies such as Humanism in Locally Agreed Syllabuses for Religious Education', *British Journal of Religious Education*, 32 (1): 5–18.

Watts, F. (ed.) (2007) *Jesus and Psychology*, London: Darton, Longman and Todd.

Watts, F., Nye, R. and Savage, S. (2002) *Psychology for Christian Ministry*, London: Routledge.

Weber, M. (1994) *Weber: Political Writings*, ed. P. Lassman, trans. R. Speirs, Cambridge: Cambridge University Press.

Weber, M. (2002) *The Protestant Ethic and the Spirit of Capitalism: and Other Writings*, London: Penguin.

Weber, M. (2004) *The Vocation Lectures: 'Science as a Vocation'; 'Politics as a*

Vocation', ed. D. S. Owen and T. B. Strong, trans. R. Livingstone, New York: Hackett Publishing.

Webster, D. H. and Tickner, M. F. (eds) (1982) *Religious Education and the Imagination, Aspects of Education*, Aspects of Education, 28, Hull: University of Hull Institute of Education.

Weiss, A. L. and Cutter, W. (1998) 'Canon and Curriculum: How We Choose What We Teach', *Religious Education*, 93 (1): 81–101.

Weisse, W. (2009) *Religion in Education: A Contribution to Dialogue or a Factor of Conflict in Transforming Societies of European Countries*, Hamburg, Universität Hamburg. Available online at http://cordis.europa.eu/documents/documentlibrary/123869721EN6.pdf

Weisse, W. (2011) 'Reflections on the REDCo project', *British Journal of Religious Education*, 33 (2): 111–25.

Wetsel, D. (2003) 'Pascal and Holy Writ', in N. Hammond (ed.) *Cambridge Companion to Pascal*, Cambridge: Cambridge University Press, 162–81.

White, J. (2004) 'Should Religious Education be a Compulsory School Subject?' *British Journal of Religious Education*, 26 (2): 151–64.

Wicks, R. (1993) 'Hegel's Aesthetics: An Overview', in F. C. Beiser (ed.), *The Cambridge Companion to Hegel*, Cambridge: Cambridge University Press, 348–77.

Wildman, W. J., Sosis, R. and McNamara, P. (2012) 'The Scientific Study of Atheism', *Religion, Brain and Behavior*, 2 (1): 1–3.

Wiebe, D. (2001) 'Ninian Smart: A Tribute', *Religion*, 31 (4): 379–83.

Wilhoit, J. (1984) 'The Impact of the Social Sciences on Religious Education', *Religious Education*, 79 (3): 367–75.

Willaime, J.-P. (2007) Different Models of Religion and Education in Europe, In R. Jackson, S. Miedema, W. Weisse, and J.-P. Willaime (eds), *Religion and Education in Europe: Developments, Contexts and Debates*, Münster: Waxmann, 57–66.

Williams, T. and Visser, S. (2009) *Anselm*, New York: Oxford University Press.

Wilson, B. R. (1966) *Religion in Secular Society*, London: C.A. Watts.

Wilson, D. (2007) *Letter from a Christian Citizen – A Response to 'Letter to a Christian Nation' by Sam Harris*, Powder Springs, GA: American Vision.

Wittgenstein, L. (2009) *Philosophical Investigations*, P. M. S. Hacker and J. Schulte, Oxford: Wiley-Blackwell.

Wolin, S. S. (2008) *Democracy Inc: Managed Democracy and the Specter of Inverted Totalitarianism*, Princeton: Princeton University Press.

Wood, A. (1993) 'Hegel and Marxism', in F.C. Beiser (ed.), *The Cambridge Companion to Hegel*, Cambridge: Cambridge University Press, 414–44.

Wood, A. W. (1992) 'Rational Theology, Moral Faith, and Religion', in P. Guyer (ed.), *Cambridge Companion to Kant*, Cambridge: Cambridge University Press, 394–416.

Worsley, H. J. (2006) 'Insights from Children's Perspectives in Interpreting the Wisdom of the Biblical Creation Narrative', *British Journal of Religious Education*, 28 (3): 249–59.

Worsley, H. J. (2013) 'Seven Years On: Insights from Children's Developing Perspectives in Interpreting the Wisdom of the Biblical Creation Narrative', *British Journal of Religious Education*, 35 (1): 55–71.

Wright, A. (2003a) *Religion, Education and Postmodernity*, London, Routledge.

Wright, A. (2003b) 'The Contours of Critical Religious Education: Knowledge, Wisdom, Truth', *British Journal of Religious Education*, 25 (4): 279–91.

Wright, A. (2004) 'The Justification of Compulsory Religious Education: A Response to Professor White', *British Journal of Religious Education*, 26 (2): 165–74.

Wright, A. (2005) 'On the Intrinsic Value of Religious Education', *British Journal of Religious Education*, 27 (1): 25–8.

Wright, A. (2007) *Critical Religious Education, Multiculturalism and the Pursuit of Truth*, Cardiff: University of Wales Press.

Wright, A. (2008) 'Contextual Religious Education and the Actuality of Religions' *British Journal of Religious Education*, 30 (1): 3–12.

Wuthnow, R. (2000) *After Heaven: Spirituality in America since the 1950s*, Berkeley: University of California Press.

Xavier Gomes, E. (2013) 'Religious Education in Brazil', in D. H. Davis and E. Miroshnikova (eds), *The Routledge International Handbook of Religious Education*. London: Routledge, 62–8.

Yarros, V. S. (1937) 'Religion and the Totalitarian State', *Religious Education*, 32 (2): 94–9.

Yates, P. (1990) 'True Stories: Science and Religion in Education', *British Journal of Religious Education*, 13 (1): 43–8.

Yob, I. M. (1995) 'Spiritual Education: A Public School Dialogue with Religious Interpretations', *Religious Education*, 90 (1): 103–17.

Young, J. F. (2013) 'Religious Education in Canada', in D. H. Davis and E. Miroshnikova (eds), *The Routledge International Handbook of Religious Education*, London: Routledge, 69–75.

Yust, K.-M., Johnson, A. N., Eisenberg, S. and Roehlkepartain, E. C. (eds) (2006) *Nurturing Child and Adolescent Spirituality: Perspectives from the World's Religious Traditions*, Lanham, Maryland: Rowman and Litchfield.

Zhou, J. (2013) 'Religious Education in China', in D. H. Davis and E. Miroshnikova (eds), *The Routledge International Handbook of Religious Education*, London: Routledge, 76–83.

Zielinska, K. and Zwierzdzynski, M. K. (2013) 'Religious Education in Poland', in D. H. Davis and E. Miroshnikova (eds), The *Routledge International Handbook of Religious Education*, London: Routledge, 264–71.

Zizek, S. (2011) *Did Somebody Say Totalitarianism? Four Interventions in the (Mis) Use of a Notion*, London: Verso.

Zuckerman, P. (2010) *Atheism and Secularity*, New York: Praeger.

Index